AMWAY
THE
CULT OF
FREE ENTERPRISE

by

Stephen Butterfield

SOUTH END PRESS   BOSTON

First edition, Third Printing
Typsetting by South End Press, U.S.A.
Manufactured in Great Britain
Cover design by R.R. Smith

Library of Congress Cataloguing in Publication Data

Butterfield, Stephen
Amway, the cult of free enterprise.
Bibliography: p. 185
1. Amway Corporation 1. Title
HF5439.H82B87   1985   381'.13'09 73   85-2133
ISBN 0-89608-254-7
ISBN 0-89608-253-9 (pbk.)

South End Press, 116 Saint Botolph Street, Boston, MA 02115

This book is dedicated to all disaffected Amway distributors: their efforts were not in vain;

And to the zealous Believers who lay up their treasures on earth: verily, they will have their reward.

TABLE
OF
CONTENTS

ONE

THE
AMERICAN
WAY

Any statistical survey of Amway Corporation is bound to be impressive. According to published Company figures, the buildings cover 300 hundred acres of riverside land in Ada, Michigan. An additional 487-acre site has been acquired near the Kent County International Airport for future expansion. A Canadian production facility was built recently on eighty acres of land in London, Ontario. Food supplements are grown, harvested and processed in California and Puerto Rico. A never-ending stream of white polyethylene bottles with bright-colored labels pours out of an automated packaging line and is carried by a private fleet of trucks to regional warehouses throughout the North American continent.

In one year, 1700 miles of paper filled the cartons of well-designed, well-financed literature that spreads the gospel of capitalism and cleanliness to millions of prospective customers and entrepreneurs. Every week, busloads of newly successful distributors—more than 8400 in 1981—drive up to the Center of Free Enterprise, a dome-shaped office and lobby complex, and disembark for seminars, tours, speeches and photography. Every day, the mails bring in bagfuls of applications from new distributors all over the world.

More impressive still is Amway's complete financial solvency and meteoric rise to fame. Privately owned, with no stocks, no outstanding debts and a balanced budget, in twenty-two years this company rose from a basement selling adventure to an empire doing 1.4 billion dollars in annual sales volume, through a vast network of person-to-person contacts in more than twenty countries. Although volume fell in 1983 to 1.1 billion, few, if any, U.S. corporations have grown so big, so fast. The manufacturing center in Ada is probably on its way to becoming one of the largest, most modern, computerized production facilities in the world.

1

This is certainly a remarkable history. How did they do it? An even more important question might be: what will they do next? For we have not yet touched upon the most impressive thing about Amway. Besides being a highly successful business concept, Amway represents a value system which has changed the lives of several million people in the United States alone.

Rich DeVos and Jay Van Andel, the founders and owners of Amway, have risen on the wave of its growth to outstanding positions of leadership in conservative business organizations. Van Andel is a Director and past Chairman of the Board for the U.S. Chamber of Commerce; DeVos is a Director of the National Association of Manufacturers. Both men are subjects of magazine articles and interviews which have appeared in *The Saturday Evening Post* (November 1979, August 1982), *Nation's Business* (May 1979), *Time* (28 May 1979) and *MacLeans* (17 November 1980).

On the surface, Amway is a company which markets soaps, cleaners, vitamins and food supplements, cosmetics, jewelry, smoke detectors, burglar alarms, hardware and software of all kinds. As such it competes with Avon, Sears, Stanley, Shaklee and many other companies which do likewise. But Amway does something else too. It sells a marketing and motivational system, a cause, a way of life, in a fervid emotional atmosphere of rallies and political-religious revivalism.

Conservative politicians speak at Amway functions to woo and manipulate the great number of voters influenced by the Amway *ethos*. Movie stars and famous media personalities, among them Lorne Green, Dusty Owens, Pat Boone, Bob Richards and Bob Hope, have joined the Amway bandwagon. Dusty Owens has risen to the top echelons of the business and his advice to new distributors is marketed by the company on cassette tape. Bob Hope actually films and delivers Amway TV commercials. Amway in turn has sponsored some of his specials on NBC. Religious leaders, Bob Harrington, Robert Schuller and others, use the massive Amway rallies to call the multitude to Christ and sell their own tapes and books extolling the virtues of possibility thinking, positive attitude, prayer and wealth to a growing force of over a million distributors. In the elections of 1980 and 1984, Amway leaders everywhere were using their tax-deductible business functions to drum up votes for Ronald Reagan.

Equally impressive is how such a large and prosperous outfit gets all its jobs done without any monkey-business from unions. The employees who run the operation are divided into a class system which excludes collective bargaining by design. At the bottom of the hierarchy are the "temporary" helpers leased from Action Services, Manpower and Kelly Girls, who often work forty-hour weeks but receive no benefits. Regular workers are first hired into a pool at slightly above minimum wage; their only benefits, as of 1982, are three paid holidays per year. From the pool they may bid for permanent jobs, but with no guarantee of acceptance. Highest on the status ladder are the long-term skilled employees, whose wages and benefits in some areas may top those of union shops. All are indoctrinated to a system of paternalism which permits them to air grievances as individuals, but not through any form of collective representation.

Here is obviously a new power in American life: a corporation with immense popular appeal, a grass-roots following among all classes and trades, an explosion of political and religious energy such as has not been released since the growth of industrial unions in the 1930s.

What makes this power all the more remarkable is that corporations have never been very dear to the hearts and minds of the American people. In the days of the robber barons, the big cartels were the villains of our literature. Frank Norris, Henry George, Upton Sinclair and dozens of other writers created the image of the impersonal "trust," using up human lives and marketing poisonous commodities in its insatiable greed for profits. This tarnished image is still the literary heritage of college students taking courses in the American novel. In fact it is not too much to say that a whole generation of writers came into prominence as rebels against the giant corporation.

In recent times we associate corporations with air and water pollution, irresponsible dumping of chemical wastes under the back yards of suburban homes, dangerous nuclear power plants, oppression of third-world peoples and political murders. The current media image of the corporate magnate is a cousin to the modernized *mafioso*: slightly gray at the temples, clad in a tie and coat, wielding life-and-death power over the world's energy and food resources, ordering the assassination of opponents in educated euphemisms such as "terminate him with extreme prejudice." In the *Star Wars* fantasy, the corporation is projected on a cosmic scale as "The Empire," inspired by a demonic Faustian connection in the person of Darth Vader, the metallic guru who goes wrong in becoming overly fascinated by power as an end in itself.

All this literary history suggests that most Americans do not revere the corporation. Even though we are bombarded every day by TV commercials and magazine images advertising the great benefits conferred on human civilization by Exxon, Weyerhauser and General Electric, there is a deep-rooted suspicion in our hearts that they are ripping us off.

How, then, do we explain the burgeoning popular appeal of Amway? What transformation does it signal in American consciousness? Attendant on these questions is a host of others: how does Amway affect the lives of the people who get in it? What changes in behavior and attitude happen to you as a result of being an Amway distributor? What do you have to become in order to succeed in the business? Why do people join? How much money can you make? What are the chances of making it? Is Amway the wave of the future, the revival of small entrepreneurship and personal freedom in a bureaucratized society? Is it, as many proponents assert, the Golden Rule in Action? The quintessence of the American Dream? Is it merely a business opportunity? Or is it something more sinister: a conspiracy, a cult, a gigantic scheme to attack the labor movement, a home-grown American brand of fascism, a "feeder" organization for fundamentalist right-wing political causes?

Imagine a tightly knit, highly dedicated group of Black Panthers, over a half a million strong, programming themselves every day with tapes and recruiting new members at an annual rate of thirty-three percent; imagine the Moonies or the Hare Krishnas filling auditoriums and coliseums with hundreds of simultaneous rallies every weekend, issuing approved book and tape lists, telling their members to read and listen only to material on the approved list, inventing chants and slogans and special in-group gestures, implanting the Leader principle in masses of followers, and actually controlling the attitudes, household product use, incomes, reading matter and social circles of a million suburban homes. The ensuing panic accompanying a revelation of this kind would make the Big Red Scare of 1919 seem like a wedding reception. Parents everywhere would be kidnapping their children and locking them in bathrooms for de-programming.

Yet since 1959 Amway has been quietly creating just such a mass political and social movement which is no less all-encompassing than Communism or Cultism. Amway offers to its distributors not only the dream of wealth, but a born-again religious experience, "a faith to live by, a purpose to live for," a new set of goals and friends and associations and beliefs, a new folklore of heroes, a total pre-packaged pursuit of happiness in which all authority comes from the top down.

The Amway movement takes in recruits from any social stratum, but its main constituency in America is the white middle class. About three-fourths of all distributorships are married couples; one-fourth are singles of both sexes. Although a few Black distributors have made it to the top levels of the business, the overwhelming majority of distributors are white. The Company *Annual Reports* do not give figures that would show the ratio of whites to minorities in its ranks, but *The Amagram*, a monthly company magazine, publishes photographs and profiles of high achievers. Information about the race and class backgrounds of Amway high achievers can be garnered from a survey of these photographs over several years. In the 1960s and 1970s, the proportion of Black faces among the Amway crowds was a tiny fraction of the total. In August of 1984, more than thirteen percent of the new Direct Distributors were Black, and over four percent were from other minorities. Nearly all of the Black distributors had middle-class professions or skilled jobs before joining Amway, e.g. business executive, electrician, barber salon owner, management consultant, salesperson. The increase of Blacks in Amway probably reflects a general increase in the Black middle class since the 1960s, as well as the efforts of many in this class to diversify their sources of income. Regionally, the business is most popular in the South, the Midwest and California.

The successful upper echelons of the movement no doubt sincerely believe that Amway has changed their lives for the better. To them it is nothing less than a liberation from slavery to freedom, a road to prosperity and paradise. They may tell the public that Amway "has nothing to do with religion or politics," but they talk privately among themselves of the day when the movement will be big enough to "turn this country around and make it what we want it to be..." — by which they mean, typically, conservative Republicans in office, right-to-work laws in every state, drastic cuts in all social services, an aggressive anti-Communist foreign policy, defeat of the ERA concept, no divorce, no abortion, prayer in the schools, a sharp curtailment of the collective bargaining right of unions, and a roll-back of all the libertarian gains made in law and public opinion since the days of McCarthyism. Moreover, to many of the leaders, anyone who sees the Amway "opportunity" and does not join is, purely and simply, a loser; and losers deserve to be broke; losers deserve to work all their lives for low pay and retire on nothing. Poverty is the fault of the poor. Wealth is a sign of Grace.

Whatever else it may be, Amway is a social phenomenon that clearly needs to be studied. Books have been written about Amway: *The Possible Dream* (1977), *The Winner's Circle* (1979), and *An Uncommon Freedom* (1982), by Charles Paul Conn, purport to be unbiased accounts of the Corporation and the careers of its entrepreneurs. Conn, who is not an Amway distributor, tells the public that he intended to write the truth about Amway; but his books are in fact collections of success stories used to recruit distributors. Every new distributor who joins Amway, in most lines, is routinely sold one or more copies of these books by his or her sponsor in the business. *The Possible Dream* was over eleven weeks on the *New York Times* best-seller list, and, as of this writing, has sold over a million copies. It does not take a mathematical wizard to figure out that at least half of them must have been to Amway people. Charles Paul Conn himself is a Cinderella to the princes and godmothers of the association, appearing at big functions and applauded by the believing multitude as a loyal spokesman of the cause. His career illustrates the profitability of writing for a guaranteed mass market such as the Amway person-to-person selling system provides. Purchase of Conn's books is not required in order to join; but the recruit who declines the purchase will probably be told that he or she might as well try building a house without a hammer as to build a successful Amway business without the proper *tools*.

The articles about the Corporation and its founders which appear from time to time in *Business Week* and *The Saturday Evening Post* serve the same function as the Conn books: they are mass distributed throughout the business as tools used in recruiting new members.

Any movement uses public relations literature and spokespeople to proselytize its views. There is nothing wrong with this, provided we are not led to confuse PR stuff with serious reflection—and provided we are able to read the views of opposing movements. A tool is not the same thing as a mirror. What is needed is a book that examines how Amway is put together, what it does to the mind, and what impact it is likely to have on the American political process. Such a book must come from a distributor, who was immersed in the whole experience and yet remained detached enough to observe it. Only a distributor can give first-hand information. But doing it might be like counting the teeth in a dragon's mouth. You either beat a hasty retreat before getting to the back molars, or you are swallowed and transformed into the dragon's voice.

The business does not lend itself to exposure from the inside. Immersion in the experience gives the sense and feel of an Amway life, how Amway affects values, attitudes and beliefs, relations with family, friends, acquaintances. But successful distributors are unlikely to want to undercut their own business by being too objectively critical about their means of livelihood. On the other hand, a critic of Amway is unlikely to reach a high level of income. To observe clearly, you must not get hooked on the Amway Dream. But to get rich, see the whole thing from every level and hobnob with the managers of the empire, you must get hooked.

I joined the business late in 1978, because I wanted to make money and learn something new. I was part of the Dexter Yager line. Yager, whose profile-biography appears in *The Possible Dream*, contributes profits from his business to Praise the Lord television and offers himself to his multitude as an object of edification and hero-worship. He is a prominent member of the eleven-person Amway Distributors Association Board of Directors. He is the head of a vast organization within Amway, which may number about 100,000 distributorships. Bill Britt, Rick Setzer, Fred Harteis, Don Held and Brian Hays, leaders in the Yager line, have also been members of the Board. Yager people occupy about one-third to one-half of the seats in the Company's top advisory body. This fact is worth remembering when we consider the relation between Yager methods and the Corporation as a whole.

It turned out that being in Yager's organization gave me an excellent vantage point for observing the cultist potentiality of Amway as a political movement. Following the Yager prescription for success, I sold products and attended Yager seminars and rallies, sales extravaganzas, free enterprise celebrations and family reunions. I brainwashed myself daily and weekly with Yager tapes and books. I showed the Amway Sales and Marketing Plan to hundreds of prospects over a two-year period and built a sales group that at one time extended into nine states. I was bitten deeply enough by the fever (and it is a fever, it invades your whole system and pushes everything else aside) to be out recruiting new distributors five nights a week for almost a year. I changed my hairstyle, dressed in a three-piece suit, counseled with the higher-ups on a regular basis, won awards. The one thing I could not do, and that my leaders told me I *must* do in order to make it to the top, is let Amway *get into me*; that is, totally commit myself, mind, heart, and soul, to the Amway mystique. They say you don't really get into Amway until Amway *gets into you*. That, as far as I was concerned, would have been perdition, the invasion of the body snatchers. If I had done that, I would have gained more treasure on earth, and traded my voice for a tape player, and my brains for a cassette Rally tape. And so I never bought a Mercedes, went on the Diamond cruise or lay on the beaches of the world with the big executives sucking ice cream pineapples and contemplating what wondrous heavenly visions are contained in a little red, white and blue box of laundry soap. But I learned enough about the business to recognize it as perhaps the most successful, and frightening, center of political reaction ever to have appeared on the American scene.

At Amway functions we were "inspired" over and over with the Personal Story, a kind of folklore *genre* in which a successful couple

gets up on stage and tells the audience What Amway Means To Us. In
a sense this is my Personal Story. I never told it, nor would I be
allowed to tell it, on the stage of an Amway Rally. Leaders in the
business do not want their followers to see how personal relationships
are converted by their brand of "free enterprise" into a circle-diagram
data base for a personal computer. Nor do they want distributors to
assess the dangerous consequences, as well as the rewards, of building
Amway. Above all, they do not want the intelligence of their recruits
to search too deeply into the aggressive, grasping, self-centered politics of private wealth which are being sold along with the products.
The function of a cult is to put intelligence to sleep.

Nobody's insights are without bias. My particular biases are
evident from my handling of the material. They might as well be
gathered together and stated plainly in one place. I think the land, air,
water and productive resources of the planet are the heritage of all the
people, not only of those private interest groups who are clever, rich,
and ruthless enough to exploit them for personal advantage. The
people may well claim their heritage through the power of the representative state, and not only remain free, but enhance personal freedom beyond anything dreamed of in the antiseptic motor homes of
Amway dreams. For the time being the labor movement, whatever its
mistakes and weaknesses, still performs the necessary function of
protecting workers from industrial serfdom, and, for the time being,
may be the only defense we have. A weak labor movement means a
weak democracy. A woman's place is wherever she chooses to make it,
consistent with a decent regard for the rights and freedoms of others.
Racism, sexism, the ideology of "free enterprise" as applied in a
context dominated by the giant corporation, the so-called "Christian" complacency of the so-called "born-again" Moral Majority, and
contempt for the poor, are forms of mind pollution, more deadly in
their ultimate effects than sulfur dioxide, acid rain and nuclear waste.
What I have written here is not only a Personal Story, but a close
encounter between these values and the world of Amway.

TWO

THE
MAGIC OF
THINKING GREEN

A person may use Amway products or see company commercials for years without ever being exposed to the Plan. You encounter the Plan when a distributor succeeds in getting you to sit still long enough to make his pitch.

There are two basic ways this can happen. One is at your initiative; the other is at his. You might have bought some products from the nice couple down the street and you ask them about the business, or you answer an ad in the paper which is plainly soliciting for Amway. Or, you are placed on a distributor's prospect list and targeted as a potential recruit. The last is by far the most common means of being introduced to the Plan. Most people are not exactly itching to see it. Amway members, like other sales types, have to go fishing for their clientele.

You never know who in your circle of friends, neighbors, enemies and other social contacts might be a secret distributor. You could be on half a dozen prospect lists and not know it. When you go to your stamp club meeting, watch out: that friendly smiling newcomer with the Dale Carnegie handshake, who wants to show how you can afford rare and expensive specimens, may already be imagining you as a link in his yet-to-be sales empire. When you stand in line at a check-out counter and the woman behind you starts talking about inflation, and then says she is *glad* prices go up because of all the money she makes, the bait is being dangled in front of your face. When an old school chum that you haven't seen in years calls you up in the middle of the night and wants to get together and discuss a tremendously important business idea, he's just been bitten by the Amway bug. If you notice someone following you and peering at you over his glasses, and leaving stores when you leave, and he's wearing a

three piece suit and doesn't carry *Watchtower*, he could be an FBI
agent or an Amway distributor.

Amway people like to remain incognito. Unless they decide
you're a hopeless case. Then they drop the mask and offer to sell you
some laundry soap and give you a product brochure. If you have any
potential as a recruit, however, they probably won't mention the word
Amway until after you see the Plan.

Most distributors, assuming they are on the move, use some
variation of the curiosity approach. The idea is to drag a lure past your
nose and take it away. The conversation might go like this:

"Jack, I've got something vital I want to discuss with you. Are
you doing anything tonight?"

"That depends. What is it?"

"Love to tell you, there's a lot of money involved. Listen, let me
ask you a question. Do you think you and I could work together?"

"I guess so. Doing what?"

"I'm really not sure you'll fit into this, Jack. I think we better talk
first and see what happens. Shall I come over at eight or eight fifteen?"

The subject of how to book a meeting with you is given extensive
treatment in Amway Seminars and cassette tapes. As we shall see in
discussing the mechanics of the business, Amway distributors must
sponsor, or bring new recruits into their organization in order to
make a living at it. Anyone can sell a few boxes of soap and shampoo
and jewelry and perhaps get some extra dollars for the cookie jar and
the kids' lunches; but to turn a respectable profit, the distributor must
persuade others to join his or her group and to go and do likewise. The
real money is made, not by what he and she personally sell, but by
what their people sell. And so new distributors getting into an active
Amway line will be encouraged to make a list of everyone they know:
friends, neighbors, co-workers, dentist, doctor, hairdresser, in-laws
and outlaws. This is how you get on their list. The next step is finding
the courage to call you up, and deciding what to say when they do.

In the Yager line, which, I was told, does close to a third of
Amway's business (I doubt this, but the actual proportion must be
large), it was considered Very Important not to mention Amway on
the phone. If Amway is mentioned, you might get preconceived ideas:
you might think that the caller wants you to sell soap; you might
decide prematurely that you don't want anything to do with it and
make an excuse to be visiting your sick mother; you might suspect that
he wants to hustle you into his business and make money off your
labor. Better to present the Plan first; and only at the very end, when
he has had a chance to conjure up dreams of Cadillacs, motor homes,
trips to Disneyworld, and covered his markerboard with fantastic

incomes, can the distributor then pull out his giant poster of Amway Corporation and open it up, like Clark Kent taking off his shirt.

The Company discourages outright lying as a method of getting meetings with prospects. Distributors are not supposed to invite people to a party and then set up a board and start showing the Plan. They are forbidden to pose as survey takers in order to get their foot in somebody's door, and they will be told not to deny they are in Amway if directly asked. The Company obeys, or, until recently, effectively circumvents the law, and publishes a code of ethics, and will revoke a distributor's authorization to sell products for blatant violations of the code. But within these limits, as every salesperson knows, there is plenty of room for fun and profit. The goal is to get the Plan in front of the prospect, and then sign him up and bring him into the fold. The best approach is whatever works best: a simple curiosity teaser that says nothing and books a meeting on the spot, without too much lead time between phone call and visit.

"Jack, listen! Money!"

"Where? When?"

"My house! Eight o'clock! Bring your wife!"

The first time I saw the Amway Plan was in 1971. My wife was having coffee with a neighbor and complaining about what inflation does to a teacher's salary, and the neighbor rather mysteriously asked, "would you like to make a lot of extra money?"

"That depends. Doing what?"

"It's legal."

"That may be, but is it moral?"

"It's not door-to-door selling."

"But what do we have to do?"

"I can't tell you until I'm ready."

Naturally we were dying to know why she had to get "ready," and what kind of venture, if it were legal, couldn't be explained in the privacy of our kitchen, and, if it worked, why this woman lived on the same street we did. Amway wasn't widely known in 1971; most people now would guess immediately at least the name of the business, even if they have never seen the Plan. We were primed with a positive-attitude book, *The Magic of Thinking Big*, and, a few days later, invited to a "get-together" at our neighbor's house to be let in on the big secret.

Up in front of her livingroom was a chalkboard with some numbers written on it. When the room had filled, about twelve people in all, and everybody was squirming around wondering why they had come here and what would happen next, a neat, slick, smiling, scrubbed young man in a coat and tie came out and began Building the Dream. This is the first phase of every competent Plan-showing. What would you like to have? A summer cottage by the lake? A cabin cruiser? A new ranch? Where would you like to travel? How would you like to have all your bills paid off? What kind of car would you like to drive? A skillful Dreamer might pass around Cadillac and Mercedes booklets, travel brochures, better homes and fashion magazines, letting his audience savor the images of wealth and status.

The second phase is a graphic evocation of the Rut. We go back and forth every day from home to work, home to work. We punch a clock morning, noon and night. We spend forty years working for somebody else and retire at sixty-five (now seventy) on enough Social Security to buy a year's supply of dogfood. We give up dreaming and learn to live, or rather die, within our means. We drive a settle-for car and live in a settle-for house, and spend our travels camping in a pup-tent, and this big old motor home pulls into the site next to ours, and the rain comes leaking through the canvas in the middle of the night, and we might wonder why we have to sleep in this little tent while that other couple watches television in their motor home. And after retirement most of us have an average of twenty-two months to live. The Plan-giver draws his own Rut with humor: "My car had rust holes in the rust holes. I pulled up to a red light and had to race the motor so it wouldn't quit. I parked on a hill every night so I could get to work in the morning. My bedroom was so small if I chased my wife around the bed I banged my shins on the bureau drawers. I took a honey-do vacation every summer—honey do this, honey do that.

"And then a friend thought enough of me to tell me about a business he was in, a way to get some of those luxuries that the budget never leaves room for. And, if I was willing to work for it, a way I could retire in five years with a permanent income that would allow me to make my Dream come true. My friend said there are only two things that make a difference in what you're going to be doing five years from now—the friends you keep and the books you read. I looked at the friends I had, and the books I read, and the bank balance I wished I had, and the future I didn't have on my job, and realized I wasn't getting anywhere. That's when I decided to take a look at this business."

At Seminars and Rallies, Amway people are taught, "if you can get someone to laugh with you, he'll cry with you, and then you've got a friend for life." The techniques for getting the audience to laugh with you are passed on and duplicated within Amway groups almost word for word, like an oral folklore tradition. You discover after getting into the business that the presentation which seems so flowing and inspired and witty and full of creative sparkle was in fact taken off a cassette tape. A good Plan-giver is so immersed in the method that it belongs to him, and he belongs to it. A good Plan is a performance, but it must seem accessible and easily learned. Even the bumblings and fumblings are often deliberately calculated. The interested prospect, watching the speaker, is wondering if he or she can give that Plan. Better not be too wise, too professional, too much in control. Drop the board eraser a few times. Trip over the easel. Get the figures obviously wrong. Make jokes at your own expense, but know what you're talking about. Have fun but don't be a clown, this is a business. While he trips over the easel, a speaker may be casting photocopies of magazine articles at the listener's feet, containing graphs on what inflation has done to home mortgage interest rates and new car prices over the last ten years.

The prologue to the circles may take ten minutes or an hour, but the purpose is to hold out the Dream and contrast it with the Rut. The Dream is evoked as something *you* can have, if you believe. The Rut is drawn as something that *I* was stuck in before I found Amway . The Rut has a powerful appeal, precisely because it is true. Millions of people, as is well known, spend year after year in boring, routine jobs that gradually anesthetize their creative abilities and trap them in lives of quiet desperation. To get out, says the Amway pitch, you need belief, a goal, and a Plan. The Plan is here in front of your eyes.

A speech that might have been used in other times to bring workers into a union, or a socialist political organization, is applied here to sell the idea of "free enterprise." The imagery of one effort has leaked into the other—the insecurity and monotony of depending on bosses for a living, the poverty of retirement, the contrasting lifestyles of rich and poor. But the assumptions have been reversed. The labor movement organizer would blame poverty on the greed and power of employers; the Amway organizer, by implication, using himself as an example, blames the ignorance and inertia of workers for staying in their Rut. From the labor movement perspective, the way out is through mass collective action. According to the Plan, the way out is through individual initiative, directed toward personal goals. Whether this Plan has anything to do with "freedom" remains to be discussed.

The marketing system of Amway, disclaimers notwithstanding, is a legal form of pyramid sales. None of the products move over the counter in retail stores. You can search all your supermarkets in vain for a box of SA-8 laundry compound; in vain go the rounds of natural food centers looking for Nutrilite vitamins. It is all person-to-person selling. To get the product, you have to know a distributor. This is one of the system's greatest strengths, and also a great weakness.

To be a distributor, you don't need store, plate glass, cash registers, employees, theft insurance, large inventory and security services. The whole thing is operated out of the home. You can do it with a boxful of products, a few basic bookkeeping forms, a telephone, a car, and that most necessary of all resources, people. After locating and servicing a small pool of personal customers, which you maintain on a regular basis, you increase volume by sponsoring new people to develop customers of their own. Your business succeeds only to the extent that those people can be motivated to sell, and recruit others to sell. This is the main reason for the constant diet of Seminars and Rallies.

The list of numbers written on the chalkboard that night was the Amway point-value, or PV scale, the system derived from earlier forms by Rich DeVos and Jay Van Andel in 1959 and used unchanged throughout Amway's rise from basement headquarters to billion-dollar company:

100	3%
300	6%
600	9%
1000	12%
1500	15%
2500	18%
4000	21%
6000	23%
7500	25%

A 26 percent bracket at 15,000 PV was later added to the scale. This figure was increased to 27 percent in 1984.

Like any application of "free enterprise," the PV scale is a means for a few people to enrich themselves on the labor of many; but a new twist is included—one is tempted to call this a stroke of psychological genius. The many know they are enriching the few; they willingly participate in the process and hope to duplicate it themselves on the same scale. The genius of the Plan, and its implications of political control over the lives of others, do not become evident until you actually experience the life that results from it. By that time the self may be taken over by it and defined in its terms.

Amway assigns to every product in its line a point value (PV) and a business volume (BV). A box of soap, for example, might be worth 5.5 points and $8.15 in BV. If you sell ten boxes, you have earned 55 points and done a BV of $81.50. The actual price you sell the box for is not determined by the Company; due to a Federal Trade Commission decision in 1979, all distributors are free to sell the product at whatever price they choose. Amway sells to the distributor at a cost slightly below BV, and recommends an average retail mark-up of 30 percent. If you buy the soap for $7.92 a box and sell it for $9.92 you make $2. You can also sell it for $8.50 or $7.50.

The point scale relates to something called a *PV bonus*. When you earn between 100 and 300 points in sales in a given month, you receive a bonus check from your sponsor of 3 percent on the BV. Point-value is nearly always lower than BV, so that 100 points would probably amount to a BV of about $180. The bonus earned on this amount would be 3 percent of $180, or $5.40. The scale escalates according to volume; at 300 points the bonus escalates to 6 percent. At 600 points it goes to 9 percent, and so forth on up to a maximum 27 percent, at 15,000 points, each higher bracket on the scale giving you a bigger percentage of the profit.

The point-value of a product remains fixed, but the BV increases with inflation. This feature protects the incomes from the ravages of a declining currency. If it took 25 boxes of soap to make 100 points in 1975, it will take about 25 boxes in 1985; the difference will be the amount of profit made on those boxes. The BV in 1975 might have been $130; in 1985 it might be $200. Getting 3 percent of the BV in both cases, the distributor's bonus has risen from $3.90 to $6.00, but he still has to move about the same number of boxes to reach the bracket.*

The larger volumes are generated by building a sales force. The only way to get into the business is to be sponsored by someone who is already in it, and every distributor, from the moment he signs his application, may sponsor others. The PV and BV generated by everyone in your *personal group*—that is, everyone with PV less than 7500 whose line of sponsorship traces back to you—is figured into your total volume to determine which bracket you are in. The simplest way to represent this concept is by means of a circle diagram. Such diagrams are so universal throughout the Amway business that showing the Plan is often referred to as "drawing circles."

The PV-BV of the 6 distributors sponsored by you is part of your total; so that, although you personally may never sell more than 100 points a month, in this example your volume is the total of everyone

---

*In 1984 the Corporation boosted the point-value of all products by 20 percent in order to compensate for increased freight charges.

in your group, which adds up to a PV of 700 and a BV of $1250. Your PV bracket is 9 percent on $1240, or $111.60. From this amount you pay bonuses to your 6 people, based on *their* brackets, that is, 3 percent of $180, or $5.40, multiplied 6 times.

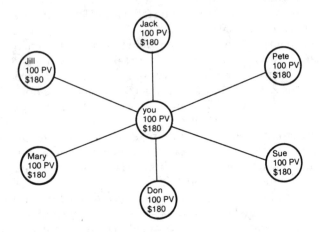

Each of the circles is a "leg" in your organization. Unless most of your volume is done by one leg, your bracket will always be higher than the brackets of the legs in your group, so that the check you receive will always be larger than the total of the checks you pay out. If the 6 legs each add 6 of their own and do 100 points apiece, your combined PV will be 4200; that combined figure determines your particular bracket. You then make 21 percent on their volume and pay out 9 percent.

As your organization gets larger, you collect more and bigger incomes. At 7500 you "go Direct," that is, break away from your sponsor and begin dealing directly with Amway. Hitherto your bonus checks and products were paid for and supplied by the sponsor; now the Company takes over. After 3 consecutive months in the 25 percent bracket, you are listed as a Direct Distributor, the first major level of achievement on the Amway success ladder. New Direct Distributors are given a special seminar by the Corporation and introduced to their responsibilities. These include maintaining an adequate inventory, supplying literature and tapes and information on new products, making sure orders are filled and bonus checks paid on time in the sales force. Directs must order everything by case lots. They may collect a warehousing fee from all their distributors, and after 6 months at 25 percent they become eligible for profit-sharing.

Theoretically there is no limit to how many new distributors can join your business. In your dreams the circles go on and on cloning more circles:

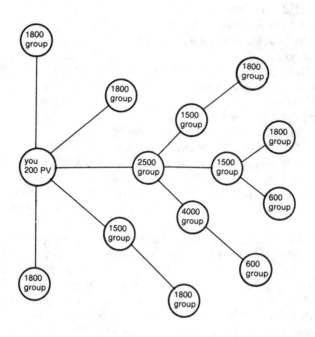

The big money starts coming in when distributors that you have sponsored go Direct. Amway pays the sponsor 3 percent on the BV of every Direct that breaks away from him. The more Directs you sponsor, the greater the number of bonuses you make on their business, and also the more types of income are added. The goal is to keep your groups duplicating themselves, so that huge numbers of people are buying and using products through an account with your name on it, which is maintained by the great Amway Computer. You are entitled to a percentage on every tube of toothpaste and every vitamin pill sold anywhere in your entire network, and all the networks descending from it.

The higher levels of attainment in Amway are named after precious jewels. They are called *pin levels*, because distributors receive a pin with the particular gem that symbolizes their achievement. For easy reference, I will list them with their qualifications in order of ascending importance:

SILVER PRODUCER: makes 7500 PV in any one month.
GOLD DIRECT: maintains 7500 PV for three consecutive months.
PROFIT SHARING GOLD DIRECT: Maintains 7500 PV for 6 months out of the fiscal year.
RUBY: makes 15,000 PV in any one month.
PEARL: has three personally sponsored Silver Producers in any one month.
EMERALD: sponsors three Profit Sharing Gold Directs.
DIAMOND: sponsors six Profit Sharing Gold Directs.
EXECUTIVE DIAMOND: sponsors seven to eleven Profit Sharing Gold Directs.
DOUBLE DIAMOND: twelve to fifteen P.S.G.D.
TRIPLE DIAMOND: sixteen to nineteen P.S.G.D.
CROWN: sponsors twenty or more Silver Producers in any one month.
CROWN AMBASSADOR: sponsors twenty or more Gold Directs within a fiscal year.

Each level adds a new type of income to those already received, and admits the distributor to the exclusive clubs, trips, vacations, and other forms of non-monetary compensation reserved only for that level. An Executive Diamond, for example, receives a regular monthly 3 percent Direct Distributor bonus on the BV of each of his personally sponsored Directs; he also receives profit sharing, which could be as high as $30,000 a year, or higher, depending on the Corporation's total volume; he gets annual Emerald and Diamond Bonuses, which are provided from funds consisting of ¼ of 1 percent of the total national BV; in addition, he is paid a cash bonus of $100 per month per Direct for each month his Directs qualify in the 25 percent bracket. If there are Directs in depth in the Diamond's organization, he may be eligible for a Pearl bonus, consisting of a ½ percent on the BV of all second-level Directs down to and including the nearest Pearl on any given line. A Diamond in Amway probably makes more than a good surgeon.

It is important to realize that every nickel produced in this system, from top to bottom, is tied to product flow. Only employees of the company are paid wages and salaries, and they are ineligible to become distributors. For the distributor, it is straight commission sales: no selling, no income. If business volume drops, income drops with it. This is one of the secrets of Amway's famed financial solvency, but in practice, as we shall see, it means that the vast majority of distributors donate a great deal of free labor to the Company and make nothing. Everything required to sell products and build a business—gasoline, sales aids, storage space, samples, telephone, tapes, training, time—is paid for by the distributors, out of their profits, if they have any; otherwise, out of their own pockets.

None of the higher incomes were explained to me, and none of the more searching questions entered my mind that night in 1971, when I sat uncomfortably in a strange livingroom, looking at the circles being drawn on a chalkboard. What I saw was a way to start with nothing and get rich. The Horatio Alger myth, brought to my doorstep.

"Amway is people helping people," said the speaker, "Amway is the golden rule in action. Back when I first got out of the Navy, and I was driving a rusted-out Chevrolet, we saw this big ol' Lincoln whiz by and leave us eating his dust. I turned to my wife and said 'Honey, someday we're gonna drive one of those.' And I'm here to tell you, we *don't* drive a Lincoln today...we drive a Cadillac. Because my wife is worth it. Amway made that dream come true."

Then he put two glasses of water on the kitchen counter. In one he stirred a spoonful of SA-8 laundry compound; in the other he put Tide. The Amway soap cleared up in a few minutes and the Tide left a film on the surface and a residue in the bottom of the glass. "Amway soap cleans without suds. Won't clog your washing machine. Use a quarter of a cup. Here's ol' Brand X, you can see something in there that isn't exactly soap. That film there stays right on your clothes." Then he proceeded to drink from the glass of SA-8.

This man was not to be dismayed by any indifference on the part of his listeners. The ones that refused to join went on his customer list. After all, we might as well be good for something.

In 1971 I would have nothing to do with either the products or the business. I distrusted salesmen on general principles, simply because whenever they arrive on the scene my money sprouts wings. Besides, I didn't spend eight years in college earning three degrees to end up selling soap. I resented the fact that this living parody of a TV commercial could make more money drawing circles on a board than I could in the disinterested pursuit of learning. I was repelled by the equation of success with Cadillacs, and moved to derisive mockery by the assumption that a woman's worth is measurable in terms of expensive cars, or in any terms whatever. The Plan fascinated me, and for that reason I hoped it didn't work, and Amway would collapse, and my neighbor would quit. Without knowing it I had been hooked.

Seven years intervened before I was brought up to the boat and gaffed. Meanwhile my neighbor did actually quit, and her whole line of sponsorship collapsed, and I assumed the Corporation must be dying out. It was a preposterous scheme anyway. Then by 1973 the gasoline panic swept over the country. Inflation went up into the double digits, and, along with other college faculty nationwide, I took drastic salary cuts and considered myself lucky to have a job. Programs were being amputated at alarming rates, colleges were shutting their doors and declaring bankruptcy.

The whole psychological process I had gone through is well known to the leaders of Amway. I wanted income security. I liked the idea of making money, lots of it, without having to show up for work. Obviously someone was making this money, because I kept seeing Amway waterless hand cleaners and Amway concrete floor compound in gas stations and auto repair shops, where I went to patch up my dying cars. I hoped it wouldn't work, but if it did, I wanted to be on the bandwagon. I wanted to be plucking the fruit from the money tree, not sitting on the outside of the circle chewing pits while others feasted. I couldn't buy a house, an airline ticket or a good suit, I *always* drove a settle-for car, no other kind existed for me, and I got used to the taste of soybeans. During that seven years Amway grew from $100 to $500 million in annual sales volume. They did it without me.

By 1978, teachers and college professors, doctors, lawyers, ministers, were getting into Amway. The great network of circles was spreading into my campus. Somebody was going to make a percentage on every tube of toothpaste that passed through the groves of academe. A scholar in my building with two published books to his credit was selling soap to the local restaurants. When he came around to my office, it was not to chat with me about Richard Leakey's latest bone-find in Kenya, but to ask me if I needed a smoke detector. "I can get them at a good price," he said. I looked around at my colleagues who had not yet joined. Suddenly, perusing a volume of Dante's *Inferno* between classes, I became immensely interested in how many others might need smoke detectors. A religion professor at a different institution, within two months, would be taking students aside for special conferences, and whispering, "How would you like to help your mom fight inflation?"

I took my scholar friend to an arbitration hearing, where I was representing a union member in a grievance against our employer. My client had been screwed out of extra pay for teaching an overload. His was one of an endless parade of grievances about money and job security. I had summoned this scholar to be a witness in the hearing; I should have been helping him rehearse the answers to the questions I was going to ask him on the stand, but instead, what I questioned him about in the car was Amway. I wanted to know who else on campus he had sponsored, how much money he made, and what it cost to join.

During the proceedings I reflected on the reason I was there. It was because I depended on a job; I was not rich. I looked at the management representative on the arbitration board, and the lawyer for the Employer. The lawyer was a member of a firm that specialized in busting unions. Maybe they might want to double their incomes in twelve months as kingpins in my future sales empire. They could certainly use floor wax. For that matter, my client might need a couple of smoke detectors. He might want to sell them to the Board. All my clients did laundry; they all needed soap. It was hard to concentrate on the grievance; I was getting *excited*.

On my way home after the hearing I was sponsored.

I would shortly learn from a cassette tape the techniques for hooking others; that is, for arousing in them the same motives that had been aroused in me: the dreams of wealth and security, the fear of inflation, the desire not to be left out of the feast, the realization that my refusal to join would in no way prevent the bandwagon from moving on.

The American child passes through a stage when it seems tremendously exciting to go around the neighborhood peddling cookies, or set up a lemonade stand on the corner, and, by brash clowning and hawking, get a few dollars in his or her hot little hand that weren't put there by Mom and Dad. What keeps the insurance man plugging away, and brings warmth to the heart of the used car salesman, must be the unconscious hope of recapturing this golden time. We may resent adult sales people, but our children are rewarded for their business adventures: the teachers smile, the neighbors buy, the parents help them save. Selling in our culture is surrounded by a whole folklore of humor and approval.

When I sat there with my Amway product kit, gazing at the red, white and blue box of SA-8, and listing who would buy my soap and shampoo, and dreaming about the faraway places I would travel to on my profits, and letting the vibrations of my own culture, the great American Way, ring my nerve centers like a tuning fork, I was probably living the archetypal first experience of every new distributor. It was a return to childhood. I had given up fighting my country. I was tired of wishing we would all be enlightened and work each according to ability and take each according to need. It was too exhausting to build movements for social change and watch the members and leaders run off to Wall Street. I was bored with political discussions of any kind, having repeated them endlessly without noticeable effect for years. It was as if Vietnam and the Bay of Pigs, the assassinations of King and Malcolm X and the Kennedys, Kent State and the black uprisings, Yankee Imperialism and the hippies and yippies had never happened, and I could go back to the malt shop with Richie Cunningham and the Fonz, as my kids were doing, and start all over again from the beginning. It was like coming home on holiday, after a long separation, to meet the family.

Soon after I joined the business, the *upline*—the leaders in my particular organization—paid me a visit. These people wore three-piece suits to come and introduce themselves to me, in my messy kitchen, while I was clad in corduroys and a flannel shirt. They dress like bank vice presidents to go to the store for a loaf of bread. They cut their hair short and smile all the time, and have impeccably clean fingernails and firm practiced handshakes. They look like Mormons. They patted me on the shoulder and pulled out tickets to an event called a Seminar and Rally. Two tickets—one for me and one for my wife. I said my wife was not interested but they told me to buy two anyway, she would come around. It was *exciting* to go to a Seminar and Rally, it would *blow my mind*. If I wanted to be successful in Amway I had to attend Seminars and Rallies. Furthermore I would never succeed unless I did. In late 1978 the tickets were $4 each. I went.

THREE

THANK
YOU FOR
TEACHING US...

"The Seminar and Rally," said my mentors, tickets in hand, "is the most important function in the Amway business." They were absolutely correct. The Seminar and Rally is a periodic mass meeting of distributors and prospective recruits, which may number anywhere from a few hundred to several thousand people, brought together under one roof to be informed, inspired, motivated and indoctrinated with the attitudes, teachings and opinions of their leaders. On any given Saturday, literally hundreds of these functions are taking place in motels, convention centers, school auditoriums and coliseums from coast to coast, and, probably, in a dozen other countries and languages. Recruits, if they have "good" leadership, will be told that Seminars and Rallies are vital to building a sound business; they must attend all of them, and persuade their distributors and prospects to attend. They may even pay for their first tickets along with their starter kits.

The Seminar and Rally is the essence of Amway: the dress code, politics, values, techniques, the full spirit of the business, all concentrated into a dramatic happening that lasts from early afternoon until far into the night, with a break for dinner. At larger functions there may not be any scheduled breaks. The audience may be expected to remain in the hall for a marathon brainwash that lasts up to twelve hours at a stretch, on hard folding chairs, without eating, sleeping, or going to the restroom. "If I answer the call of nature during a Seminar," say the speakers, "I might miss the very thing that will enable me to go Crown." Going Crown is comparable to attaining the peak of Mount Everest, trailing clouds of glory, accompanied by the Mormon Tabernacle Choir.

What the revival meeting is to evangelical Christianity, the Seminar and Rally is to the world of Amway: a microcosm, a mold, a powerful social reinforcement, a mighty coming together of the chosen to celebrate their salvation. To understand the dynamics of the Seminar and Rally is to grasp the *ethos* of the whole movement.

Appropriate garb for this occasion is a coat and tie, preferably a three-piece suit for men and a dress for women. The precise dress-code may vary with time and place. In the early days of the company, the "in" costume at many Rallies was a red, white and blue outfit. Then as the organization began reaching out to attract professionals, dress became more conservative. Different lines of sponsorship have different practices, but the important common element is that dress expectations come from the top down. The leaders tell you at the function what clothes to wear. The code may be enforced by public humiliation. Men who show up looking like workers are taken aside and advised to get a suit and polish their shoes. Women are admonished from the stage that pants-suits may be very nice, but only a dress will fit the proper image of success. One of the "positive" books marketed to distributors is *Dress For Success*, by John T. Molloy (Warner Bros., Inc, October 1976; September 1978), a prescription for how to project a clean-cut, conservative business image to the world through clothing styles.

In the sixties and early seventies, young people wore Indian jewelry, tie-dyed shirts and flower-patched jeans to symbolize their repudiation of Middle American values. The Amway dress code conveys the indirect message that the era of radicalism is dead; the fifties are back.

At the front of the auditorium, a red, white and blue banner is inscribed with a huge welcome for the couple who have been brought in, sometimes flown from a great distance, to address the crowd: "TO JOHN AND MARY DOE, THANK YOU FOR TEACHING US TO BE FREE." The host appears on the stage first to do the warm-up. The host/hostess team will usually be a local couple who have just made it to the level of Direct Distributor. Husband and Wife come on together. Both partners speak; wife first, then husband. The lion's share of the time usually goes to the man.

Speakers are groomed and tested carefully for commitment to the value system before they are allowed to conduct a Seminar and Rally. Hosting is one of the means by which the upper echelons prepare the new Direct Distributors for their leadership roles.

Picture yourself in a huge theater, packed with sales people smiling and shaking hands, many displaying pins on their jackets to identify their award level. Some put business cards and clothing down on seats to save sections for their particular groups, although the host may take the microphone to discourage saving of seats. The local leaders stand at the door and shake hands and wave, and pat new-comers on the shoulder: "How ya doin'...glad to see ya...great you could make it." Music by the Sammy Hall Singers is usually piped in over the P.A. system. Sammy Hall is a born-again ex-hippie who writes songs specifically for Amway functions, such as "I'm Excited, How About You" "Don't Let Anyone Steal Your Dream," and "Circles, Crazy Circles." The music helps create a revivalist atmosphere.

Some time after 2 p.m. the host walks on and the whole congregation breaks into applause. "Are you excited?" he asks. "I'm excited! Show me how excited you are! What a sharp bunch of people! Look at the tremendous growth we've had here since the last Seminar! Next time we'll have to find a bigger place!"

Now the audience is led in prayer. This is a typical prayer, with no exaggeration or parody: "O Lord, we thank you for this great Country of ours, and for this opportunity to build our Amway business. We know there are many countries where we would not be allowed to have this wonderful opportunity, Lord, and we ask Your blessing so we may build this Business strong in order to keep our Country free." Following the Prayer is the Pledge of Allegiance to the Flag. After a lead-off like that, to find fault with the teachings would be like putting down the Boy Scouts.

When a school auditorium is used as a meeting place, to pray on the site from which the Supreme Court has banned prayer expresses the contempt that many leaders feel for the absence of prayer in the public schools. They do in their meeting what they would like to see done in the classroom.

The host eulogizes the main speakers for a few minutes: "They really know how to put this thing together; let 'em know how grateful we are that they came all the way out here to share their love with us..." In a marvelous bit of irony, the people who pay this leader's travel expenses and a good deal more besides in ticket sales, and who, if he is in their own upline, have made him rich by building his organization, are asked to be grateful because he is willing to give them a Seminar on how to build it even bigger. They respond, not only with gratitude, but wild enthusiasm. It is magnificent to watch. When the host shouts the names of the speakers—"Diamond Direct Distributors...John and Mary Doe!"—the entire crowd gives them a yelling, stomping, whistling, standing ovation as they run onstage from the wings.

At the bigger functions in 1979-1980, the introduction of the main speaker was sometimes accompanied, significantly, by the music from *Rocky*. Sylvester Stallone's hero is the prototypical

American winner, the poor boy who believes in himself enough to seize his opportunity when it knocks. To succeed, Rocky must be totally committed to his goal, he must work hard, train rigorously, be willing to defer sensual gratification to the future and do whatever it takes in the present to win. All this is part of the Amway message.

For the next three hours, the speakers tell the audience what they have to do in order to be winners. You must have a Dream. You must Believe. You must have faith in the products and the Corporation. You must have faith in your leaders. You must do everything they say. They have a vested interest in your business and they know more than you. They have only your success at heart; because, you see, if you understand this business, you realize that no Direct is going to tell his distributors anything that would hurt them, he would only hurt himself. So before you buy a house, check it out with your upline. Before you get a motor home, ask them what kind to buy and when. Before you read a book, find out if it's on their recommended list. Buy tapes and listen to them every day. Get a tape player for your car and plug in a tape on the way to work. Listen to tapes before you go to bed. Stock your bathroom with the "positive" books from the list. Take in Positive while you're eliminating Negative.

"You've got some fantastic leaders here...you've got the best upline in the business...they really know what they're doing...listen to them, don't go off on your own trying to re-invent the wheel." Now, just as the host eulogizes the speakers, they in turn will praise the local leadership, and the crowd applauds on cue. Directs, Silvers, and anxious go-getters lead the applause.

The Seminar covers the basics of the Amway business: how to call on prospects; what to say and what not to say; how to overcome the fear of using the telephone and talking to strangers; how to recruit people and how to help them "stay plugged in."

But none of this effort will get you anywhere if you don't have the Dream. Your Dream is the reason you are in the business. Much of the Seminar, like the Plan, is devoted to building the Dream. It is a thoroughly consumerist and materialist craving which the leaders do everything possible to instill into their distributor force: driving Cadillacs and motor homes, owning a twenty-bedroom house in the richest part of town, arousing the envy of neighbors, spending a month on a Caribbean Island, travelling first-class to Hawaii and being waited on by servants, wearing furs and diamonds, hob-nobbing with movie stars, having lots of status and money in the bank. A dream that could not be satisfied with money, such as wisdom, or co-operative ownership of industry, would have no place here. Altruistic dreams are mentioned strictly in the context of accepted middle-class formulas: giving money to a church, for example, or providing jobs for maids, are acceptable Unselfish Dreams.

There is no conflict between being rich and being saved. God wants you to succeed. If there were anything wrong with diamonds, God would not use them to decorate Heaven. You must have money to perform good deeds. "Without materialism," the speaker might add, switching off the microphone to dramatize his point, "you could not even hear my voice." Thoreau's concept that it might be more unselfish to employ yourself in your kitchen rather than accumulate wealth to employ someone else there, would seem incomprehensible within this flag-draped hall.

Once you have a Dream, you must transform it into a Goal. Cut out pictures of your Dream and put them on your refrigerator: the Cadillac, the new furniture, the new home, whatever it might be. Then transform the Goal into a Burning Desire. It is not enough to want something; you have to need it. When you *need* a Cadillac, when you put pictures of the Cadillac all over your house, when you ride in the Cadillac and smell the leather and push the buttons and sink into the comfortable seats, then you will have a Cadillac. Whether you will be happy after you get it is not a question that troubles Amway people. The fact that goals, once achieved, turn to ash, giving the achiever a momentary bitter taste of the futility of all earthly goals, is already foreseen by the Dream-builders: merely set a bigger Goal, a better house, a more luxurious bathroom, a whole collection of Cadillacs and then a Rolls Royce.

The ABCs of Success (spelled $U¢¢E$$) are Attitude, Belief and Commitment. These are some of the attitudes expected of a successful distributor: Amway is the greatest Corporation in the world; the products are the best products in the world; the free enterprise system is the best system in the world; your particular upline is the best leadership in the business; anybody that wants to be rich can do it; those who are not rich are lazy or stupid; poverty is the fault of the poor; there is no excuse for failure; only losers complain and criticize; when faced with insurmountable obstacles you will not quit; there are no problems, only challenges; winners never quit and quitters never win.

You must guard your Attitude as if it were a casket of precious jewels. Don't let anyone steal your Attitude. Don't listen to anyone who might weaken your faith in the business. If your friends disapprove of Amway, do not associate with them: they are not walking the winner's path. Your paths will diverge sooner or later anyway, so you might as well leave them now. They are losers, and, by joining Amway, you have chosen to walk with the winners.

Believe you will succeed and you will. Believe in yourself, believe in God and his Church, believe in people, believe in your Country, believe in the Corporation, believe in your upline. Faith will move mountains. If you say you can't do it, then you won't. You never "try"; you either do it or you don't. The past tense of try is tried; the past tense of do is did. One is action and the other is an excuse. Thomas Edison believed he would succeed; so did Henry Ford and George Washington. You are snared by the word of your mouth. You are hung by the tongue. Never confess doubt. Say that you will go Direct, set a date when you will go Direct, talk about going Direct and you will go Direct. The speaker leads the audience in chants: "I'm gonna be a Diamond, period!" Whatever the mind can conceive and believe, it can achieve. "Some of you are sayin' 'We don't want them big old Cadillacs and motor homes.' And God is up there sayin' 'I hear ya! I hear ya!' If you don't ask for it, you won't get it!" You get what you ask for. "I'm gonna make it, *period*! No ifs, ands or buts. Say it! I'm gonna do whatever it takes! Say it!" The speaker works on the group until they are on their feet shouting in unison: "I'm gonna be a Diamond *period*! Whatever it takes! I'm gonna be a Diamond *period*!"

A short part of the Seminar is given to warnings against the dangers of Negative. Whatever influence weakens your belief and commitment in the business is Negative. The brother-in-law who laughs at you is Negative. The "friend" who says it won't work is Negative. Expressions like "I'll try," and "I'll never own a nice home," and "Maybe I'll see if this works, and if it doesn't, I'll quit," are all Negative. Argument and criticism are Negative. Any product which competes with an Amway product is Negative. Failure to attend any function put on by your upline, or to follow all of their instructions, is Negative. Refusal to buy a tape when recommended by the upline is Negative. It is Negative to complain about the expense of functions, or find fault with the speakers, or make the excuse that you can't go to Seminar and Rally because you can't afford a babysitter.

During two years of Seminars, I heard statements like these, repeated over and over by speakers at various high pin levels:

"I cleared all those Negative products out of my home: all the Crest, and the Prell, and the Spic-and-Span, we put all the Brand X in a big box and gave it away...I don't allow any Negative in my house."

"When we were new in the business, my sponsor came to our house and went into our bathroom, and found my tube of Crest. I didn't like Amway toothpaste, and I decided that I wasn't going to use it. And she wrote on the mirror with the Crest, 'I love Amway toothpaste.' Then she came out and said, 'I want you to go look in your mirror.' Well, that day I learned my lesson.''

"Tide won't put your kids through college. Tide won't buy you a Cadillac and a new home. Tide won't give you a retirement income. So get rid of it. Every new distributor should have his home completely converted to Amway products within three months of getting in the business.''

"There's a very simple principle about reading; it's called GIGO. Garbage in, garbage out. If you read garbage, that's what will come out of you. I got rid of *Playboy*. I read what my sponsor tells me to read. If I have any doubts about whether to read a certain book, I check our approved reading list.''

"God is Positive, and the Devil is Negative. The Devil wants people to have jobs and worry about money and be under financial pressure...people out there are prayin' the Lord will show them a way out. And you know what? This business is the answer to those prayers.''

To use competing products, to question the Amway system, to associate with friends who try to steal your Dream by deriding Amway, is, by implication, allying yourself with the forces of darkness and despair and poverty against the forces of light and hope and wealth.

The commitment required of a distributor to achieve the profitable pin-levels is implied in the phrase "Whatever it takes." Amway people, according to Dusty Owens, a top sales performer and Country Western singer, are never asked to give up anything important in life, such as devotion to God, Country and the Family. Indeed, these devotions are inculcated, reinforced, and assimilated into the business as part of the motivational package. It will be necessary, however, to give up your recreations and friends. These needs will then be met by activities within the business. Amway offers new friends; Amway functions and trips provide new recreations. The new friends might eventually include the high pin levels; if you work hard and achieve those pin levels, you may look forward to lounging "the beaches of the world" with the top leaders. The new recreations cost money, and are held out as carrots to motivate performance.

No one tells these facts to new distributors; they are eased into the funhouse gradually, through the tapes and Seminars, and through the actual practice of building a group. A recruit is told only that the business may demand ten to fifteen hours a week of his spare time; not a bad investment for a chance to make an extra fifty to a hundred thousand dollars a year. But at Seminars he will be encouraged to spend five or six nights a week "drawing circles," or showing the Plan to prospects. On that schedule it is impossible to have many other interests in life besides Amway. I have seen speakers work their audience into chanting "Five and six! Nights a week! Five and six! Nights a week!" At the larger functions, which go on and on long after midnight, crowds sometimes pour into the streets at three in the morning still chanting "Five and six! Nights a week!"

There is no specific time requirement imposed on the sales force by Amway Corporation, as the Company maintains the legal fiction that this is "your business." No distributor is an Amway employee; you are free to choose your own hours and level of commitment. In practice, however, your leaders, if they are sufficiently zealous, and if they think you have any promise, will do everything they can to extract a maximum performance out of you. This is not necessarily bad, provided that you don't mind eating, sleeping, living and dreaming Amway for the rest of your life and are possessed with a burning thirst to be rich, and a religious conviction that Amway is the highest path to wealth and happiness.

Most Seminars cover the important topic of how to strengthen the commitment in a group. The essential ingredient is for the leader to be totally committed himself. It will be the objective of the upline Directs, in their association with a potential leader, to find out his "hot button," that is, his particular needs and greeds. If he likes cars, they take him to a Mercedes or Porsche dealer and have him test-drive the most expensive models. If he likes homes, they take him on tours through wealthy neighborhoods. If he wants to escape his nine-to-five job, they might visit him at two in the morning and invite him to a pool-side party; then suddenly look at their watches and exclaim "Oh no! We forgot! You've got a job!" And spin off in their Cadillacs in a cloud of dust. Or they help him plan his retirement parade, in a fleet of Cadillacs through the center of town, with a plane overhead, flying a banner that reads, "Ain't it Great." This kind of manipulation may be accompanied by a rich sense of humor, but the message is clear: for the time being, give up golf, give up bowling, give up television, give up fishing, give up karate and music. Do Amway. Later you might return to some of your recreations, with Amway friends, in the context of the Amway business.

By the same token, distributors are told not to waste time on people who refuse to commit themselves. "Don't try to run a race with a dead horse. If you get on a horse and the bell rings and he runs a few yards and falls down on the ground, don't stand there and beat him. Go get another horse. If you drop in on one of your distributors and he's on the couch with his feet up watching the boob tube, fold his hands over his chest and put a daisy in his hand and say a few words over him and go find somebody else." Likewise apply the same standard to yourself. If you steadfastly refuse to be totally committed to the business, expect no help from upline. You are on your own. The friendly smiling upline leaders will shun you. As we shall see, the more successful you are in Amway, the more you have to lose by getting out and by being ostracized. The leaders acquire power over a distributor's life, which is not to be lightly resisted, and which, in many ways, for many people, is more complete that any power exercised by a boss over his employees, even in the age of the robber barons.

Committed distributors are ones who "duplicate properly," that is, do precisely what they are told. They cut their hair the way they are told to cut their hair. They spend a minimum of three nights a week recruiting, a day for product flow and a day for retail sales. They follow directions exactly as given. They call their leaders frequently, usually late at night, after they finish drawing circles. Committed distributors "stay plugged in." They cut down on sleep. "Pretty soon we find that we don't need all that sleep, we're on the road goin' someplace, man, we're excited!"

Committed distributors are expected to attend every function put on by their upline. The functions are crucial, because it is by means of them that "correct duplication" takes hold throughout the group. Distributors buy tickets, meals and lodging, and they drive, or fly, sometimes over thousands of miles for Seminars and Rallies, leadership training, Family Reunions, Extravaganzas, Free Enterprise Days, and Dream Nights, all at their own cost. They must be willing to invest in "their" business, but if they deviate from the leader's advice, they are told it is the leader's business too, and if they want help they better learn to conform. Up to twenty-six functions are held in a year. If anyone has a problem getting the money for them, the solution is simple: sell some vitamins. Sell some cookware. Sell a few boxes of soap. Sell your color television. Do whatever you have to do, but get there.

A major objective of the Seminar is to make the audience commit themselves publicly to the expense of the next big function. This is done in stages: first you are shown a movie of scenes from last year's bash—the leaders playing golf and riding horseback, the women wearing gowns and diamonds, the executive motor homes of the upline, the chandeliers in the dining hall, smiling faces, crowds of excited, happy people. Then the Pearls and Emeralds come onstage and describe how much the event meant to them, in terms of love, goodwill and friendship. And where else can you get a vacation as wonderful as this which is also tax deductible? Then the main speaker narrates how, when he first got in the business, he didn't understand the importance of Family Reunion, Free Enterprise Day and Dream Night, but he wrote a check for the cost weeks beforehand, not knowing how it would be covered; but he believed that if his sponsor said he had to be there, then he'd better go.

"We went to our first Free Enterprise in a dented Volkswagen and ate peanut-butter sandwiches and slept in a tent...." Now they fly first-class or drive in their motor coach. The lesson: you get to be a Diamond by making sacrifices right from the beginning, even when you have no money. When you reach the top, you too can go in style. If you don't go to the functions, you probably won't do anything with the business and you might as well drop out.

The final stage in extracting the commitment is for the speaker to ask, "How many of you are planning on being a Direct? Stand up." Not to stand up is a confession that you are just playing with the business, you are not serious about it, you don't plan to make any money; or worse, an admission that you are a loser and have not read the "positive" books. Then: "How many of you are going to Free Enterprise Day? Remain standing. You Directs, look around. Remember this. As soon as you leave here this afternoon, write a check and get your money in. If you don't do it now, we can't guarantee there will be any tickets left at the last minute." Although I never knew of one major function, during three active years in Amway, that was completely sold out in advance, where Directs were not trying to unload tickets at the last minute, and oversold distributors were not standing at the gate offering excess tickets to the crowd, the speakers inevitably repeat this technique of "buy now while they last."

The speaker may also take a shot at television soap operas: "Who wants to watch a program about some guy running around with some other guy's wife?" Attacks on television usually get an outburst of spontaneous applause. The criteria for rejecting the soap opera is not the mass-produced plot situations or the stereotypical and shallow characterizations, but simply the subject matter. A strong sentiment exists in Amway crowds to censor literature—to remove offensive books from public schools and "immoral" themes from television screens.

Television programming is made symbolic of everything that is Negative in American life: laziness, beer-drinking, adultery, high divorce rate, creeping Socialism. The leaders know that if a distributor is to build a solid sales organization he or she must quit watching television and go out there and show the Plan; but this also removes an influence on the mind that might contradict the programming of the Seminars. Presumably, when Seminars, like Amway commercials, can be televised, and the channels, like the Mutual

Broadcasting System, are owned by Amway, and the PTL soap-testimonial has replaced the soap opera (SA-8 would be the soap in question), then television will be welcomed back as a Positive.

With admonitions to keep the hall clean ("remember, we're in a soap business"), the audience is released for dinner, at regular small-scale functions, between five and six o'clock. "Do you know someone in your group who isn't here? Go call them up and get them to the Rally at eight."

FOUR

RALLY
FEVER

Charles Paul Conn, in *The Winner's Circle*, thought that Rallies "seemed natural and wholesome and—well, for want of a better word—fun!" (see page 8). He observed a "holiday atmosphere" of convivial, cheerful, boisterous crowds that "didn't fit my mold—or any other mold." The people, relaxed and smiling, "seemed to know one another on sight, and were eager to mix and mingle."* A "natural" and "wholesome" Rally; like a breakfast cereal that uses honey instead of sugar. The Seminar is only the appetizer; the Rally is the main course. It is by this means that Amway "gets into you."

The hierarchy of pin levels is stamped on this ceremony in all kinds of ingenious ways. The curb space around the convention center is reserved for the Cadillacs and motor homes of the Emeralds and Diamonds. Lowly distributors making every sacrifice to come to the function carrying peanut-butter sandwiches in their battered Volkswagens had better not pull up in Cadillac row; one or more of the Directs and Silvers, the ushers and altar boys of the event, will appear promptly to chase them off. At a large Extravaganza, even the Pearls may be forced to scramble for a parking space blocks away from the building. The purpose is two-fold: to exhibit the visible emblems of wealth to distributors entering and leaving the center, and to suggest in every way possible that achievement in Amway means recognition, privilege, a softer life, less far to walk, higher status, greater wealth and power.

At dinner the hierarchy is observed by choice of restaurant and company. The Directs eat together. Ordinary distributors are not allowed to eat with the Directs. On special occasions, Directs may not be allowed to eat with the higher pins. These make a point of dining at

The Winner's Circle (Berkley Publishers, 1980), p.8.

what they conceive as the most exclusive places—a tax-deductible expense because it is used to motivate the rank and file. If by chance some regular distributors appear at the same restaurant, the Directs may seal themselves off in a special room or turn their backs.

Distributors approaching a table full of Directs may be asked, "When are you going Direct?" This question, from a higher pin, is a way of asserting rank; it reminds them that they are not yet Directs. The right answer is to come back with a specific date, no more than ninety days in the future; an individual or uncertain response shows that they do not set goals, do not follow advice and are therefore fools, unworthy of attention.

"June first."

"Come back in June, then, you can't sit at this table until you reach 7500 PV."

Conversation at the dinner table of an Amway group runs in predictable grooves:

"What's your dream?"

"I went to look at Cadillacs this morning...fantastic! I couldn't figure out what all the buttons are for."

"Did you prospect the salesman?"

"Got his name and phone number right here in my book."

"Where's Pete?"

"He's over there prospecting the waiter."

"Darn! He got there before I did."

"How's Jack doing?"

"He drew the circles on his own four times last week. He says two couples are getting in for sure, and two others want to see it again."

"Ain't it great! When are you going Direct?"

"Ninety days. Got the date on my refrigerator door."

It is an unwritten law that alcohol and business do not mix. In the Yager line, this law extends even to meals; distributors with a glass of wine at their plate during dinner are breaking a taboo. They may as well pick their noses and wipe the contents on the table cloth.

The most bizarre display of dining hierarchy that I witnessed was at the Bryan Family Reunion in 1980, a huge Rally held at the Place Bonaventure convention center in Montreal and attended by perhaps four or five thousand people. Dinner was catered in the center itself, buffet style, the tables covering a city block of floor space. Above the main floor was a mezzanine balcony set with tables. The distributors thronged into the hall and stood in long lines to get their second-rate food (pre-paid, with the tickets, at Filet Mignon prices), mass-produced in the characteristic institutional mode, ladled onto their cheap plates from big steel pots. The Directs, wearing sky-blue tuxedoes with ruffles at breast and cuff to distinguish them from the regular rank and file three-piece suit, went from table to table, greeting and ushering the members of their groups, flashing the ubiquitous Amway smile, before assembling in their own section at the head of the floor.

Then a Direct appeared and unrolled a wine-red carpet from the door, along the wall, and up the stairs to the mezzanine, where the tables, set with linen cloths and crystal glasses, were just barely visible over the railing. A herald entered and announced, "Ladies and gentlemen, the Pearls and Emeralds of the Downeast Direct Distributors Association!" Accompanied by actual trumpet fanfare, the Pearls and Emeralds, wearing black tuxedoes to distinguish them from the junior baby-blue of the Directs, marched in order of pin level along the carpet and up to the balcony. Each was seated by a waiter. Thus exalted over the heads of the sales force who put them there, the jewels ordered from a menu and were waited on by a team of servants, in full view of the masses standing in line at the pots below. Occasionally a leader (always a man) would walk over to the railing and look down, and be greeted by a few whistles and cheers, especially from his own group.

In the entryway to the building, people at literature tables pass out leaflets from "Citizen's Choice," a right-wing political pressure group founded by Jay Van Andel in 1976, whose main purpose is to lobby for a complete dismantling of the New Deal and Great Society programs passed by Democratic administrations in the last fifty years. "Citizen's Choice" worked very hard to get Reagan and a Republican Congress elected in 1980, and, as of 1981, boasted a growth rate of 100 per cent within twelve months and a membership of 70,000.[*]

Vendors also hawk sweatshirts at the doors inscribed with the familiar circle pattern and slogans like "I'm excited!" and "Keep on doin' it to it!" Ticket takers demand that you smile before they let you in.

Crowds begin filling the auditorium sometimes as much as an hour before the Rally, which usually kicks off at 8:15 with a mighty burst of applause. Distributors wear Amway jewelry and conspicuously squirt their mouths with Sweet Shot, an Amway aerosol breath-freshener in a pocket-size cartridge. Waves of reciprocal chanting sweep back and forth over the hall, one side shouting "Ain't it Great!" and the other answering "Ain't it Though!" In a regional event, thousands flick their Bics, or other brand-name propane lighters (Amway does not yet manufacture one) and whirl the flames in a circle

---

[*]Says the December 1981 issue of *The Amagram:* "Citizen's Choice is determined to turn the tide and *keep it turned,*" p. 16.

to symbolize the mystical force of the Plan. In a dark hall, row upon row of little flames spiral in the air, to the beat of "Circles, Crazy Circles." Slogans and circles are flashed on a huge video screen at the front of the amphitheater, strobe-light style, in time to the music. The planners of the Rally borrow crowd-hypnosis techniques of this kind from the rock concert, but with a specific political objective. Rock musicians only want the crowd's money and applause; Amway leaders, in addition, want their loyalty, commitment and belief.

The use of rock music at Amway Rallies is profoundly ironic. Leaders in the business openly attack the culture of rock as "liberal decadence," corrupting the minds of the young with drugs, loose morals and Satanism. But what they borrow from that culture is precisely the noise, lights, herd instinct, hoopla and emotionalism which deaden wakefulness and blunt the capacity for intelligent thought. Part of the Amway purpose is to provide an alternative to rock-rallies by emptying the *content* of any ideas that might question the private profit system, and using the *form* to convey the Amway pro-corporate ideology. From the leaders' point of view, this is changing the Negative into Positive.

The appearance of the host and hostess is greeted by a standing ovation. Indeed, the entrance and exit of every speaker calls for a standing ovation throughout the entire night. At Extravaganzas, people sometimes stand on seats and clap with their hands over their heads. But the standing ovation is not quite a spontaneous, natural, wholesome, cheerful outburst of convivial admiration; Silvers, Directs, 4000 pins and distributors eager to impress their groups form a claque; they stand in the aisles and at the front and back of the auditorium to bring the crowd to its feet. Always the distributors I could observe and overhear found the fifth, sixth, seventh, eighth and ninth standing ovation tiresome; you begin to feel like a jack-in-the-box. The pressure of mass behavior, led by the claque, keeps pushing your button. If your sponsor stands up, not to follow suit would be Negative; it would imply disapproval of the Rally. It would set a bad example for the people in your group.

In Step One of the introduction, the host works to excite the crowd: "Are you excited?! Show me how excited you are! Make the chandeliers rock! What's that? You call that excitement? All right, the left side of the hall. Only the left side. Let me hear it! Now the right side! Are you excited?!" He plays one part of the crowd off against the other part until everyone in the room is committed to yelling, in unison, "I'm excited! Yes! I'm excited!"

Step Two could be titled The Description of the Food. In this phase the host draws a word picture of the opulent surroundings and

luxuriant gourmet banquet just enjoyed by the Directs during dinner
break. "Just imagine this thick juicy steak...and the salad bar, wow!
It must have covered half the floor! We had at least four courses.
Wouldn't you like to go out to a dinner like that every week and not
have to think about the price? How many of you would like to dine at
a banquet like that in the company of Tim Bryan or Bill Britt and
Dexter Yager? These are the kind of people I'd like to spend the rest of
my life with. How about you?"

One realizes only after a diet of many Rallies that these steps are a
planned, orchestrated format, a kind of drama-pageant observed and
duplicated strictly in widely separated functions from Nova Scotia to
Florida.

In Step Three, the host goes on to ask, "How many people here
are under twenty? How many are over sixty-five? How many drove
more than four hours to get here? How many drove eight hours? Who
do we have from Connecticut? Anyone from New Jersey? Anyone
from Massachusetts?" Each question is a cue for shouting, whistling
and vigorous applause. The extremes of age are recognized, and the
extremes of distance and the identity of state. Not only is the crowd
encouraged to develop *esprit de corps*, but they are taught that you can
build the Amway business at any age over eighteen, in any area where
products are shipped. Age and distance are no excuses for staying
home.

For the Rally the leaders usually change into evening clothes: the
men wear lighter colors and put carnations in the lapels of their coats,
the women wear sumptuous gowns. Speakers who have attained the
Diamond level bedeck themselves with diamonds and furs.

At large functions, the wives may come out to the microphone
and sing songs. The type of song is in the Pat Boone Baptist choir
mode, like a musical Hostess Twinkie, filled with natural and
wholesome Whisker Whiz, surrounded by a halo, served in the top
floor dining room of the Sheraton Christ-the-Crown Motor Church.
Rallies provide an opportunity for ordinary housewives and secre-
taries to dress up like movie stars and command standing ovations for
crooning "You Light Up My Life" before a captive audience.

Following the "entertainment" is the giving of awards. In my
line of sponsorship, the first pin that is awarded and recognized on the
stage is the 1500 pin. For this you must achieve 1500 PV in any one
month. The 1500 couple go across the stage, state their name, address
and occupation, and get brief applause from their group. The 4000
pin is the same scenario, except that, at smaller Rallies, distributors at
this level may be allowed to sit on the stage with the Directs. Not until
they receive the Silver Producer or 7500 pin are the distributors

permitted to "say a few words" at the microphone. Public speaking, like dress, dining, parking and the possession of luxuries, is subject to a rigid status hierarchy. An additional reason for the control over who speaks is that the leaders want no one at the microphone until he or she has been tested and observed for complete loyalty. Recognized last are the leaders who have broken into the higher pin-levels—the Gold Direct who just made Ruby, the Pearl who now qualifies for Emerald.

The message conveyed by the awards is that only one kind of achievement matters in a distributor's life: high PV. This is the only source of income, until distributors get big enough to put on their own functions and sell their own tapes. This is also the reference point for the hierarchy, and the awards, and the reason for being of the entire world of Amway. When Amway "gets into you," and "correct duplication" has captured your brain and heart, and you depend on Amway bonuses for a living, PV becomes the reason for being of your own existence as well; PV is like salvation, or the path to Enlightenment in yoga. "Let me tell you...my PV last week was ten thousand. All I can say is...thank God for this great Country of ours!"

The conferring of a high pin makes a hero out of the recipient, a model of duplication, to be emulated as an authority on marriage, human relations, politics and leadership. People with no talent or wisdom, by repeating the Plan hundreds of times and correctly doing everything they are told to do, may rise to eminence on the graph of their PV, convinced that they have unlocked their "hidden potential." They then have a chance to live out their ego fantasies before an adoring multitude. A "plain Jane" can be Queen of the Prom. A walking parody of Jerry Falwell can advocate banning abortion and jailing homosexuals from an Amway pulpit, and be cheered into believing he is an important cultural pace-setter. Couples who know nothing about family therapy can give lectures on how to attain harmonious marital relations. Despite the prompting of the claques, distributors do show genuine enthusiasm for this weird world, in which one of their number, perhaps one or two in a hundred, if they faithfully persist and obey the system in every particular, can realistically hope to get onstage someday and deliver speeches like the very worst pep-talks in high school assemblies; and the audience, instead of throwing spitballs, will stand and applaud.

The main event of the evening is the Personal Story. The speakers appear, one at a time, first wife, then husband (hierarchy also, and especially, applies to the relations between the sexes) to narrate what they were doing when they first saw the Plan, what they thought of it, what they wanted from it, why they got in, what obstacles they had to overcome on the road to success, and how Amway has changed their lives and improved their marriage. Over the course of many Rallies by various speakers, the Personal Story is seen to be a definite *genre*, a confessional autobiography, similar in purpose to the testimony of born-again Christians on PTL television programs. This is a rough outline of the form:

1. Before Amway, we worried about money. The husband drank too much. The wife, bored and unfulfilled, was thinking about divorce. We were both stuck in a rut, going back and forth between home and work. There was too much month left over at the end of the money. Our job, or business, was on the rocks. The government took a huge bite of our income for taxes. We had to put down other people in order to make a living. We were shy and afraid to speak in public. We had little time for each other. Our kids hardly knew they had a father.

2. We saw the Amway Plan—a bunch of crazy circles on a board. I didn't want it but my spouse did, or vice-versa. I thought it would save him/her from alcohol, despair or a bad investment. Our thinking was small; we wanted a chainsaw, washing machine, dryer. We were cynical and Negative and our attitude stank. But our sponsor, and/or the sponsor's upline, had faith in us even though we had no faith in ourselves.

3. We floundered around doing the business our way and didn't get anywhere. Then we went to our first Seminar and Rally and things really began to happen. We plugged into the system and learned to do exactly as we were told. When we duplicated properly, our volume went up and we grew fast. We went to all the functions, that is, after we wised up. We listened to the tapes and read the books and got excited. Finally we went over the top. We missed our goal a few times but we hung in there and persisted.

4. Now we have money in the bank, jewels, beautiful clothes, a nice house with a swimming pool, nice cars. We take vacations in Hawaii. We spend lots of time with each other. We stopped drinking and we work together on common goals. We love to speak in public and we have hundreds of new friends. We get up in the morning at the crack of noon. We earned our freedom and now it is ours to enjoy. No boss controls our destiny any more. The neighbors look out at the great big motor home parked in our yard. How sweet it is to be married to a winner.

5. Our friends who laughed at us are still living in the same dumpy neighborhoods and driving the same rusted-out cars. We had a retirement parade through the middle of town in a fleet of Cadillacs. Everybody was watching and wondering "Who's that, some foreign

diplomat?'' We gave a retirement present to our ex-boss. We ought to thank him for being such a tyrant; by this time he must be making almost as much money as we are. The few friends that got in with us, who were smart enough to see the potential of this business, are just going Direct, and they will travel with us to the beaches of the world.

6. Some people say that we got in on the ground floor, when the time was right. But the right time to get in is now. Amway is going to be the largest Corporation in the world. (Loud cheering.) You people getting in now have all kinds of support that we didn't have. You've got television commercials. You've got all the latest research and development. You've got a system already built for you. It took us over a year to make Direct; you can do it in ninety days. In the future, people will be making Diamond in less than a year. (Applause.) So realize what you've got in your hands.

7. Although we have all the money we want, the most important thing in the Amway business is Love. Amway taught us how to love people. Amway saved our marriage. Our kids, growing up in an Amway household, are learning to set goals and be positive thinkers. True success is founded upon the success of others. We made it by helping people, not by putting them down. Only in Amway could we have found the opportunity to change people's lives in such positive ways. That's something you just can't buy.

8. You can have anything you want from this business. You can have furs. . . (the wife casually drops an expensive mink on the stage floor). . . you can have fancy cars, you can travel, you can have your own plane, you can have freedom—but you have to be willing to pay the price. You have to show the Plan when you would rather be watching baseball. You have to suffer temporary inconvenience to get permanent improvement. But I'm here to tell you, it's worth it, believe me, we know; we've been poor. Successful people make a habit of doing what unsuccessful people are not willing to do. So keep on keeping on. Keep on doin' it to it. And we'll see you on the beaches of the world.

By stripping these confessionals down to their essential form, I do not mean to imply that they are all insincere. Some are obviously smug and slick, but many are moving accounts of the moral chaos, uncertainty, and psychological suffering which have accompanied the economic decline of the middle class over the last fifteen years. Husbands and wives bare their souls to their audience, with tears streaming down their faces, as they recount the tensions and quarrels that divided them before Amway came into their lives. In each case, it is the Amway opportunity that leads them on to eventual prosperity and triumph. Their naive cynicism about the business when they first saw it is recounted with humor: "I threw our sponsor out of the house...I was a classical pianist and this man wanted me to go around the neighborhood peddling soap...at my first Rally I thought all the people were squirting drugs into their mouths." The distributors in the audience laugh knowingly; these are precisely the negative attitudes which they encounter when they go looking for recruits.

But whether sincere or not, the Personal Story is a product of duplication, a consciously arranged narrative, always similar from Rally to Rally and place to place, always leading to the main theme: Amway saves. There is hope with soap. You can do it too.

A regular monthly Rally ends shortly after the Personal Stories of husband and wife are concluded. All the Directs come up on stage and join hands, and the rows of people join hands in the auditorium, and the whole crowd, swaying gently back and forth, sings "God Bless America."

Then the speakers form a receiving line, and the couples in the audience line up to shake their hands. Up and coming distributors, new 1500 and 4000 pins, have a chance to prove their loyalty by cleaning the hall, taking the banner down from the stage and putting away the folding chairs.

Extravaganzas, Family Reunions, Free Enterprise Days and Dream Nights are special functions on a grand scale, and have multiple sets of speakers, each with their own Seminar and Personal Story. None of them seems to be under much constraint of time limit; they go on talking as long as the spirit moves. Some wait at the microphone for the Lord to tell them what to say. The Lord usually puts into their mouths a string of banalities about attitude and commitment, which they offer like pearls of prophecy, and the audience, incredibly, keeps on standing and clapping. Interspersed with these ego trips are fashion shows (a Dream Night special), musical performances and speeches by prominent right-wing political and religious leaders.

The Extravaganza is larger than a regular Rally but follows the same format (for twice the cost). Where the monthly Rally is located within a hundred miles of the distributor's home, and draws mostly a local crowd, the Extravaganza is intended to bring together all the distributors of a multi-state region, and is held in a civic center of an important city. These functions are scheduled in Spring and Fall, coinciding approximately with Easter and Thanksgiving. An additional one may be given in February.

Family Reunion, Dream Night and Free Enterprise Day usually involve a package price of $200-$300, which buys hotel accommodations, entrance to all the events and one meal for two to three days. Other meals are in addition to the tickets. Distributors were not allowed to cut costs by foregoing the hotel reservations even if they had relatives and friends in the area to stay with. They had to buy the entire package. Family Reunion fell around the Fourth of July, Free Enterprise Day was planned—no doubt deliberately—to correspond with Labor Day, and Dream Night was placed near the Christmas season. Every major holiday of the American calendar is thus made to correspond with an Amway function. For committed distributors, taking to heart the admonition that every function is vital, and wishing to "stay plugged in," the claim of the organization on their time and interests is total. As they rise on the PV scale they become eligible for "leadership" training Seminars, which they must attend *in addition to* the regular functions and spectaculars. What is taught in the leadership Seminars will be covered in a later chapter.

Amway Corporation does not sponsor all these gatherings, or make the arrangements for them, although one often sees Company representatives present and speaking from the stage. The relationship between the Company and any Direct Distributor is controlled legally and officially by the Amway Code of Ethics and the Direct Distributor's Manual. Neither of these documents contains a prescription for how to run functions. The big organizations within Amway compete with one another economically, put on their own functions and sometimes even maintain their own warehouse and shipping facilities for the products. It is questionable how much the Corporation can be held responsible for the cultist hoopla of the Yager Rallies. In 1979 and 1980, while one leader was leaping out on the stages of mass Extravaganzas brandishing a gold crucifix, and others stood at the microphone calling on the Lord to tell them what to say, the Corporation was publishing editorials in *The Amagram* defending the principle of diversity in religious and political beliefs. Rallies put on by non-Yager Amway groups may not correspond to every detail reported here—some provide more outrageous examples of cultism—but there cannot be great variation from group to group.

The Corporation itself sponsors regional conventions, which were, interestingly, not advertised by the Yager people during the time I was in the business. Free Enterprise Day, a Yager special held in Charlotte, North Carolina, was ballyhooed for months in advance at every Seminar and Rally; the pressure to attend was intense; distributors were told that if they didn't go to Free Enterprise Day they would never make Direct, they would probably quit the business within a year, and if they wanted any help from upline building their groups they better get their checks in for Free Enterprise. Every counseling

session with a Direct invariably began with the question, "Are you
going to Free Enterprise Day?" Not to buy a ticket meant that, among
other inconveniences, you could no longer borrow jewelry and
cosmetics and cookware from your Direct to show to a customer, you
had to buy your own; and if you returned merchandise or kits, the
Direct would refuse to take them. People drove or flew to Charlotte to
be at Free Enterprise Day from as far away as Nova Scotia and Texas.
But the Corporation Northeast Regional Convention in Hartford,
Connecticut was never mentioned by Yager people, even to New
Englanders, although Rich DeVos, one of the founders and co-owners
of Amway, was the featured speaker. Tickets were not available from
Yager Directs; the only way a Yager distributor could learn about the
Corporation conventions was by reading about them in the Company
magazine, *The Amagram*, and sending directly to Amway in
Michigan for the tickets. Amway, like every movement, has internal
politics, which the leaders try, unsuccessfully, to conceal from the
ranks of the membership.

Out of curiosity, I attended the Hartford Convention to hear Rich
DeVos, a charismatic and warm-hearted entrepreneur with a tough,
twinkling, Dutch-uncle style of delivery, somewhere between the
Army sergeant of a TV comedy series and the high-school football
coach. Generally the atmosphere was more professional and less
hysterical; much more time was spent on advertising products, and
the films gave more support to retail sales. However, despite the lower
profile and the more evenly modulated tone, the basic ideology and
value system were the same. A prominent Board member, one of the
earliest distributors, who is currently at the level of Crown Ambassador, made the gesture of casually dropping her furs on the stage. The
appeals to God and Country, the resurrection and propagation of the
American Dream, the teaching of positive mental attitude, the
encouragement of the nuclear family unit, the corporate-modified
Protestant work ethic, the importance of duplication and commitment, the right-wing political indoctrination, the Personal Story, the
middle-class consumerism and materialism—all this is not an aberration of the Yagers but the mainstream of the Amway business as a
whole. Dexter Yager and his Diamonds have a block of positions on
the Corporate Board of Directors. If there is any serious conflict
between Yager's practices and Corporation policy, Rich DeVos and
Jay Van Andel are just as silent about it as he is.

What we have to look at now is how building the business
actually affects distributors' lives, and what is demanded of them as
they rise on the PV scale toward leadership: what happens to their
relationships with family and friends? What does Amway do to the

mind and heart? How many people really make money? What human values are lost, or gained, in the process? What kind of "love" is practiced and what "freedom" achieved?

Can you use Amway for your own ends? What is the price-tag attached to that income? Is Amway a road to freedom, or do you slide into a totalitarian enslavement worse than any conservative's nightmare of Communism? Does your livelihood, if you succeed, become so parasitically dependent on the Amway system, and your thought so conditioned by tapes and books and functions, that you are no longer capable of critically evaluating the business even if you were courageous enough to risk losing the income? These questions remained with me as I moved deeper into the world of Amway.

FIVE

STARTING
RIGHT

The various Amway lines have definite ideas about how a new person should be sponsored. Starting off on the right foot is a good motto in any undertaking, but in Amway whatever foot you use will be copied in your group. Wittingly or otherwise, you become a role model for the people you bring in. Distributors who march to the sound of a different drum screw up the tempo for everybody who follows them. If you come down on the left foot, you tend to start other people as left-footers. If you put your foot in your mouth, and manage to sponsor anybody in that condition, chances are they will gag along with you.

The ideal way to be sponsored in my line was according to a prescribed series of steps: the new prospects first attend a get-together to see the Plan. Never call this a "meeting." The guests might smell out commitment emanating from the very texture of the word. No one should hear or guess the word "Amway" until the Plan-man unfolds his poster at the end, showing a blown-up color photograph of the 300 acres of Corporation facilities in Ada. Then he passes out the literature. *Amagrams* and a compendium titled *Profiles of Success* go around the room, while the prospects gaze wistfully at all the rich, successful couples in the pictures, surrounded by their luxurious homes and expensive cars:

> Gary and Diane have realized many of their dreams...
> Parked outside their new 5000 sq. ft. home is a Cadillac and
> a 28 ft. motor home...Their motto in the business as well as
> life is, "SEE IT BIG!"

This business is more than just the financial gains of being able to keep our dream home, trading our old Pontiac for a gold Continental, traveling to places never thought possible and having extra land to help a widowed neighbor, to purchase extra land and new home furnishings, to hire a housekeeper, to support missionaries...

Now that Dave has retired from his position at the University and Mary is a full-time wife and mother, they are free to enjoy traveling. Whether it's in their Mercedes or by yacht to St. Thomas and the Caribbean...

Hank and Alicia have gained many material benefits in the short six years of their business, including a Cadillac Brougham (their second) and their mountain estate. A modern four bedroom home with six car garage (three antiques) and large workshop, all on 56 acres.

Today Rick says, "We're enjoying our third new motor home, our sixth new Cadillac, our lakeside vacation home in North Carolina, and a mountain-top retreat home in Georgia. We're able to wear stylish, quality clothes and travel a lot."*

Over in the corner, out of sight, the Plan-man has stacked a row of plain boxes. While prospects are poring over the *Profiles* he breaks for coffee. The ones who stand at his elbow and ask questions during the break will get in. From the corner he gives each couple a *decision pak* to take home, a cardboard box with a handle, containing three cassette tapes, a tape-player, two or three *Amagrams*, a copy of Conn's *The Possible Dream* and a few sample products. Yager likes to insist that his book *Don't Let Anybody Steal Your Dream* also be included in the pak. The contents are more or less duplicated from the top. The Direct sells the decision paks already made up to the distributor, for use in lending to prospects after the Plan-showing, and the distributor is not supposed to add to or subtract from whatever is in that box. This policy must be very good for the royalties on Yager's and Conn's books. My upline would not sell me the box with the handle on it as a separate item, but insisted that it could only be obtained complete with tapes, books, *Amagrams* and products. I wanted the empty box in order to compose my own pak at less cost. This maverick impulse was precisely what they intended to discourage.

The object of showing the Plan once is to get it in front of the new couple twice. The Plan-man opens his little date book (Yager sells date books, too, at $4 a copy) and says, "When would you like to see

* *Profiles of Success*

this again, tomorrow or Tuesday?" He is taking control; he does not ask whether his targets want to see the Plan again, but offers a choice of two times. If they back off then he takes it away.

"Gee, I've got bowling tomorrow night, and Tuesday I'm watching a movie."

"Well, my calendar is pretty full until the end of the month. I wish I could fit you in somewhere else, but these other people are too important. Unless you could cancel your bowling."

The cardinal rule is to follow up within two days. If a prospect is not seen again the same week, he or she is lost for months, maybe forever. The Take-It-Away technique has a good rate of success; people don't want to be passed over. In addition, the distributor must act from the beginning as if he does not need anyone. Even if a couple cannot be committed to a second meeting, he sends them home with a decision pak anyway; it must be retrieved, and he then has an excuse to see them again. When he drops by for the pak, he may invite himself in for coffee and start drawing the circles a second time. "If you can get those circles in front of a person twice, you will sponsor that person."

For the next forty-eight hours after the first Plan, the new couple are supposed to look over the books and the *Amagrams* and listen to the tapes and keep dreaming about the Mercedes, the cottage on the lake, the escape from the Rut. The successful couples in the pictures look like everyday people: dentist, plumber, teacher, electrician. "If they can do it, why not us? Look at that ugly Joe, how did he get to be an Emerald?" The tapes and products involve all of the senses in this so-called decision process. One is intended not only to see Amway, but hear it and smell it and touch it as well. The soap smells like lemon. The LOC feels like coconut oil. The speakers on the tape are funny and warm-hearted, like Howard Cunningham in "Happy Days." Everything looks innocent and clean and straight and wholesome. "Cleanliness is next to Godliness." "The Devil waits for idle hands." Childhood sayings, the strings in the collective unconscious of the culture, begin vibrating in tune with the images of "success." And look at the money! Yager's motor coach, antique Rolls Royce Silver Ghost, red brick mansion in Charlotte with the four white columns along the portico, very tall at the angle of the camera; and the numerous Yager children lined up on the steps. A wife may think, wouldn't it be nice to have a huge family like his and hire somebody else to clean up after the kids.

At the second Plan-showing the distributor says to his prospects, "There are a few things you need to know in order to be successful in this business." He does not ask if the couple are getting in; he assumes they are, and goes on to the next step; teaching them how to duplicate.

He has already made the decision for them. If they make a decision, it will have to be to resist him. They will have to say no; a negative choice that most people find difficult to make. "They are not saying no to Amway," the Seminars teach, "only to their own dreams." Saying no makes them look negative and the sponsor look positive. So they are in a corner, without quite knowing how they got there. He nods his head: "Yep, here's what you need to know." The only way out of the corner is to follow him.

"You need a list of names. Now which of your friends and relatives do you think would be most excited about this business? Write them down on that sheet of paper. Where are you from, originally? Where have you worked? I'll bet you know a lot of people there, don't you?" He nods his head. The questions are framed to elicit positive replies, and the head-nodding is to suggest that they agree, and he approves.

"The next thing is, we're gonna ask you to read some books, and listen to tapes, and come to Seminars and Rallies. You would agree it would be pretty foolish to go trying to build a house without a hammer and saw, wouldn't you? Well, this business is like anything else. To do it right you need the proper tools. It's only smart to take advantage of the training that we provide for you." He nods. They nod.

"One thing I must ask is that you have complete confidence in everything I do and say." The demand for "complete confidence" is much more than a sales technique for radiating positive magnetism; it is central to the whole Amway business. If the prospect could foresee where this demand leads, she might jump up from the table and hustle her would-be sponsor out into the street.

"Our line is the best and fastest-growing organization in the whole world of Amway. The people that are getting into this business now are gonna be millionaires five to ten years down the road. I tell you, it's exciting! Wait till you come to the functions! They'll blow your mind!" The Seminar teaches the distributor to act *excited* about the Plan, even if he doesn't feel it at first; the act will eventually bring on the feeling. The banalities are comfortable and familiar. They grease the wheels of the caravan. They are easy to duplicate.

He prompts the couple into a list of fifty or sixty names. "What you want to do (he knows what they want) is have a little get-together here in your livingroom, and I'll come over and show the Plan. Give some of your friends a chance to see it."

"Well, I don't want to impose on my friends."

"Hey, chances are, some of your friends are going to get into this business and go Direct. It's just a question of whether you sponsor them or somebody else does."

"Well, I really don't have the time."

"How many hours a week do you work? Forty?"

"Sometimes it's fifty."

"Okay. And how much do you sleep, about eight hours? That's fifty-six. What do you do Monday nights?"

"That's bowling night."

"What do you do Tuesday night?"

"That's my night with the kids."

"What do you do Wednesday night?"

A relentless distributor never accepts the time excuse; he will sit there until he has scheduled every night of the prospect's week, and every hour of the 168 hours from Monday to Sunday, and he will find fifteen to twenty unused hours. "Fifteen hours a week is all you need. Would you use these fifteen hours to give your wife income security, to give your kids a college education, to have your cottage by the lake? Would you give up bowling one night a week for the chance to have your own bowling alley in the basement of a new home by the seashore?" It is vital, when he makes these arguments, that the wife be sitting beside the husband at the table; most men do not like to say in front of third parties that bowling is more important to them than income security for their family.

"When you have this get-together, don't put yourself out or go to any trouble, leave the room just the way it is and if we need extra chairs we can bring them in as people arrive. Serve store-bought cookies and coffee in styrofoam cups for refreshments, nothing fancy. Here's a tip: when you make a call, don't mention Amway, products or selling. Just say something like:

" 'Jack, are you and Jill busy tomorrow night?'

" 'No, we don't have anything planned, why?'

" 'I'd like both of you to come over around eight, it's very important.'

" 'What's it all about?'

" 'Love to tell you, listen, I'm in kind of a rush, get a babysitter and we'll see you tomorrow night and I'll tell you then.'

"If somebody says 'I'll try to make it,' that means they're not coming. So you say, 'Jack, I've got a tremendously tight schedule this week, I'm sure you can appreciate that: will you definitely be here?' Get them to say it's definite."

Telephone approaches now are reduced to booklet form, and a prospect may simply be given a booklet with suggested openers. Totally patented approaches are discouraged. If the party on the other end does not say the right lines in the script, you sit there with your mouth open wondering what should come out next.

"Be sure and put your kids to bed by eight. Do you have any pets?"

"We have a dog."

"That's great; what kind is it?"

"He's a mongrel."

"Put him in the cellar or outdoors during the Plan. And take your phone off the hook around quarter of eight."

The next move is up to the new couple.

If the meeting takes place, the distributor repeats exactly the same routine with the couple's friends: show them the Plan, get a follow-up meeting at their house, lend them decision paks. At the end of the night, when the friends have left, he goes out to his car and brings in a kit. He never asks if the prospects want a kit either. He will graciously offer to take a post-dated check for it. His wife will talk to the recruit's wife about how to retail products while the husband opens the application form and receives instructions concerning the importance of functions, books and tapes. Both partners sign on the dotted line.

The Amway Sales and Product Kit, which is prepared by the Corporation, lists for $76.00 in the 1 September 1984 price list. The PV on the kit, which goes to the credit of both seller and purchaser for that month, is 34.75. The price includes all the paperwork necessary to start a distributorship, but the major portion of the cost is the sample products. Purchase of products is not required in order to join Amway; every kit is stamped "Product Portion is Optional." But in practice, Yager lines sell to the new distributor, not only the whole product portion ("Only a rookie would split up a kit"), but four Yager tapes, three books—*The Possible Dream, Don't Let Anybody Steal Your Dream,* and *The Magic of Thinking Big*—two Seminar and Rally tickets, a Yager date book and a board and easel. This package costs in the vicinity of $150. A sponsor must buy the kit from the Direct first in order to sell it to the recruit. The kit is sold with all the extras as a complete unit; if the sponsor does not convince the new couple to take all the extras, he or she will be stuck with loose boards, easels, tapes, books and products. Only the products are refundable to Amway.

Moving the whole unit is the "correct" way to start a new distributor; you are not told that the extras are optional. If you ask, the response might be, "I want to help you in every way I can, it would be a disservice not to sell you the tapes and books and tickets. Hey, you'll be moving dozens of these down through your organization in a few months. You're gonna be showing the Plan, you'll need a board and easel." The sponsor has already demanded your complete confidence.

The duplication motif is irresistible; if your sponsor says you need the package to do the business correctly, then who are you to refuse? She knows and you don't.

In the ideal pattern, the sponsor has already conducted the first meeting for the new couple by the time they sign the application; then he or she does the follow-up on the people who came to that meeting. In practice, Murphy's Law creeps into this system, like any other, and the ideal pattern has to be repeated and repeated from tape and Seminar to be kept alive. People get sponsored in snowstorms and hospital beds. One spouse joins and the partner refuses to have anything to do with it. Thirty friends are invited to a "get-together" and they all say they will definitely be there and nobody shows up. A new distributor, sponsoring a poor relative and wanting to give her a break, decides not to sell her the books, tapes and tickets. Then the poor relative sponsors *her* people without books, tapes and tickets. I have drawn the Plan on a napkin over lunch. On one occasion, showing the Plan for a new person already in the business, I got the follow-up meeting with an eager couple, lent them the decision pak, and went down again three days later, driving forty miles, expecting to find a houseful of new prospects; the eager couple had locked all their doors, and were in the livingroom watching television, and would not answer the doorbell or the telephone.

There is also more than one ideal pattern. Ultimately the ideal is whatever works, but it has to be reduced to a pattern in order to be duplicated.

The single most important word in the Amway business is Duplication. What mass production is to the Ford Motor Company, what reproduction is to the world of biological organisms, duplication is to the Amway system. A successful distributorship is a self-contained economic unit, totally dependent on the Corporation, which takes in products, moves them out, makes a profit *for the Direct Distributor*, and duplicates itself *ad infinitum.* You build the business by copying exactly the system recommended by your upline and then teaching others to copy you. Faulty systems reap the consequences of their mistakes by dying out. Successful systems bring more and more distributors into their magnetic field. Distributors proliferate in them like flies in the summer heat.

A variant on the home meeting is to bring friends to the Direct's home, or to a rented conference room at a Motor Inn, and watch the Direct draw the circles. However they get in, recruits must, as quickly as possible, be secured before they drop out. The way to do this is to get somebody in under them, teach them to show the Plan on their own and bring them to functions. Amway has an enormously high dropout rate. If these things are not done immediately, the distributor will quit within six months.

Amway begins to change your life the first time you approach your friends and family members to sell the products or recruit them into the business. Hitherto you related with them as friend, brother, sister, son, daughter. Now you are relating as salesperson to customer. As soon as you list all your friends in a notebook as potential customers and distributors, they become *prospects*. With a friend there is no ulterior motive for your association: friends get together to enjoy each other's company, play games, play music, climb rocks and share secrets, have a few drinks, go on a trip. But when you put a friend on a prospect list, then you are guiding the friendship in a preconceived direction; the friendship is no longer primary, it is a means to an end. You want something from that person; you want to sell her soap and show her the Plan. You want to get her into the Amway system and change her life; but she should not even hear the word "Amway" until after she is already hooked. She meets you to go bowling, while you are rehearsing in your mind the script from a tape which will arouse her curiosity and get her talking about business and money. She is chatting about her kids, but you are waiting for the right moment to say, "Isn't it tough nowadays to support kids on one income?" They think you are interested in their lives when you ask them about their schedule, but you are looking for a free evening to invite them over at eight o'clock to discuss an Exciting Idea. This is not a relationship of equals, but of manipulator and manipulatee. If you sponsor a friend, then the relationship is *upline* to *downline*—a completely prefabricated business association in which honest friendship gradually becomes impossible.

This danger of turning friends into customers and prospects is keenly felt by new people; in my experience, the biggest hurdle a distributor had to overcome was the fear of calling everybody he knew to organize a get-together whose purpose would only be revealed after they arrived. We may call friends a dozen times a week for recreation, gossip and mutual aid, but as soon as the ulterior motive enters in, most of us instinctively feel ashamed. We don't like other people to think we are taking advantage of them.

For a sizable number of recruits, the Dream is shipwrecked on this rock before it ever gets out of the harbor. They call two names and the frosty response on the other end of the line immobilizes them. Their sponsor comes twice, three times, expecting a full livingroom, and finds only the sheepish distributor and his wife sipping coffee from styrofoam cups: "Yeah, I made some calls, they said they would try to make it, I don't know why they didn't show up."

Seminar leaders are fully cognizant of this fear, and spend a great
deal of time teaching the distributor how to conquer it. You are not
taking advantage of your friends, say the leaders, but doing them a
favor by giving them this wonderful opportunity to make their
dreams come true. If your friends discovered a money tree, wouldn't
you want them to tell you about it? Then if you have any respect for
your friends' intelligence, of course you would tell them about this
business. Amway is love; it only grows by being shared with others.
How would you like to meet your friends at a Rally, and find out they
were sponsored by somebody else? Your friends will either join, or buy
products, or wish you success in your new endeavor; if they don't do
any of these, then they're not your friends, so why care about their
opinions? Will your friends pay your bills if you become disabled and
can't work? Will your friends provide you with a retirement income?
Do you consult your friends when you get sick, or go to a doctor? It's
the same thing with business: when you want to make money, do you
listen to some guy who makes $12,000 a year or do you listen to a
successful businessperson? If your friend starts putting Amway down,
ask him "What's your PV?" Ask him to explain the 3 percent
retirement income. If he's not an Emerald, don't listen to him; he
doesn't know what he's talking about.

Before distributors can sell their friends and family members,
they have to believe that they are right. The source of that belief is the
Organization, the lifeline of the upline leaders, pumping conviction
into the new couple through the propaganda. This is the beginning of
a total change in political consciousness and must be analyzed to
understand the power of Amway as a corporate movement with a
grass-roots base. We derive identity and self-concept from our
friendships. We depend on friends and family members for a good
opinion of ourselves; we want them to like and respect us and feel
good in our company. Suddenly we have put them on a prospect list,
and now we want them to do their laundry with SA-8 and wash their
dishes with Dish Drops and eat Nutrilite food bars for lunch so we can
make a profit; then we want them to sell products and show the Plan
and sponsor others so we can boost our PV and rise to bigger incomes.
They might correctly surmise that we are using them. They might
criticize and reject us.

The identity and self-concept that we derive from our friends
must be supplied as quickly as possible by the upline leaders. All
kinds of events in Amway are planned for that purpose. For
sponsoring one to four people the first ninety days in the business, we
receive a silver Believer's Pin. For sponsoring three in the month
before Dream Night, we might be invited to sit up front in a group

called The Winner's Circle. For sponsoring five in the first ninety days, we win the gold Inner Circle award and get our names listed in *The Amagram,* and are asked to stand up and be recognized at a Rally. We receive honorable mention for retailing 200 PV in any one month. The Directs give us the arguments to justify the business; they keep feeding the Dream, providing the covered-dish suppers and Rallies (paid for by our tickets), the smiles and handshakes and head-nodding and other forms of approval, selling us the literature to reinforce their teaching, and, in short, surrounding us with a whole new support group.

If we examine what attitude the recruits are taught to adopt toward friends and family members, it becomes obvious that they are being prepared for the parting of the ways with anyone who might hold them back in Amway. This fact is not stated in so many words until much later, perhaps not even until the first leadership training functions, when the recruit is irrevocably committed to the business. It is a *favor* to offer Amway to a friend, even an act of charity; but if the favor is refused, don't listen to that friend; the potential recruits know nothing and you don't need them anyway.

The theme that you don't need any particular person is repeated often at Seminars. Ostensibly it means that, if any one person or group refuses to get in, they are not rejecting you, they are rejecting themselves; never let yourself be stopped by rejection, find somebody else. Amway will succeed no matter what; there will be a Ford dealer in your town, a Cadillac dealer in your town, a McDonald's in your town and Amway in your town; the only question is who will make the money, will it be you and your friends or somebody else and theirs; if your friend doesn't get in, she made a choice that somebody else will make that money and not her. But you are not bound by her choice.

This outlook has a more basic meaning which reveals the effect of Amway on the consciousness of the distributor. We need human association and approval. If these needs are no longer met by our friends, then they have to be met by the business; and, for those who stay in and achieve the higher pins, this is precisely what happens. We no longer need our former friends; we need the business instead. We need the approval of the upline Direct and the leaders of the Seminars and Rallies. "I lost my father and mother," said a prominent Emerald. "My father still won't speak to me. But in Amway I acquired a whole new family."

Amway leaders, however, set rather different terms for their association with us than ordinary friends. They have very specific ideas about what they want us to become. Their approval depends upon whether or not we fulfill these ideas. They have befriended us in order to enlarge their business. Their friendship is measurable in terms of duplication and PV. The process can be very succinctly summarized: no duplication, no friendship. They will tolerate low PV for a long time if a distributor makes a sincere effort to duplicate.

Need works the other way around: our friends need us too. If we cut them off and won't listen to their criticisms of Amway, or listen only in order to turn them around, and no longer have the time to bowl and have fun with them because we are out showing the Plan, "on the road going someplace," then they must get along without us; on the other hand they might ask, "How's that Amway thing doing? You get rich yet? Where's your Cadillac?"

Behind these questions is a thinly veiled resentment at being abandoned, but also a curiosity, envy, and a desire for continued friendship. These motives can be used to *pick them off one by one*. And the technique for picking them off is explicitly taught through Seminars and tapes. I must be totally positive. No matter how I feel about the business, in response to questions I must always say, "It's doing great! Fantastic!" Before Amway I might have been able to discuss feelings honestly with my friends; now I say what is best calculated to sponsor them.

Equally important is to withdraw from my former social group. "When you join Amway, you have chosen to walk with the winners." Amway is my social group. Only as part of that group can I risk a foray among my old cronies to pick them off and convert them into distributors. The sheep and the goats are absolutely separate.

One of the doctrines of Amway is that I am responsible only for myself, my wife and my children. I am not responsible for my friends, brother-in-law, extended family, co-workers or humanity in general. Since my friends won't pay my bills or provide for my retirement, their opinions about my sources of income are meaningless. I share this wonderful opportunity with them, but *I* want to sponsor my friend; I don't want him to sponsor me. The sharing is a one-way process. I will share my time teaching my friend to go Direct, but only if I am the one collecting the 3 percent bonus on his organization.

Before Amway, if I go to his house and his feet are propped up on the couch and he is watching the Super Bowl, I might bring a six-pack and watch it with him. After Amway, every contact with a sponsored friend is a "get-together." I can no longer drink with him because we are not supposed to mix alcohol and business—a sound principle, but in Amway, *all* time spent with my distributors is business. I visit my friend in the first place to see if he is drawing circles, and to help him do meetings. In the second place, I would watch the game only to motivate him with the idea of how great it will be to travel to the Super

Bowl and watch it live after we both go Direct; and finally, if he is not out showing the Plan, I follow the teachings of my Seminar and "fold his arms over his chest, put a daisy in his hand, say a few words over him and go find somebody else." I don't have time for this loser any more.

Starting a new recruit, then, is not a process of giving people the chance to make an intelligent choice about their future. You must *appear* to be offering an intelligent choice, and support that appearance with facts, figures, graphs, statistics and a professional image. But what you are actually doing is playing on their emotions, feigning excitement in order to arouse their interest, making all their choices for them in advance, and hastening them from one step to another before they have time to say no. In the case of friends, you are taught to use their trust to get them to a meeting and convert them into prospects, under the pretense that you are doing them a favor. If they resist then you simply take it away, or convert them into customers. You circumvent their intelligent choice by involving the senses. You frame the context of the questions so that they will give the answer you want. You present a completely patterned method of approach which at once begins to separate them from their own world and draw them into a dependence on the world of Amway.

Most salespeople use most of these techniques; indeed, they might respond that the economy could not well get along without them, and they might be right. The watchword of our system is, after all, "let the buyer beware." But Amway recruiters do not just want your money. They want your whole life.

The distributor cannot see in the beginning how far-reaching and irreversible this transformation will become. "If you could only look down the road and see all the fantastic things ahead for you," say the Emeralds and Diamonds on the stages of their functions. "You don't know the half of what this business will do for you if you just believe; if you could only realize what a powerful force you have in your hands..."

SIX

PROSPECTING

Before long I discovered that most of my friends and family members were not climbing the walls with excitement at the vision of the Plan. Higher pins admit candidly that very few of the Directs in their business were drawn from the pool of friends they had before they joined. A Diamond asked a Seminar audience, "How many of you have sponsored a close friend or a family member?" Only a few scattered hands were raised. It seems that, typically, the tactic of inviting friends to a home meeting for an unspecified purpose is good for two or three Plan-showings. Then the word gets out and the attendance dries up.

Some of my friends bought the products, some looked at the Plan and turned it down but remained friendly, and some avoided me as though I had just contracted a virulent new strain of Herpes II, communicable only through the medium of handshakes and Amway soap. An occasional friend will buy a kit. It is unlikely that she will do anything with it. After showing the Plan to twenty-six friends and family members without sponsoring a single one, I went to my upline Pearl for counseling and asked him what to do.

"Flush 'em and find twenty-six more."

"How long does it take to go Direct?"

"Ninety days."

"But at this rate it will take me ninety days to get one distributor."

"Jeff Professor showed the Plan thirty-eight times without getting anyone. The thirty-ninth guy is an Emerald today. The thing of it is, the no's don't matter. Only the yes's matter."

"But I'm running out of friends."

"Your business won't take off until you start working with strangers."

"Really?"

"I prefer strangers myself, it's less complicated."

"Do you pick names out of a phonebook?"

"I've done that, but I don't recommend it. Look at this." He gave me a business card. On it were printed his name and phone number and a single word; rather than give away his game to a prospect pool of millions, permit me to use the fictional term *Intergram*.

"What does it stand for?"

"International Retirement Income Program."

"What do you do with it?"

"The other day I pulled up to a gas pump and I said to the attendant, 'How ya doin', great day isn't it?' And he said, 'Yeah, for you, but not for me, I have to work here.' So I said, 'Gee, that's too bad, have you ever considered early retirement?' He laughed and I said 'No, I'm not kidding, I specialize in setting people up in retirement incomes of fifty, sixty thousand a year.' Then his face lit up like a Christmas tree and he said, 'I wish you could give me more information on that!' Then I gave him my card. I said, 'Well, I can't promise you when I can get back to you, but if I'm ever in the area again I'll stop by.' He's seen the Plan already, he's getting in this week."

One thing that will always motivate an Amway distributor to gnaw on his heart is a tale of a hot prospect getting into somebody else's organization. I wanted an immediate crash course in how to approach strangers. My Pearl got out his tape rack. "Here's a good tape on cold contacting. Here's a great one, you'll love this. Here's another, it's right up your alley." Before I left his house I had bought $30 worth of new tapes.

I had passed the test of retailing products, learning the Plan and toughing it out through twenty-six rejections, and now I was being introduced to how the business is really built. Most people exhaust their initial list of friends and relatives quickly, and to keep their caravan on the road they have to find a never-ending stream of fresh contacts.

The cold-contacting lore in the Amway business is like the hunter's repertoire of big-game stories. Here is a little decision-pakful of samples, paraphrased from tapes and Seminars:

1. *The Expansion of Gamelin Enterprises*
   I saw this sharp-looking guy behind the counter, and I started walking back and forth, looking at my watch like I was waiting for somebody, walking back and forth and up and down. So I went over to the counter and shook my head and I says, "You

know, I can't understand some people; you'd think a guy that was interviewing for a position that paid $30,000 a year would show up on time, wouldn't you?"

Then I waited some more and I said "By the way, what do you do?"

He said "I'm the hotel manager."

And I stuck out my hand and said, "My name is Fred Gamelin, I represent Gamelin Enterprises; we're in distribution and supply for several big corporations and we're thinking of expanding in this area." That's the truth, see, 'cause wherever I happen to be I'm expanding in that area, I don't care where it is. And I said, "We're looking for a few sharp people that might be interested in heading up their own business."

"What kind of business is it?"

"We need somebody with a lot of ambition who's not opposed to making some real good money over and above what they're making now. Do you know anyone like that?"

"I might. What sort of merchandise do you handle?"

"Just about everything, as long as it's legal and honest. Where did you get your Master's degree?"

"I don't have one."

"Oh. Well. You're a pretty sharp looking feller, I thought you might have a Master's in Business Administration. Where did you get your Bachelor's?"

"I don't have one."

"Oh, I guess..."

"But I managed a supermarket for five years."

"How many employees did you have under you?"

"Five."

"Oh."

"But each of those five had thirty."

"Well listen, I can't promise you just when we're gonna get started here, but if I'm passing through this way again, is there any reason we can't get together?"

"No, let me give you my name and phone number."

"I don't know if you're just what we're looking for, but it can't hurt to sit down and talk. Here's my card, and if I don't call you in a couple of weeks give me a ring."

And you know, that feller called me up twice long distance to find out when I'm gonna pass through his area again. He said, "I know you haven't forgotten me, it just seems that way."

2. *I Love Inflation, It Makes My Wallet Fat*

What me and my husband like to do when we go to the Mall

on weekends, we take three hundred dollars out of the checking account after 3 p.m. on Friday afternoon, so it's not charged to the account until Monday morning. Then we get these three hundred-dollar bills and fold them and put them inside the billfold so the tips of the hundreds are showing, and then I ask my husband at the checkout counter, "Honey, can you pay cash for this one, I left my credit cards home." When he opens that billfold, you ought to see the eyes in the checkout line. Then I say "Well, honey, prices went up again, we should go out and celebrate, we're gonna make another bundle."

Sure enough, pretty soon somebody's gonna ask, "Do you folks own the store?" Then you want to answer a question with a question, be careful and don't jump in too fast. Always answer a question with a question, like, "Are you from around here? What do you do?" Like that, just get a conversation going, get the person talking about themselves. 'Cause what's everybody's favorite subject? Themselves. Then you say, "You seem to be able to relate pretty good with people, I bet you know a lot of people around here." Build them up a little, see, and you smile, and nod your head. Ever notice when you nod your head people start nodding their heads.

You can always talk to anyone if you just remember four letters, F-O-R-M; that's Family, Occupation, Recreation, Money. That's what you talk about. You just remember you want to FORM that conversation in a positive mold, you do it with those four subjects. Then after we get that person warmed up and friendly, my husband says, "Gee, it's funny we should meet you like this, 'cause we're expanding a business in this area and we're looking for someone who might want to develop a good second income."

Now when you get those questions, that's the time you want to back off. When he asks "Doing what?" or "What's the product?" Then you say "Well, I'm not in a position to offer anything definite right now, but is there any reason we can't get together and talk about it?" I tell you, we've got a whole drawerful of phone numbers we've never even called, we just don't have the time to get to them all. Then Monday morning we put the three hundred dollars back in the bank.

3. *Only A Fool Pays Taxes*
The main thing is to keep your ears open, just relate with people, smile and shake hands and say "Hi, nice day, isn't it?" You ought to practice that smile every day. If you go out contacting and you feel like you have to make a contact, you're

turning it into work. You're scaring yourself to death before you even start. You gotta hang loose and have fun with this thing. Be open and friendly, the contacts will come; you know, there are 220,000,000 people in this country; all you need are six Directs to be a Diamond and you never have to work again for the rest of your life.

I was sitting in the barbershop and my barber was complaining about taxes, and I said "What? You pay taxes? How come?" And he laughed and said "Well, I wish I knew. Everybody pays taxes."

"Not in my business."

"What is your business?"

"I help people develop second incomes."

"How do you do that?"

One thing you never want to do is let your prospect ask all the questions while you sit there giving answers, 'cause he's in control. And you want to control that conversation. So what you do is turn it around. I said:

"Ever take your kids to Disneyworld?" Well no, he never did, but he was planning to, someday. Then I said, "You know, last summer I took the family to Disneyworld in our motor home and wrote off the whole trip as a tax deduction."

"Really? How did you do that?"

"The best part was, I got the Government to make the down payment on my motor home."

Now, don't get me wrong, I believe in obeying the law; I think the Government should get everything the law entitles them to, but not one penny more. You don't want to misrepresent this business as a tax shelter, but the tax advantages are there for you, and a sharp businessperson will know how to appreciate that.

Then when I saw that I had the barber's interest, I took it away from him. I said, "Look, I'm pretty busy, I'm booked solid for a couple of weeks in advance and I don't know if this is for you anyway; but if I get a chance during the week I'll give you a ring. Which days are best for you?" He gave me a list of five days when I could call him at home. That barber just went Direct last month.

4. *Playing the Dumb Wife*

Gals, you can help your husband a lot of times making contacts if he's the shy type, but you have to be careful not to take the leadership away from him. It might be hard for a man to talk to somebody like a doctor, because a doctor has status, and you might think, why would a doctor be interested in Amway. But let me tell you, there's plenty of doctors getting into this business; doctors are smart enough to know the value of having a cash flow income that's not all tied up in office equipment. Then if you think about estate taxes, in most occupations if you have a cash income of $100,000 a year it takes about $2 million worth of estate to generate that cash flow. The tax consequences on that $2 million are tremendous. In our business you can have a cash flow of $100,000 and your estate is a couple of file cabinets and a calculator and a product shelf.

We got the Plan in front of my doctor because I asked him one day, "Gee, you're doing pretty good in this town, are you planning to expand?" Then he started telling me how expensive it is to set up a medical practice, and I said, "Well, my husband is in a business helping professional people diversify their income. I don't know if this would help you or not, but maybe I can ask him to drop by and talk with you."

Then you get the questions, what is it, and all that. But being a woman makes it easy, gals, you aren't expected to know how to answer them. Just play the dumb wife. I said "Gee, I really don't know much about it, I'll have to let my husband explain it to you 'cause I'd just mess it all up." That does two things, that lets you off the hook, and it lets your husband be the leader. You know that doctor today has fourteen Directs in his organization. I cry all the way to the bank.

5. *I'll Bet You Make A Lot of Money*
Be careful never to tell a prospect that he could use some extra money. That makes him defensive; he's likely to come back at you and say "I don't know about that, I'm doing all right." Then where are you going to take it from there? What you want to do is start out with a positive. Ask him "What do you do for a living?" Then when he tells you, say "Oh, I bet you make a lot of money at that." And you know, most people don't wait very long to tell you how much money they aren't making. That's just what you want to hear. I walked into a little plant store in a Mall, and I struck up a conversation with the owner, I said "This is a very attractive shop you have here, you must do a very good business. Then he started telling me how expensive it was to rent floor space in a Mall, and how the rent was going up, and he didn't know how much longer he'd be able to hang on.

Then I said "Have you ever considered income diversification?" And he said "You mean like stocks?" And I said "The way big business weathers a recession is to diversify; it makes sense for us to do it too." And we talked about stocks and marketing for a few minutes, and I said, "You know, a couple of things that impress me about you: you're not a quitter; and you relate well to your customers. Ever been involved in corporate management?" I made him feel like I was interviewing him for something, he didn't quite know what, but whatever it was he didn't want to make a bad impression. You just keep asking the questions and that puts you in control. He was convincing me how good he was. I asked him, "Could you find ten to fifteen hours a week to put into a second business if the money was good?" And he said "I could find a lot more than that if I liked what I was doing."

You know what he did? He took all his own excuses away. The biggest excuse you're gonna get is time; after you're all done showing the Plan, the prospect leans back and says "That's all well and good, but I just don't have the time." How was he going to turn around later and tell me he didn't have the time when he just told me he could find a lot more than fifteen hours a week? And how was he going to give me the excuse that he didn't have enough ability in sales when he had just sold himself to me for the last half hour?

You have to make people feel like you have something they want. Never chase anybody. You start chasing and they'll lead you in circles.

When I began working the business with strangers, everybody became a prospect and every situation was a potential contact. For a distributor out to build a group, there are only four categories of people: prospects, distributors, customers and losers. A prospect is what a person is before he sees the Plan. A customer is what he becomes if he declines to join. "Sell him soap and clean him up." If he won't even buy the products, then he is one of the vast mediocre majority who will never make anything of themselves and are fit only to be employed by the winners.

Some leaders warn their people against judging anyone as a loser just because she declines to be involved in Amway. One distributor's "loser" might be another's Pearl. Betty Smith might be hostile when I show her the Plan, but when you show it she might get in. She might turn both of us down this year, but next year she might be hooked by the guy who runs the plant store in the Mall. If I peg her as a loser and somebody else sponsors her and she goes Direct, my hasty judgment will have cost me a quarter of a million dollars in 3 percent bonuses over a twenty-year period.

Two anecdotes were often told in my line to reinforce this

teaching: the tale of the bearded art professor and the tale of the negative friend. The bearded art professor looks like a hippie. His hair hangs down past his shoulders and he never uses shoe polish, deodorant or a comb. Most distributors would take one look at him and decide that he would be among the last people on earth that they would want in the business. But a colleague in his Department sponsors him, and within two months he makes 4000 PV. Of course he has to cut his hair and start wearing a suit, but we all have growing to do.

The negative friend is a "welfare bum" who drinks and smokes pot and watches the boob tube and puts everything down. "I didn't think he would ever succeed in Amway, so I never showed it to him. My sponsor had more faith in him than I did; *he* sponsored this guy on a separate leg. Today there are nine Directs in that leg and this ex-bum just went Pearl."

Conn repeats a variant of the Bearded Art Professor in *The Winner's Circle*:

> Bill Britt once held an opportunity meeting into which walked a "scraggly looking fellow" with shoulder-length hair, an Indian headband, glassy-eyed look—all the marks of a confirmed hippie. After the session, he walked around and around the blackboard, muttering, "Man, that's cool." To Britt's surprise, he got into the business; and, three years later, that distributorship which he represented is still a large, secure Direct leg.*

His purpose in repeating this tale is to illustrate that Amway is democratic; anyone can succeed in it, regardless of race, religion, age, education or pre-Amway lifestyle. Not mentioned is whether the man continued to dress like a hippie after he joined, or was forced out, and the "distributorship which he represented" kept by the sponsor.

But whether these stories are true or not is irrelevant. They function as folklore: they project the longings and fears of the distributor into ritual and form, they provide a model of what is expected and how to succeed, and they mold and shape behavior toward the desired goal.

The prospecting stories have certain common elements. As a distributor, I am in possession of secret knowledge which the prospect will not realize until the appropriate moment. This secret knowledge is nothing less than the American Way, the key to salvation, the

---

The Winner's Circle, pp. 127-128.

means of making Dreams come true; it is the realization of the pursuit
of happiness: material prosperity, positive attitude, cleanliness, hard
work, devotion to God and Country. It is the Amway version of
Dante's heavenly rose, opening in the last ring of Paradise, with
Diamonds and Crowns flitting to and fro among the petals like
angels. I manipulate the expectations and perceptions of my prospects for their own good, because my objective is to trick them into
being winners.

The techniques give me control over the situation: I ask the
questions, I maintain the format of an interview, I have the power to
build up or squelch the prospect, I can offer Salvation and take it
away, and I alone know where the conversation is going. Moreover, if
something goes wrong I can break it off and move on to another
contact. By this means I build the illusion of control over my own life.
All of my experience is simplified into the goal of making it to the
next pin level, and all human contacts are reduced to the four
categories of prospect, distributor, customer and loser. The manipulation and the trickery are justified by the belief that prospects will
benefit; when they become distributors they will employ the same
methods themselves. They will understand it better by and by. In the
meantime, their naivete is a good subject for humor. At their expense.

The caution against pre-judging other people as losers has
nothing to do with respect for the complexity and innate worth of the
person. This caution is meaningful strictly in the context of business
success. Innate worth is equated in all kinds of direct and indirect
ways with high PV. A winner is someone who has what it takes to earn
a high pin, even if she is not actually in the business at this time. It is
not considered a mistake to divide people into the categories of winner
and loser; these categories must be evoked to explain poverty, to blame
social oppression on the victims, to justify and rationalize the
fundamental parasitical character of Amway incomes and to reinforce
the distributor's commitment. The danger is that we might put
somebody in the *wrong* category, not that the categories themselves
are false. We might peg Joe Low as a loser merely because he wears
long hair and puts down the rich. Then somebody else might sponsor
him and turn him into a Direct and we would lose money because of a
hasty judgment.

It is also instructive to note the value assumptions of the
supportive folklore. The "hippie" art professor and the "welfare
bum" both represent groups traditionally hostile to the middle class:
intelligentsia and unemployed poor. The distributor is taught not to
write off individuals in these groups as hopeless, but to identify their
potential for conversion. They are losers as long as their conscious-

ness belongs to their respective groups. But if they can achieve high PV, then our opinion of them must be revised according to their pin level. PV, and, more indirectly, the ability to make money, is the final measurement of personal worth.

The fever struck me when I followed exactly the teachings of the tapes and Seminars and then began to score meetings with strangers. Within a month I had sponsored three people. Not only that, but the contacts known to these three swelled my prospect list with over a hundred new names; to be sure, any names that were supplied by my distributors would have to be sponsored under them but everyone in their groups was also in mine; and if all three went Gold Direct, I would be an Emerald.

I had been given specific behavioral objectives—this is what you say to a stranger, this is how you interest him in the business, this is how you get an appointment and a follow-up, this is how you sponsor her—and I had correctly duplicated the behavior and been reinforced. Now I was molded by what I had done. I "got excited." In fact I drew my three people out on a sheet of paper in the form of three circles, projecting from me, the center, and I added circles from the new prospects I had met that I thought might get in. I stayed up late, tossing and turning in bed, fantasizing about who I would sponsor next and how I would hook them. I ransacked my memory for more names. The unions, churches and chess clubs I had served or belonged to appeared in my imagination as fields full of ripening prospects. I no longer cared anything for their goals, except as a means of accomplishing mine.

My ear picked up any theme in a conversation that I could FORM. In talk about Family, I listened for how I could use the natural family loyalties of a prospect to get him interested in the business; I wanted to know what he hoped to achieve for his family, and whether his brother, sister, parents or children were the ambitious type. In talk about Occupation, I listened for any job dissatisfaction or longing for security which the job did not provide; then I could scan my date book and suggest that it might be a while before I could show that person a way out of his dilemma, because I was Very Busy and kept a full calendar. In talk about Recreation, I prodded my target into describing his dreams and material desires, and then at the appropriate moment I could ask, "Do you really want these things?" Money was the most straightforward subject, and led right to the point: "How would you like to double your income in twelve months?" Within a few weeks I was showing the Plan every night, and had a drawerful of phone numbers I would never have time to follow up on.

From this process I gained a sales force; I rose up the PV scale to the four-figure brackets and received bonuses that I could brag about. All my bonus money, and more besides was spent on functions, tapes, books, inventory, sales aids and gasoline, but I looked on this as an investment in "my" business and I kept believing in the golden future, when the bonus checks would surpass the expenses, and I would be a jewel.

I learned how to strike up acquaintances with total strangers, hold their attention and discover their needs and greeds without revealing my ultimate purpose. It was Negative to think about what I lost in this transformation, and I drove those thoughts away so I could climb the scale faster. But in retrospect, what I lost was much more important than what I gained.

Many of the contacts initiated by prospecting could have ripened into genuine friendships. I met all kinds of people with all kinds of talents. Vietnam veterans, construction workers, carpenters, grocery store proprietors, musicians, salespeople, managers, professionals, each with a story to tell, an experience of life, a consciousness formed by that experience, a frustration and a dream, a mind and a soul. It was a tremendous opportunity to dissolve what so many writers, from Marx to Fromm, have described as the alienation of modern life, the fear and loneliness that divide us into separate capsules and reduce us to numbers in a computer program. In order to be effective, I had to put my stereotypes aside.

But my interest in these people was channeled strictly according to the requirements of the business. I merely replaced one stereotype with another. If I met a musician, I could not enter deeply into music with him; otherwise we might end up jamming, and form a band, and I would never get him to sell soap and learn the Plan. What I had to do instead was dream with him about expensive instruments and sound systems, and then make an appointment to draw the circles and show him how he could make the money to buy that sound system; and if I sponsored him, then I became his *upline*, a relationship which is governed by correct duplication. If he refused the Plan, then he might become one of my customers, but I could not afford to waste time on his friendship; I had to move on to the next contact.

In each case, friendship was limited only to what I could use to accomplish my goal. The justification given by Amway would be that in order to realize my Dream I must help the prospect realize his. But the Dream had to cost money, otherwise it would not be useful; and I had to play that Dream like a fishline, specifically to bring the prospect into my group. If he could realize his Dream by selling T-shirts and ski hats, I would make no profit on him, and our

Dream-building association quickly evaporated. In the end, "prospecting" was more alienating than loneliness. The capsule that divides us took on tangible form; it began to look more and more like a three-piece suit and a red, white and blue box.

The most amusing illustration of this point is what happens when two Amway distributors unknowingly meet in a Mall and begin prospecting each other. Some tapes work out comedy routines around this situation; Amway people are not without an appreciation of the ironies in their game.

"Is this a growing area?"

"I was wondering that myself. Are you from around here?"

"Where are you from?"

"Springfield."

"I'll bet you know a lot of people there."

"Say, that's a very perceptive comment. What do you do for a living?"

"I'm in distribution and supply for several large corporations. What do you do?"

"I'll bet you make a lot of money at that."

"We do a fantastic business. Matter of fact we're expanding right now."

"Really? We're expanding too."

"What's your business?"

"We specialize in helping professionals diversify their incomes. Right now we're looking for a few sharp people that might be interested in heading up a multi-state operation for this area."

"Is that right? You know, what I like about you is that you seem to relate real well with the public. We look for people like that. What's the name of your company?"

"Diversigram. What's yours?"

"Replicom."

"Didn't I see you at the last Seminar?"

"Wanna sell soap?"

General laughter highlights the mutual revelation, and after a little shop talk the distributors would go to opposite ends of the Mall to ply their trade. Being in the same business does not bring them together in mutual assistance and humanity. Besides being competitors, they are forbidden to *crossline*—a concept which will be explained in due course. An upline friendship is conditional, manipulative and insincere; a crossline friendship is simply impossible.

All sales personnel have to deal with the public as customer; commodities are distributed in our system by means of sales, and one of the valuable lessons I learned from being in Amway was to purge my snobbish pseudo-radical contempt of salespeople. This contempt is an occupational hazard for academics. Living in a world of ideas, we tend to look down from our ivory towers at people who live in a world of commerce. Sales personnel are the workers who distribute those things necessary for our own use: food, soap, clothes. Although sales, like many occupations, can be dehumanizing, there is no justification for dismissing salespeople as less human than ourselves.

What makes Amway different from most other sales work is the total, twenty-four-hour-a-day obsession with Building the Dream. The insurance person or the used car salesperson practices manipulation to sell policies or cars, not to save the world from Communism. They do not have to convert the customer in order to move the product. The cars may be lemons, and the sellers may lie, and cheat, and conceal facts to make a commission. But at the end of the day they go home and do something else. Selling cars is not a path to salvation, but only a way to make a living.

The Amway distributor is a convert who wants to convert others. He wants the whole town to be in Amway, provided they are all under him. Amway is a cause, a calling to "return to the values that made our Country great." Human relationships outside of Amway have no meaning and are eventually dropped. In Amway I must do more than sell a product; I must duplicate my sponsor; and I must demand that my prospect duplicate me. Above all, I must Believe.

SEVEN

UPLINE, DOWNLINE, CROSSLINE

The genealogy of the Amway system is like a military chain of command:

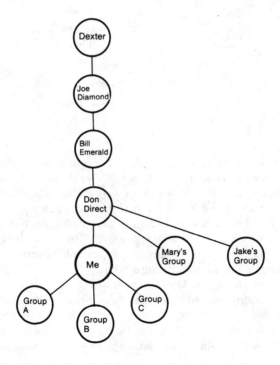

The line of authority goes from top to bottom. Dexter sponsors Joe Diamond, who sponsors Bill Emerald, who in turn sponsors Don Direct. And Don sponsors Jake, Mary and me on separate legs. My *upline* includes Don and everybody above him all the way to Dexter. This is also Jake's upline, and Mary's. My *downline* includes only the groups that came in under me, Groups A, B and C. Don's downline includes not only me and all my groups, but Jake and Mary and all theirs. Dexter's downline includes everybody in the diagram.

Crossline from me would be Jake and Mary, who are neither over nor under me but are sponsored on parallel legs. We all have the same Direct, but my business is separate from theirs. Likewise, my three groups are downline from me, but crossline from each other.

A leg *in depth* is one removed from the sponsor by intervening legs. I am four legs deep from Dexter; Bill Emerald is two legs deep from him. *Width* refers to the number of parallel legs personally sponsored by a distributor. For example:

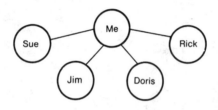

In this diagram I have a group which is four legs wide: Sue, Jim, Doris and Rick all being part of my width. For the sake of simplicity, each circle includes only one name; but in practice, a married couple generally operate a single distributorship as partners.

Around these teams is woven a complex system of human relationships which gradually replaces the ties formed with the outside world. Not only do circle diagrams resemble family trees, they become a substitute for the extended family.

In the mythology of Amway, the upline is the distributors' life source, the umbilical cord that plugs them into the great heart of the system, without which their business would have little chance of survival. From the upline come books, tapes, functions, "positive" attitude, belief, commitment, vital information, counseling and assistance. Until they go Direct, distributors also depend on the upline for products and bonus payments. Challenge Directs with the inference that they are exploiting their groups, and they will respond that their role is to help all their people succeed; without the Direct they would have no business. The mythology faithfully mirrors the general corporate argument that without rich owners and managers, the workers would have no one to give them jobs and could not feed themselves.

The distributor is indoctrinated, by means of the books, tapes, functions, attitude, belief, etc. so benevolently provided from above, to revere and obey the upline jewel. My responsibility to my upline, in exchange for all their help, is to follow their instructions, duplicate correctly, retail products, get my group to the Seminars and Rallies and build my own business, which is also their business. I am not supposed to be interested in how much money they make. I look upline only for teachings, inspiration and role models. My inquiries about their pin levels and their other legs are discouraged, unless the answers excite me to greater effort. My curiosity about their internal politics is ignored, and, at Seminars, politely squelched as Negative. My ear should be cocked upline to receive advice, but my attention should be focused downline, on the growth of my own people.

Anything I learn about upline will be revealed and selected, not at my option, but at theirs. When they move to a higher pin level, I will find out about it by watching them receive the award at a Rally. This arrangement is to motivate me to strive for my next pin. But if I ask them, in a spirit of friendly conversation, "When are you going Emerald?" I might be told, "Don't worry about me, you just concentrate on when you're going Direct." Above all I am not to get the notion that my upline *needs* me for anything. It is especially desirable if I see them change pins on the stage and realize it was not my group, but somebody else's, that pushed them over the goal. I should feel that I need them, or my business would collapse, but they could get along fine without me; I am only a small part of their volume, and if my whole line quit tomorrow they could replace me within a month.

Furthermore I am not to interfere with anything my upline does in my group. If a Direct or an upline Pearl comes down and works with my distributors, and sells them tapes and tickets to functions, and shows the Plan in their homes, and teaches them correct duplication, this is a great honor to me. To regard it as interference in "my" business is childish possessiveness that will only slow me down. I haven't got a business worth mentioning at least until I go Direct.

Even if new people that I worked hard to bring in start quitting after they get visits and phone calls from zealous leaders, I should not question or disagree with what they do, but have complete confidence in my upline's judgment. Those who quit because they get too much pressure to buy tapes or attend functions would have quit anyway, and I am better off without them. Some actions of my Direct may puzzle me at first, but I must believe that he would never do anything harmful to my business. Even though he doesn't need me, if he harmed my business he would only hurt himself. He must know what he is doing; he is the expert and I am the novice. Whenever I have doubts, I should plug in a tape and listen to it before I go to bed. Whenever I'm tempted to criticize and find fault with the business, the answer is to plug in a tape. After I have been to enough functions I'll understand the system and learn to do it Dexter's Way. My way is like driving in the ditch; Dexter's Way is the paved road. Dexter is the final authority, not only for how to build "my" business, but for all the major decisions of my life.

Of course I will never even get to meet Dexter at least until I make Direct, perhaps not until Pearl. Dexter has a special telephone number known only to Pearls and above. Mere Pearls are not allowed to enter his motor home; the qualification for this privilege is Diamond. But I can listen to Dexter on tape, and when I counsel with my upline Direct or Pearl, due to the duplication system I will be getting Dexter's Way by proxy.

The proper attitude toward the upline is not usually stated so bluntly, but conveyed little by little as the distributor becomes more and more entangled in the system. A Seminar speaker may be blunt, but a good Direct, having read Dale Carnegie, will use phrases like "I suggest" and "I recommend," interspersed with positive strokes: "Hey, I'm only trying to help you out, if I didn't tell you these things it would slow you down; we know you're going to make it, you're doing a fine job." Not until the distributor has invested heavily to build a group, and cannot easily quit, will the upline enforce conformity by getting tough.

The resemblance of a line of sponsorship to a family tree is much more than a figure of speech. The psychology of upline/downline relations is a form of paternalism which reduces the distributor to the status of a dependent child: the wise, successful, benevolent leaders can do no wrong, do not need me and only have my best interests at heart; my business is theirs, but their business is their own. Dexter is not so much Big Brother as Big Daddy, the *pater-familias*, and my immediate parent is the Direct who descends from him and has made it to Direct by following the Way. Having been robbed of an autonomous adult selfhood, I can get it back by "growing up" again in Amway. But for this process I need the care and guidance of my Daddy.

As in the military, one becomes a leader only by first becoming a follower. I learn to command by learning to obey. My effort in the beginning should be to show the Plan and build a group and plug them into the system; I should not attempt to "manage" my group, but get out there and recruit; leave the management to the leaders.

One of the carrots held out to motivate me is the privilege of being permitted to attend "leadership training functions" when I reach the appropriate pin level. The minimum qualification for the first leadership function is usually 1000 PV. In addition, there are special Seminars at which no one below 1500 is allowed, and smaller ones for the 4000 and 7500 pins. Part of the reason for establishing PV qualifications to these events is simply to pique the curiosity of the distributor; when I heard about "leadership" Seminars, where I was not allowed until I reached a certain level, I wanted to earn the pin just so I could go and find out what went on. This curiosity is teased further by the progressive-departure meeting, which is held typically on the Sunday after a big Rally. You must have earned 1000 PV in a single month to get in. The Diamonds who spoke the previous night from the stage appear at this meeting more informal and human, sometimes getting physically closer to the people by walking into the aisle to answer questions. At a certain time everyone below 1500 is asked to leave. Chairs scrape and feet shuffle and the lines of the freshmen depart into the corridors, and the diminished group draws closer to receive the intensified lessons on the attitudes expected of leaders. Then everyone below 4000 is asked to leave. Friends and upline sponsors bid so long to their juniors, and competitors snicker as they part company. The inferior pins are exposed to public view as insignificant; it is always humiliating to be asked to leave a meeting, even if the whole scenario is planned and everyone knows what will happen. With the 4000 pins, the Diamond may talk on a person-to-person basis. Then they in turn are invited out, and no one is left but Silvers, Directs and jewels.

Teasing the distributor is not the most compelling reason, however, to restrict attendance at leadership functions. Many of the lessons taught in leadership training are reserved for higher pins because the upline does not want new people to know them. "There is a right time for your people to be given certain information," say the Diamonds to the 4000 pins and Silver Producers, "and you have to learn when that time is."

The primary purpose of leadership training is to achieve total control over rising distributors. When this control is achieved, then they are acknowledged as leaders; slowly, they are trusted to begin speaking to small gatherings—to introduce the main speakers, to give brief testimonials.

The secondary purpose is to teach them how to strengthen their business and manage their downline. In my experience, the former always took precedence over the latter. If that control is not achieved, then the distributors' business, together with their entire downline, if necessary, will be ruthlessly sacrificed; their group is raided for more pliable leadership material while they themselves are by-passed and cut off.

An amusing little skit I saw performed at a 1500 leadership meeting was used to convey these priorities. I had been primed for the meeting a month in advance and was eager to learn the new techniques that I thought would enable me to make Direct within ninety days. "Wait till you get to 1500 and find out what goes on at leadership training, you'll take off and fly!" I was so hot to trot that I would have bought a roomful of products myself just to reach the bracket, but, thanks to the performance of my fledgling group, I qualified with minimal financial loss.

Instead of teaching technique, the jewels called their Directs on stage and lined them up like "chorus girls." "You realize that the most important lesson in this business is Duplication," said the Diamond. "Bill Emerald, I want to find out how well the Directs in your organization have learned this key principle." The Diamond asked the Directs one by one, putting the microphone to their mouths for their response: "Don, you have some 1500 pins from your group in the audience, don't you? What would you do to show them how well you practice what you preach? Would you do anything your sponsor told you to do, without question?"

"Anything. I have complete confidence in him."

"Is that right, Bill? Why don't you test him? What would you like him to do for us here today?"

"Well...I think I would like him to sing a song."

"What do you want me to sing?"

There was an upcoming function in Bermuda for Directs who could break two new Silvers by the qualifying date.

"Sing me a song about Bermuda. Sing 'I'll see you in Bermuda with two.' "

"Any particular tune?"

"Make one up."

After the singing, the Directs were made to go through a series of clown routines, which included hula dances, plunking on imaginary ukeleles and gambolling around the stage like elephants. Finally the Diamond called up a prominent Pearl, one of Bill Emerald's personally sponsored legs.

"Does Tom Pearl do everything you tell him, Bill?"

"Well...I don't know if he's learned yet."

"What would you like him to do?"

"I want him to take off his pants."

At this point the audience began to protest.

"Do you really want him to go through with this?"

"No!" said members of the audience.

"Absolutely," said the Emerald.

Tom Pearl unbuckled his belt.

"I notice the ladies are sitting expectantly on the edge of their seats," said the Diamond.

"All right, Tom," said the Emerald, "drop them."

Tom dropped his pants. He was wearing a bathing suit. The whole room exploded with laughter.

"How many of you thought we were going too far with this thing?" asked the Diamond. Several hands went up. "Tom, did you know why we told you this morning to put on your bathing suit under your pants?"

"I had no idea."

"But you did it anyway."

"Sure, I knew you had a good reason."

"See," the Diamond said to the crowd, "there may be times in your business when you think the upline is going too far with something, but you have to trust that they know what they're doing. Your leaders will never tell you to do something that is bad for you. Why is that? They would only hurt themselves. Isn't that right?"

The Diamond, who had been on the verge of alienating the entire audience a few minutes before, now brought them to a spontaneous burst of applause. It was a masterpiece of brinksmanship. The butt of the joke was not Tom Pearl and his chorus line but our own distrust. When we learn Tom's unquestioning faith, we will be rich like him.

Leadership functions also teach techniques, but the information is not especially restricted. I heard the same techniques explained at general Seminars and on tapes available to anyone. A vital concept for insuring the long-range health of a business is building depth.

The method of building depth is inherent in the ideal pattern for starting new distributors, which is described in Chapter Five. When sponsoring a new person, my objective is to work directly with her contacts. Since she knows nothing, I cannot trust her to do follow-ups and move tickets and tapes; as quickly as possible I introduce her to the Seminar and Rally system and then start doing meetings for her best prospect. I keep repeating this process until I carry a leg to a dead end, or the ends of the earth, whichever comes first. If I have a line which is ten legs deep, the place for me to work is on the tenth leg, with the brand new person. The last thing I should do is try to motivate a personally sponsored distributor by sitting on her like a mother hen, hoping she will hatch a group. Tuesday I might show the Plan in Jack's livingroom, but Wednesday I want to be in the next town showing it to Bob and Donna, who came to Jack's place on Tuesday; and Friday I want to see Bob's friend Pete, who might live twenty miles away. Then after I have sponsored Pete under Bob and Donna, and that couple under Jack, I return to him and say, "Look how your business is growing, Jack, it's about time you learned the Plan." If he should quit, the Donna-Pete-Bob leg remains mine.

Building depth is a mystically inspiring game which, to me, became fascinating for its own sake, as a convoluted expression of material desire. The legs of an Amway business are like the roots of a gigantic money tree; some tendrils wither and die, while others twine through the population in such sinuous entanglements that your next-door neighbor's upline might include the Ku Klux Klan, Black Muslims and your own cousin all living in different states. The trunk of this tree is the Corporation. The products and tapes and the kinetic energy that we know variously as hope, faith, dreams and work, move down toward the roots. The money, however, moves toward the top.

Working depth on a single line accomplishes five important goals:

1) The line is secured from collapse in case any particular leg drops out. If I sponsor a line under Jack which goes down to ten legs deep, and Jack quits, I still have nine other legs on that line. Moreover, Jack will think twice about quitting if people under him plan to stay in.

2) The way to motivate a personally sponsored leg is to build a fire under him. Business volume comes from the bottom up. If I keep adding new people under Jack in a straight line, his volume grows but he will not be able to keep the bonus money on that volume. When all your volume is done by a single leg, you and that leg are in the same PV bracket. You might receive 18 percent but you have to pay out 18 percent to the person doing the business. You only make money if your bracket is higher than his. Otherwise your PV bonus goes right through you and on to him. Jack must build side-ways in order to lift

himself up to a bracket higher than his deep leg. By deepening the leg further, I make it necessary for him to add more width in order to profit from the work I have done for him.

3) I keep in constant touch with his downline by working at the bottom of the group. I want to make sure that the entire line conforms to Dexter's Way and that the tapes and teachings are not being held up by some Unbeliever in between. If I want to know whether Jack is following my advice, I don't ask him directly; he might lie or get defensive. Instead I befriend his downline and find out from them.

4) Jack may not be a leader; he might take years to become one, and I would rather not wait that long. By working depth, I can identify the potential leaders in his group. "Every loser knows a winner." I am in effect diving for Pearls in his ocean; but his business is mine and my business is my own. Only a fool would resent this practice, because Amway is love, and Jack should realize I would never do anything to hurt his interests; I would only be hurting myself. Then if Jack is intractable and decides to run his own show, I can groom the leaders downline from him and teach his people Dexter's Way whether he likes it or not. In fact I can force Jack out entirely and still get a Direct from one of his legs. If Jack really understands Amway, he might be grateful that I forced him out.

5) The corporation pays an extra commission, called a Pearl Bonus, for volume in depth. The amount is ½ percent on the BV of all Directs down to and including the nearest Pearl on the line. To qualify for it I have to be a Pearl. This concept may sound more complicated than it is. It works as follows:

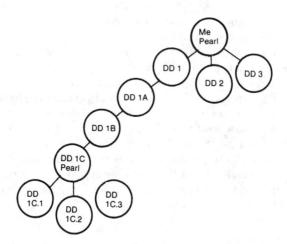

My Pearl bonus is not paid on the volumes of DD 1, 2 and 3, because they are personally sponsored by me. Depth begins with DD 1A. On her, and on everything below her down to DD 1C.1, 1C.2 and 1C.3, I get the ½ percent. But since DD 1C is a Pearl, *she* receives the bonus on any Directs in depth below her three Direct legs. The percentage may not sound like much, but in this example, with every leg doing a minimum volume of $12,000, the Pearl Bonus would amount to $360 per month, in addition to the 3 percent commission paid on the volumes of my personally sponsored Directs. From an upline point of view, it is a very sound policy to teach my group to build depth on a single line.

In the beginning I may see a few big pins showing the Plan at my house, giving me personal instruction and inviting me and my wife over to their place late at night for coffee. The reason is not hard to guess: as a new recruit, I am the depth, the outer fringe, of their business. As soon as they find another good prospect from my list, they will sponsor her under me and move on down the line. After I have acquired a group and been in the business for a while, these big pins are not so visible; I have to make appointments to see them and earn their attention by doing what they do; I have to know my place on the hierarchy, and, eventually, they will not even counsel me until I reach 4000 PV.

Leadership functions also teach the proper methods for controlling a group. It is always considered highly dangerous at any level to switch from showing the Plan to managing a group. At 1500 or 4000, the distributor is not supposed to be concerned with management at all, but leave that task to the expertise of the Direct and get out there evenings and draw circles. Nevertheless, drawing circles leads to acquiring a downline, and, once acquired, a downline must be supplied, trained, motivated and molded.

"By encouraging your distributors to duplicate your efforts," says a Company publication, "you build the organizational depth that leads to high volume."* In the Yager business, a great deal more is "duplicated" besides effort. Emeralds have said that all they have to do is watch a distributor for a while and they can tell who his upline Direct is. Distributors tend to copy the walk, mannerisms, voice inflections, body language and cliches of their Directs. Duplication sometimes extends all the way down to the brand of shoes, and all the way up to the hairstyle. When Dexter Yager got an Afro hairstyle, throughout 1979 and 1980, some Directs in his organization began curling their hair in the same style.

The Amagram, December 1981, p. 31.

How I am taught to deal with my downline is simply a duplication of how my upline deals with me. I must not let them think I need them for anything. When they ask for my help, before granting an appointment I should imply that I keep a full calendar and they are lucky to see me at all. When they come to my house for products, I should sponsor new people and have new faces come at the same hour, so that each knows she is only a small part of my group. I should be familiar with the goals and dreams of every one of my personally sponsored distributors, everyone that I work with in depth. If downline people ask me about my business, I should respond, "Don't worry about me, when are you going Direct?"

I should not tolerate any excuse for failure to conform. My distributors must buy upline-approved tapes, books and marker boards and they must attend the functions and keep products and sponsoring kits and decision paks on hand. Amway Corporation does not require any of these things as a condition of being a distributor, but the leaders teach me how to move the material over the objections of my people. The accessories, especially tapes, books and marker boards, are "the mortar that holds the bricks of a business together." Without mortar the bricks will sooner or later fall down. The amount of money a distributor spends on accessories should be 20 percent of the total product volume. I should program my distributors to buy a minimum of one tape and one approved book per week for everyone in their groups.

"I can't afford tapes."

"Do you have a color television?"

"Sure."

"Would you sell your television to add an extra hundred thousand a year to your income?"

"I can sponsor people without listening to tapes."

"Would you let a surgeon operate on you who hadn't read any medical books or attended seminars on anatomy?"

"I can't find a babysitter for the day of the Rally so I guess I won't be able to go."

"You'll go if it harelips the king."

"What do you mean?"

"How do you think it looks for me to be telling your people to come to a Rally and you're not there?"

Downline management in Amway is an excellent example of behavioral psychology in action. This fact is not without irony.

Rich DeVos, in *Believe!* (Pocket Books, 1975), a collection of the Founder's opinions on God, America and free enterprise, disassociates himself from B.F. Skinner and behaviorism, on the premise that it represents a "no-accountability" point of view; Skinner, the most influential psychologist in America, and the chief architect of modern behavioral science, is made a symbol of the whole liberal idea that society, not the individual, causes bad actions:

> Man is not responsible for his behavior, Skinner says. He is constantly being manipulated by his environment and all his actions are forced on him by the conditions under which he has experienced life. No matter what he is or does, Skinner says, he could do no differently . . . He is never good or bad; he merely behaves according to the conditions that exist in him and around him.*

DeVos then announces sagely that "a society built on that premise will never work." Against this fuzzy socialistic utopianism he offers belief in the "freedom" and "dignity" of the individual. We must each be accountable for what we do. We must accept responsibility for our deeds.

But the system which DeVos co-founded for recruiting and controlling Amway distributors is a spendid application of all the behavior shaping techniques which Skinner discovered and taught. This is the reason for its phenomenal success. Upline leaders identify specific behavioral objectives: make a contact, use the telephone, get a meeting, get a follow-up. They use graduated positive reinforcement and successive approximations to mold their people toward the desired goal. They extinguish unwanted behavior, or nonconformity, by withdrawal of attention and rewards, and by changing the environment of the subject. Among the most powerful of their negative reinforcers is social ostracism.

The PV scale itself is a prime example of graduated positive reinforcement; it is easy to reach the lower brackets of 100, 300, 600, and the rapidly escalating percentages give immediate and realistically attainable reward. This is not the same thing as making money; as we shall see later, very few people make any real money in Amway, but it is nonetheless reinforcing to go from 3 percent to 9 percent on the scale; the hope is thereby kept alive. Then the gaps between brackets get larger and larger: 1000, 1500, 2500, 4000, 6000. A more and more intense level of commitment is required to reach them.

A vigorous organization also reinforces distributors with pins, attention, approval and social life. The social life, as seen in the Rallies, is a carefully controlled environment which amplifies the

*Believe!, pp. 44-45.

total reinforcement structure with a hierarchy of status and recognition appropriate to each new behavioral goal. A 4000 pin is allowed on stage and given a counseling audience with his upline Emerald; a Direct may eat with the leaders; a jewel may park her Cadillac in front of the convention center.

In short, the distributor is conditioned to the Amway lifestyle, just as certainly as a Marine recruit is conditioned to the *semper fidelis* of the Corps.

Distributors who refuse to conform should be ignored. I am not home when they call. I don't give them appointments or draw circles for them. I don't buy back their products and tapes. I charge them $10 for each error on their order sheet. Through working depth I influence their people to have nothing to do with them. I arrange to have their downline pick up products at my house and pay the bonus checks directly, and then charge the nonconformist a bookkeeping fee. If the group is affected beyond redemption, then I cut off the whole line and pressure the people in depth to quit. Better to lose one member than that thy whole body should perish.

Among the things I must never do with my downline are criticize a product, function, tape, policy or upline leader, socialize during prime evening time (8-11 p.m.) when we should be drawing circles, or allow distributors on different legs to get friendly with each other. No matter what happens, the products are the best products in the world; the tapes are all fantastic; the functions will blow your mind (if you have any mind left to blow, after the first year); the leaders are super people and we're lucky to have them, and I would give a month's bonus for an hour on their calendar.

If someone complains that she got a warped marker board, I should say "How would you like to be able to buy a new board every week and take it as a tax deduction? That's your goal, right? Don't let details hold you back." If the nail polish chips or the soap turns clothes gray, or the products are too expensive, I tell the distributor, "Look, will Revlon and Tide put your kids through school? Amway did over 1.4 billion dollars in retail sales last year, they must be doing something right."

The standard formula for inverting Negative is called *feel, felt and found:* "Hey Joe, I understand how you feel, I felt that way too, but let me tell you what I found." If I'm selling tickets to a Rally in my group and someone says that Rallies are repetitive and boring, the formula gives me a quick and ready comeback: "I used to feel that way too, but then I found that all the Directs made a habit of going to Rallies before they went Direct."

How is the contradiction between the official pronouncements of DeVos against behaviorism and the actual practice of downline management to be explained? Does he not understand Skinner? Is he being deliberately dishonest?

Only for the naive is there any real contradiction. The test of all "truth" in Amway is whether it strengthens the business and increases PV. Dishonesty is such a routine and formulaic practice that the jewels probably do not even recognize it. Just as they can reduce feeling to the stock response of "feel, felt and found" without any sense of alienation from what is genuinely felt, so "freedom," "dignity" and "responsibility" can be used as catch-words to control thought with no perception that the ideology they express kills freedom. Skinner is merely a "strawman," a convenient symbol for the Enemy. Few Amway people are likely to study Skinner and learn how they are being manipulated, any more than they will study Paul Sweezy or Karl Marx. The goal of the ideology is to transform, not merely behavior, but consciousness.

And this is indeed what happens. It is not possible to achieve a high level in Amway without a transformation of consciousness. Human relationships are altered by the programming and the upline/downline/crossline context, and this effect needs to be examined and weighed as part of the total price of the jewel.

EIGHT

SO
MUCH LOVE
IN A SOAPBOX

Smile at everyone. Shake hands warmly. Don't be afraid to talk to people, no matter how important they are. Even the Governor puts his pants on one leg at a time. Learn how to relate with all kinds—black, brown, yellow or white, Christian, Muslim, Klansman, doctor, lawyer, Indian chief. Be friendly, even if you feel down; it's better than crying in your milk.

This sage advice describes the *funnel concept,* one of the teachings programmed into the distributor through the audio-visual techniques of the mighty mind-blow. If you try to fill a bottle with sand using a very narrow funnel, you might get a few grains in there, but a wide funnel will do it a lot faster. Stay in the mainstream, don't get out on the fringe looking for weirdos and freaks. If you sponsor a freak, you have a distributor with a very narrow funnel. "And who will he sponsor? Other freaks like him; people who can't relate to the mainstream." A person like that will take forever to go Direct, and he won't duplicate properly, and neither will his line. So learn to keep a *wide funnel.* Stay in the broad current of humanity.

Perhaps the advocates of the Amway system would argue that I missed the point by comparing the lines of sponsorship to a military chain of command. The whole business, they say, is animated by Love. Drawing circles is The Golden Rule in action. ·

The funnel concept is a good example of Amway Love applied as a prospecting technique. Although I have abandoned the "losers" among my former friends, I must still *seem* to be old warm-hearted Joe, willing to put my feet up on the stove and get out the cornbread when I'm not drawing circles. If I can't *play the role* of old warm-hearted Joe when the occasion demands, I am limited in who I can sponsor; people who eat cornbread and put their feet up on the stove will not trust me. But my purpose is to build the business. Being Just Folks is cultivated as a means to that end.

My "true friends" are my upline, who give me this wonderful opportunity to realize my dreams. They spend time working in my group, keep extra products on hand so I can fill rush orders in a hurry, counsel me all hours of the night. Their burning desire is to help me go Direct.

To be a Diamond, all I have to do is find six ordinary people and "transform their lives." At Family Reunions, the love theme is sometimes ritualized by the passing of the Flame: thousands of distributors bring candles, and the highest pin lights the candles of the Directs, who in turn light those down the scale, until the Flame passes out to the farthest reaches of the crowd. "Who would ever have thought," says the high pin over his microphone, "that so much love could come from a little box of soap?"

But I soon discover that every hour spent in my group by a jewel entitles him to pull my strings at some time in the future. I might get a phonecall at midnight telling me to stock more decision paks and tapes.

"I can't afford it."

"You can't afford not to. You want your business to grow, don't you?"

"Sure, but I got in to make money, not to go broke."

"You have to spend money to make money. Don't get hung up on details, it will only slow you down."

"Well, Amway doesn't require me to buy decision paks and tapes. They say so right in the literature."

"Listen, if you want our help you have to learn to take our advice. We would never do anything that would hurt your business. Do you have confidence in us or not?"

The message is clear: they love me if I do what I'm told. The jewel wants to pass the burden of carrying supplies to his downline so that *his* money will be freed up for other uses. He is my true friend and only has my best interest at heart.

With my downline I learn to repeat the same routine. I feed them only the "love" which brings them along up the scale, and only if they conform to the mold. Moreover, the mold is not subject to change by us. We are the *tail*, and our leaders are the *dog*. The dog always wags the tail, not the other way around. I know my group's PV, personal goals, even the conditions of their marriages, but they know nothing about my total business and nothing Negative about my life; for I never let Negative go down in my group.

At the Rallies, speakers talk about how Amway people stick together when one of them is in trouble. A Direct is killed in a car accident and the funeral is packed with members of his group; distributors help the wife and children, move the furniture around, make arrangements to ease the burden on the family. Violins play somewhere offstage during these touching stories; but a distributor below the level of Direct, unless she is a new favorite, and rising fast, and a perfect model of duplication, should not hold her breath waiting for an upline Pearl to move her furniture.

The Pearl, on the other hand, has a free labor force to call on when he needs wood-cutters and water-carriers. One Vermont jewel, moving in a rented truck, called a dozen people from his downline to carry the furniture for him. Answering a call like this promptly and cheerfully might mean a spot as ticket-taker at the next Rally. It shows Good Attitude. Being a ticket-taker is a visible position, reserved for go-getters. You know a distributor is really making it when you see him taking tickets; it means he is rubbing elbows with the jewels, and being tested for the role of Host. After drafting his own downline to do his work for him, the leader may then advertise the event as an *exemplum* of Amway love.

An experience I had with a leadership Seminar will further illustrate the proper etiquette of "love" between upline and downline. A prominent jewel high up on the line had come over to our territory to speak with a few selected 4000 pins. He had come specifically to help somebody else crossline from me, one of my competitors, and my Direct made a point of letting me know this. I had languished at 4000 for months without showing any signs of meteoric upward thrust. In fact I was wondering if I should quit. The hope was that this important personage might jar me out of my "rut."

The jewel led off by telling us that he does not help just any group, he considers carefully where to spend his time; he had discussed us with his wife, and decided that, based on the signs of good duplication he had seen, it was worth his while to make this trip. He praised J. Paul Getty and Howard Hughes as heroes fit to model our lives after, and then launched into specific advice: we must focus our attention on the growth of our own people. Never mind wondering how much money *he* made; that was irrelevant to our success. And we must not listen to anyone who talks against Amway or men of great wealth. In fact do not even converse with a critic. "Would you let a friend come into your home and empty a bucket of garbage on your livingroom floor? Then why would you let her dump garbage into your mind?"

This admonition had a hauntingly familiar ring. I had heard it expressed in the 1960s by communists of Stalinist persuasion who worked around the peace and radical student movements of that era: "Do not let so-and-so speak, he is a fascist pig, he is an enemy of the people, shout him down."

During a break I was introduced and shook the leader's hand—distributors crowded around him as if he might any moment start handing out hundred-dollar bills—and he said "You look sharp in that suit."

"Well," I said, "you look sharp in yours."

"When are you going Direct?"

"When are you going Diamond?"

A dark cloud passed over his face, and he said "See, you weren't listening to what I said. Don't focus your attention upline."

Later, my local leaders castigated me for my impertinence. They told me that if I ever get such a priceless opportunity again to meet a high jewel, *I better show more respect*. I had violated the hierarchy by treating him as an equal. I was supposed to say "Ninety days, sir," and give a specific date. Instead I had reflected back to him the patronizing stroke about my suit and the needle about my pin-level, and he was outraged. He would not even convey his displeasure personally, but used his intervening legs to do it.

What does Amway have in common with the Golden Rule? Do leaders help their legs put foundations under their castles in the air?

At every Seminar, distributors are urged to write down their personal goals. We were supposed to cut out pictures of our goals from magazines and tape them on the refrigerator door. Leaders are taught to become familiar with the goals of their people. My Direct asked to see my written list and came to my house to check the refrigerator.

One might argue that to help a person visualize and achieve goals is a plausible good deed. Instead of giving my hungry friend a fish, I teach her how to catch her own. But in Amway I do it only if I make a percentage on the fish. And what I want her to catch is not fish anyway, but motor homes and Cadillacs—or other luxuries that she can only afford by playing my game for the rest of her life. Moreover, I do not wish her to see the little plastic bubble that this game puts over the human spirit. In fact it is unlikely that I will see it myself, except in dreams of my face, trapped inside the circles on my marker board, drowning in LOC.

By writing down a list of goals, I begin to nurture the illusion of personal destiny. Even though my goals may be cars, boats, homes and clothes, all the pre-masticated stock pablum of the commercial media, to write them down and make a career out of achieving them gives me a sense of importance; I am somebody special because I have this picture on my refrigerator. Then to own the actual object justifies my self-definition as a winner.

But the lust for objects is a parching wind; the heart is dried by it like a pod, and the goals rattle inside like mockeries of electronic happiness. Amway jewels know, as all true believers in the Protestant ethic have known since Puritan times, that mere wealth without soul is a tasteless carrot to dangle before a donkey. If it is sugared with religion, perhaps the donkey will believe in the race. "True success is founded on the success of others. Amway is people helping people. You just keep giving this thing away, keep on giving it away, and after a while it will come back." In the new Gospel according to Amway, the Good Samaritan sponsors not only the wounded person in the ditch, but the Inn-keeper, the Pharisee and the Governor—especially the Governor, who is a winner, and understands tax advantages. If the 3 percent bonus is not forthcoming, he returns the wounded person to the ditch, who , after all, "chose" to be there.

The major goals of life, the Dream, the big motor home, the mansion, cannot be taken until they are "earned." It is unwise to purchase a motor home without permission from above. One should have approval, not only for the timing of the purchase, but the style and make.

This is an Emerald's advice on motor homes, paraphrased from a 1500 leadership function:

"When I first made it to Direct, I wanted a motor home so bad I could taste it. Dexter told me it wasn't time, but I had no patience, I wanted to do it *my* way. After all, this is 'my business.' I know none of you have ever said that to your sponsor. Well I couldn't afford a coach like Dexter's, so I went out and bought this little Winnebago, it wasn't number one, but I thought it was cute. A cute little box on wheels, is what it was. I was actually proud of that thing. I was so proud that I went and took it to Dexter's place. That was my second mistake. I knew right away something was wrong when I pulled into that parking lot. Here's Dexter's coach, and here's this little kiddie cart, I left it way over in the corner, hoping he wouldn't see it; and Dexter was talking to some people, and I waited, and waited, and finally he came over. He said 'What's that?' And I said 'That's my motor home.' And he said 'Oh.' And just walked away. He didn't even laugh. I mean, at least he could have held his nose and snickered, I wouldn't have felt so bad. I got rid of that thing. I didn't make any more ventures into motor homes until I got the word from Dex. The one I have now takes up the whole yard. The neighbors complain that it

blocks their view so I park it right out in front, where they'll be sure to
see it on their way to work in the morning.''

At a leadership function in New Hampshire, my upline jewels
came onstage and wept into the microphone as they described the
"love" they had learned to give and receive in the Amway business.
One after the other they choked up, and the tears coursed down their
cheeks, and their voices trembled as they gave instructions to the 1500
pins in the audience.

"I asked Bill's oldest boy how his father had changed since he got
into Amway. And he said...he said...I'm sorry, I can't speak. He said
before Amway he didn't know he had a father.'' The father had been
an alcoholic.

"Your people are looking for you to help transform their lives.
And the only way you're going to do that is by transforming your own
life. And if you're not willing to change...if you're not willing to listen
to somebody that knows more than you...then you're just stupid and
selfish...and the only thing you can do for your people is get out of
their way...because you're just holding them back.''

"Dexter and Bill and Tom, these men are my heroes. I pattern my
life after them. I'd stake my life on their word. What kind of hero do
you want your kids to worship? Some doped-up rock musician? Or do
you want them to worship men who have achieved success for their
wives and families by hard work, like Dexter and Bill and the other
leaders in this business? Men who believe in their country and believe
in God? You've got to worship these men as heroes, you set the
example for the people in your group. How many of you would like to
sponsor seven Dexters? Would that set you up for life? Then *edify your
upline*. They're super leaders, aren't they? If you don't believe that,
then what are you doing here? Dexter is Our Leader.'' The crowd went
wild.

"When you're lounging around the house on a weekend and you
go out for a gallon of milk, put on a coat and tie. You might meet one
of your prospects at the store. How will it look to him if you come
slobbing up to the counter in your old flannel shirt? To be successful,
you have to look successful not only when you're showing the Plan,
but every time you appear in public.''

"This is a very important piece of advice, gang. You meet other
distributors at these functions. And it's nice to say hello, but don't
crossline. When you travel to functions, go with your own upline, if
you have to ride with someone, but the best thing is to go by
yourselves. When you go out to eat after the Seminar, don't sit with
people from different lines. It won't do your business any good to
wonder what someone else on a different line is doing. Socialize

upline. The upline will always give you straight information. Why is that? Because it's in their interest."

I was not introduced to the prohibition against crosslining until after I had earned my 1500 pin. I thought my business was really cooking, there were ten or fifteen couples in my group and some of them had bought boards and easels and were drawing circles on their own. My volume was jumping a new bracket every month. I decided to pull them all together for a meeting to discuss what we wanted from the business and how we could best put the idea across to new contacts. At that time I looked on Amway as a kind of people's distribution system, a wonderful tool for self-help, a way for the working-person to take advantage of tax laws that favored income derived from profit. Some of my new distributors were shy about retailing products, and I thought I could show them from my own experience how to overcome that particular block.

Inadvertently I mentioned to my Direct that I was planning a small-scale seminar at my house. I had already invited the members of the group. They were enthusiastic about coming; they wanted all the help they could get. Within the hour I got a call from my upline Pearl telling me to cancel the meeting.

"Why?"

"That's crosslining. We don't do that in our line."

"Explain this to me, I don't understand."

"You shouldn't bring distributors on different legs together for social occasions. It could slow them down. If you want them to learn the business, get them to the regular Seminars and Rallies."

"How would it slow them down?"

"Well, some people in one of my legs went to Free Enterprise Day once with distributors from another line; they rode down to Charlotte in the same car, and they were hot and tired, and they started complaining about the trip, and the cost, and the food and the speakers. And they talked themselves right out of the business. They all quit. Nobody was there from upline to set them straight."

"But I want to talk with my distributors. Can't I do that?"

"Sure, that's fine. Talk with them one at a time on the phone. Late at night, after they finish drawing circles."

"But I want to talk with them all at once."

"You shouldn't be trying to give seminars at 1500 anyway. That's why we have functions. Get them to the functions, let the Directs teach them."

"I thought this was my business."

"Well, it's our business too."

I persisted that I was free to invite anyone I wanted to my home, for any legal reason, and I would go ahead with the meeting. Then the Direct called every couple in my group and told them not to come, the meeting was cancelled, and there would be another meeting they could attend at *his* home in two weeks.

At 4000 I was taught the "correct" way to handle different legs. Let them encounter one another at my home only during product pick-up, so they can see that they are merely a small part of my business. Promote competition between them by casually and privately mentioning to Distributor A the tremendous growth enjoyed by Distributor B. Make sure that when one couple wins an award at a Rally, the other legs are there to watch them go up on stage and get their pin.

Do most Amway groups operate like this? Was my upline an especially authoritarian and fanatical aberration from the norm within Amway? The highest accessible jewel on the line was the person who told my Direct to cancel my meeting, a man well known and respected in the business throughout the Northeast region, who speaks regularly at functions attended by thousands. He assured me, and I believe him, that he duplicates Dexter's Way to the letter, and that was the secret of his personal success.

When I thought about it, the ban on crosslining makes sense as a means for achieving complete control over a distributor force. I had approached the business as a *cooperative* enterprise, by a group of equals, to better their circumstances, every person free to apply their own method and swap ideas with others. But the purpose of Amway is to sell, and reinforce, a *competitive* class system, with a status hierarchy; the ultimate hope of each Believer is to rule over thousands of subjects, like a king. The highest pin is a *Crown* full of diamonds. The lure of the rewards—the voyage on the Amway yacht, vacations on Peter Island, membership in exclusive clubs—is that only a very few can have them. For the jewels, Amway is a fantasy world in which they can play at being aristocrats. The idea that any distributor is their equal would destroy the whole point of the fantasy.

The ban on crosslining, if correctly duplicated, would limit most human contacts to upline, downline and prospects. The upline manipulates me; I manipulate my downline and my prospects. "Association should be vertical, not horizontal." No friendship can develop, therefore, which is not conditioned by the Amway context. I say hello to crossline distributors, but cannot meet with them or befriend them. Even if I could, they are competitors; I want to sponsor their prospects and they want to sponsor mine. The lines are kept apart. The business is thus made impervious to any kind of collective action from distributors below the level of Direct. A rebellion, or movement for change, on one line would be restricted only to that line, and could not spread to others. The infected line is then cut off, the uncorrupted customers and distributors are salvaged through working depth and the agitators pressured to quit.

A community deeply penetrated by the Amway system is, in effect, fragmented into separate psychological compartments, corresponding to the separate distributorships, and then reconstituted along the lines of the Amway genealogical tree. I actually observed this process happening on the campus and neighborhood level. Two friends get into Amway on different lines; they have many of the same contacts; they inadvertently take prospects and customers from each other; each wonders if the other is deliberately stealing his or her people; soon they are not speaking anymore except to needle one another about their PV. Then they encounter the ban on crosslining and cease altogether to be friends. They compete to see which one will be first to win the various pins. The sponsor watches them from the wings, gleefully rubbing his hands. This kind of antagonism was promoted by my upline, who took special delight in sponsoring my neighbors and colleagues before I could get to them. One way to destroy a union local, I would think, is to sponsor a few members on separate legs and let them compete for the rest.

One does not have to be a robot to stay in Amway (but it helps). Thousands of distributors probably receive no pressure to conform, because they have no ambition in the business beyond selling a few products. But when the Dream bites into the brain, and you get big ideas, is when you start to become "transformed." The process is gradual. You do it to yourself. You fasten the puppet strings onto your own hands and feet, and then dance out on the stage singing "Born Free."

It is not my intention to stereotype all Amway leaders as puppets, or greedy hypocrites incapable of opening their hearts to their fellow humans. The most indoctrinated fanatics probably pat their dogs and show genuine tenderness to their families. Intelligence and generosity flourish within the worst systems in the world. Out of three or four dozen Directs whom I saw regularly at Seminars, I felt real affection and respect for at least two. They were open and decent, with a rich sense of humor, and a clear knowledge of how to use Amway for sober, practical ends, like education, family travel, job independence. Their identities did not seem to depend on Amway, and they did not attempt to convert their audience into Believers and worshippers.

One was from rural Nova Scotia, a hunter and fisherman who seemed relatively uncorrupted by attachment to commodities and did not appear to judge anyone for being different. "When you show the

Plan, it's like wounding a deer," he said. "You can't just let it run off and bleed to death, you have to bring it in." After a saccharine diet of "love" sermons, honesty like that was a fresh fall of snow in the northern woods.

The other Direct was himself ostracized and bypassed by the jewels above him. He was an embarrassment to the whole local organization because he had risen too high to be ignored. His failure in duplication was to tell his people that they were free to use the business for their own goals, schedule their own time commitments, and use what methods seemed best for them, consistent with the law and the Amway Code of Ethics. He stayed friendly with the dropouts and nonconformists as well as the go-getters. He was not allowed to speak at functions. His upline told me that he knew nothing about the business and I would surely fail if I listened to him. He made Direct because two of his legs, heeding his upline's advice, bypassed him and became products of Correct Duplication and pushed him over 7500 with their volume, and held him there long enough for him to qualify as a Voting Member. It was partly my endless delight at his presence in the hierarchy that kept me in for so long. Probably he will learn to conform or quit.

Yager himself is praised as a man of love by many of his Directs. "Dexter didn't need my business," said one of his public relations agents, "he was already a Triple Diamond before he sponsored me. He taught me because he loved me, he wanted me to succeed." But this anecdote, told to a coliseum full of Yager distributors, had the obvious function of helping to maintain their belief in him.

Amway "love," like "freedom," is simply part of the doctrine that holds the business together. Genuine love is willingness to give, intelligently, without expecting anything in return. Nothing could be further from the reality of the Amway system. Distributors on the bottom are certainly programmed to give, and give and give, but it is not an intelligent choice, it is a conditioned response. The leaders give in order to increase their bonus checks and propagate the gospel that maintains their territories. "Love" is an aspect of their total ideology. The ultimate goal is not love at all, but power.

NINE

IN
FOR
LIFE

A combination of sacrifices and results hooks the distributor by increments into the Amway circuit. In the beginning the sacrifices predominate.

Compared to most small business ventures, which may require an initial investment of thousands, the cost of starting an Amway distributorship seems risk-free. It is low enough to be within reach of virtually anyone, no matter from what class or section of town. Still, for working people it is not cheap. The kit, tapes and books, marker board and easel with which to show the Plan, and first Rally tickets add up to a commitment of $140-150: a strain on the budget roughly equivalent to an unexpected major car repair.

Naturally one wants to get this investment back as quickly as possible, and the most obvious way is to sell. But never mind the investment. It could take a week of selling just to pay for the gasoline required to deliver five boxes of soap. Trying to break even by retailing Amway products is like trying to climb out of quicksand. Perhaps some distributors make a living at it; the Corporation magazine reports occasional record-breaking enthusiasts who become Silver Producers on their own sales. But in fact the average monthly retail sales volume per distributor in 1981 was $150. The Corporation itself calculated this figure by including only "active" distributors, that is, ones who had

> engaged in at least one of the following activities during the month for which sales data were sought: (a) attempted to make a retail sale, or (b) presented the Amway Sales and Marketing Plan, or (c) received bonus money from Amway or his/her sponsor, or (d) attended an Amway meeting (one

conducted by Amway corporation or one conducted by an
Amway distributor).*

We doubt if anyone doing this volume could ever make enough in
retail profit to justify the time, trouble and expense of taking and
filling orders.

To begin with, the Corporation does not make sample sizes of
most items in its line. If you want to show something to a customer,
you have to buy it first—in the full size container. To market jewelry,
you should own a demonstration kit full of jewelry, each unit of
which costs anywhere from $5 to $50. To sell cosmetics, you should
have the cosmetics display case. To sell the cookware and smoke
alarms, you need some cookware and a smoke alarm.

The official Corporation policy is that no one below the level of
Direct has to stock inventory as a condition of being a distributor. And
this is true; my application was accepted without proof of inventory
purchase. But it is difficult to sell goods without having them around.
Moreover, distributors come under intense pressure to convert their
homes totally to Amway products within a few months of signing up.
The initial "investment" figure is deceptive; the inventory which you
are not required to purchase can easily double and triple that figure.

A second drain on the profits comes from the expense of literature
and sales aids. Every time I went to the home of my mentor in the
business, new publications were laid out on the table: fact sheets,
advertising brochures, compendia. Everything costs money; even the
one-page flyers that went with new products were a dime or twenty
cents apiece. Then the hand was placed on my arm, and the white
smile would flash: "I've got a fantastic new tape; it'll *blow your
mind.*" The tapes were $3.50 each. It was like being caught in a
spider's web. I might have made $5 that day selling soap, but before I
could extricate myself from the web and go home I had written a check
for ten. "You ought to firm up that handshake," said the Mentor,
"and smile, the business is fun."

The profit margin in retail sales is supposed to be an average 30
percent. For me, every penny was eaten up in costs, not counting the
hours spent securing the customers and persuading them to buy. For
the few months when the account book actually showed a profit in
retail selling, if I counted the value of my own time I made about a
dollar an hour. I deliberately did not include the cost of changing my
house over to Amway; the figures would have wiped me out of the

*The Amagram, Feb. 1982, p. 39.

business, and given me more than a glimmer of suspicion that I was being had. I told myself that I would have to buy soaps and cleaners anyway, and I had to eat lunch; I might as well eat a Nutrilite food bar. But in fact Amway products are much more expensive than comparable fare in the discount markets, and being in the business, I tended to buy a lot more than I would ever use.

To look at these facts honestly is considered Negative, a sign of "stinking thinking." They are all explained away by various means. Buying samples, literature, tapes and sales aids, paying for gasoline to find customers and deliver products to them, are forms of "investment" in "my own" business. Think what I would have to pay for a Wendy's franchise; if I nickel-and-dime this thing I'll never get anywhere; besides, selling soap is child's play.

The expense of the products hits most new people the minute they open a price list. I infer this from the fact that all of the distributors in my group were deeply concerned about it; rationalizations for the high prices were constantly being given at Seminars; evidently other lines had the same complaint, although, of course, I could not find out what other lines thought unless I, and they, disobeyed the ban on crossline socializing. The usual way to account for the high prices was to point out that Amway products are concentrated, and that, on a per-use basis, they actually cost less. But it takes time and skill to persuade a customer that he or she is getting a better bargain to pay $6.25 for a quart of Amway Dish Drops and wait a week or two for delivery, than to stop at the household supplies counter of a local supermarket and pick up a quart of no-brand dish liquid for $1.39. With the cosmetics, the concentration argument did not apply; one simply had to explain that Amway nail polish cost more because it was better; a position which became embarrassing when the customer discovered that it chipped off the nail in less than a day.

Whether Amway products are good, or mediocre, is really an unimportant question. The soap cleans; the vitamins provide the RDA amounts listed on the labels; the smoke detector works. The company scores points with environmentalists by being one of the first to offer a no-phosphate laundry detergent. The money-back guarantee in case of customer dissatisfaction was, to my knowledge, always honored, although it is the distributor who must pay the bill to ship the unwanted product back to ADA. Most items perform well; the defective stuff is usually pulled off the market and changed. Beyond these few remarks, we may be content to let the Corporation make its own case for product quality. The point here is how the pricing affects the distributor's chance to make retail money. I found it to be almost prohibitive. Large commercial establishments, cleaning contractors and institutions, as a rule, were not interested in doubling their bill for floor wax in order to get a product which far exceeded Federal quality standards. Even if the wax is superb, few business concerns wish to spend their overhead allowances on a search for the ultimate shiny floor. Household customers had to be constantly wooed with attention, discounts and deals to keep them from buying their soap at the supermarket. I could not charge friends and family members a full retail price and still maintain their friendship, much less their patronage.

A good salesperson is not deterred by customer objections to price. "I don't give any discounts," said a Ruby at a Seminar, "the products are already a bargain at the recommended retail." The person who can sell refrigerators to Eskimoes will be able to make Amway customers feel that their money was well spent.

But Most Amway distributors are not sales people by trade; they are teachers, carpenters, factory workers and a thousand other occupations, and their chances of landing big commercial accounts for floor cleaners, or even sewing up a blockful of household orders, are about as realistic as being the first to extract petroleum from dandelion greens. The products will sell; but in small amounts, chiefly to friends, neighbors and family members. A school might buy a drum of LOC for the walls and bathrooms, if you know the custodian; a gas station might buy the concrete floor compound. Accounts like this don't come often. For the average distributor, the profit margin from retail sales, if looked at coldly in black and white, is simply not worth the effort. Minimum wage as a floor sweeper, or tips from waitressing, give a much higher return on the same number of hours. Below the level of Emerald, the real hope of income in Amway is the PV bonus. The fabled riches to be had from the 3 percent and other bonuses become significant only at Emerald and above.

A jewel with a downline of thousands need not worry about customer opinion; as long as the *distributors* keep on buying, and recruiting, she will keep on collecting her checks ("so keep on keeping on"). The Corporation requires even jewels to have a minimum of ten retail sales to ten different customers per month, but a Diamond busy enjoying the life of leisure can always hire the person down the street to sell a few items off the shelf at a reduced price.

Why would a distributor convert his home entirely to Amway products when they are more expensive than what he would ordinarily buy? And why does he tend to purchase in excess of need?

I was told from the beginning that to be able to sell the product I had to use it; if I used it, I would believe in it, and then I could retail without difficulty. But the trap is the PV scale. Every product bears a point value. A distributor wants to make a bracket, even if she becomes her own best customer to put herself over the rung. If I make 80 points on retail sales, I get no bonus, but if I buy 20 more points, a month's supply of vitamins, for example, I go over 100 and receive that little check for 3 percent of the volume. I might miss a high bracket such as 2500 or 4000 by some ludicrous amount which could easily have been made up in self-use. To achieve brackets like that, at various times, I bought smoke detectors, cookware, jewelry and whole cases of foodbars.

Once you acquire a group, it is more than imperative to use nothing but Amway. It becomes a moral duty. "Every distributor should order something every week, whether you need it or not," said a Diamond at Seminar. "Would you like all your people to do that? Would it boost your PV for every member of your group to order something every week, whether they need it or not? Can you imagine the cases and cases of products going down through your organization? You have to set the example. If you don't do it, neither will your group."

No more Spic and Span, no more Prell, no more Dial and Johnson's Wax and Gillette shaving cream and Scope mouthwash. How will it look if people in my downline come to my home and go in the bathroom and see a tube of Prell? Or wash their hands with Dial? What if they tell *their* downlines that I use Prell? How many cases of Amway Satinique Shampoo will that cost me? If I want them to use Amway products in order to boost my PV, then I should have Family Bar Soap, Whisker Whiz and Mop Mate out there in plain sight. I have to *believe* in those products. My commissions depend on it.

Little by little, the distributor sinks into the world of Amway. No spider is necessary to turn her over and over; she jumps in the web and wraps the strands around her own body. The initial investment is the first strand. No one told me, and I told none of my legs, that "retail profit" is a phantom, which, the harder pursued, the more expensive it is to catch; as soon as I learned this lesson from experience, I went on to the next stage, the effort to build a group; that is, laying the web for others, so that I might get free of mine. Let them do the work, I would collect the bonuses. But to sponsor is only to go more deeply into the web. Every person I sponsored was another strand on the cocoon.

Naturally you don't feel trapped at the time; you feel excited. The trap was my job, and here was a way out of the rut. I didn't imagine that I was laying webs for people but helping them to meet their particular financial needs ("meeting needs" being the jargon that currently rationalizes professional bureaucracies of all kinds). I was a public benefactor, spreading the gospel according to Rich and Jay and Dexter.

Let us now trace step-by-step the process by which an otherwise lively and multi-dimensional human being (me in this case) turns himself into spider food.

It takes an enormous amount of time and money to build a profitable group. Below 4000, most of the bonus goes right back into the business. It is not so much wisely and deliberately re-invested, as eaten away, by the tapes, accessories, decision paks, phone calls, travel expenses and functions. My upline was usually honest about paying the bonuses on time; but they might as well have put a tube in my pocket on the way out the door and sucked the money back. Unlike investment in other types of enterprise, few capital goods are purchased by this money that could be resold in case of withdrawal; they are pure liquid expenditures, necessary to prime the pump, but a dead loss if you quit.

Yager tapes are not required by the Corporation; but they are certainly required by Yager and his jewels. The first three or four are included with the starter kit. After that I was expected to buy a tape every week for myself, and one "positive thinking" book per month. The cost of a Seminar and Rally was $8 to $12 for tickets and $10 to $20 for travel, or, if the location was out of state, up to $80 for travel and overnight accommodations. Just the personal indoctrination represented a regular monthly expense of between $40 and $90—as much as a payment on a new home appliance. This figure does not include the costs of leadership training and major functions, not to mention the open meetings and covered dish suppers, all of which had a door price to get in.

At 1000 PV, I was manipulated not only to buy tapes and books for my own consumption, but to stock them for my people. The tapes and books had to move out through the group. Increasing tape flow was considered a sign of health; scanty or absent tape flow meant that your business was, or soon would be, sick. Duplication was not taking hold. My people would not buy tapes unless I had them available at my house, in quantity. Once again I had to set the example. Now I was the one who kept the dozens of tapes spread out on a table; if they didn't move, and fast, I would be in the hole for hundreds of dollars; and when someone came for product pick-up, I touched his or her arm, flashed a smile, and said "I've got a fantastic new tape; it'll blow your..."

"But I can't afford it."

"Tapes are the key to success in this business. Tapes are the mortar that holds the bricks of your group together. How long do you want to spend going Direct, ten weeks or ten years?"

The programming that tapes are vital to the health of a business was so insistent that one comes to believe it without question. I spend a month building a line, four legs deep, which is beginning to show some volume, perhaps a hundred PV in a week. The Emerald above me says that if I don't move tapes into that line on a regular basis, it will be gone in four months. Who am I to say otherwise? An Emerald must know the business. I sit up late at night learning techniques to sell tapes because I do not want to lose that weekly 100 PV. But then some of the people are turned off by the tapes and quit anyway.

In truth, the Yager tapes are overpriced, often poorly engineered and give precious little useful information. Amway markets a high-quality instructional cassette tape for half the cost, but we were discouraged from relying on Corporation tapes. I never knew that Yager tapes are not Corporation tapes until months after I joined. Amway tapes have blue and white labels decorated with the Company logo; the engineering is professional and usually flawless; if it is not, a money-back guarantee covers the product, no questions asked. Yager tapes have white labels, beneath which I could often read the nearly invisible letters "Made in Mexico." Defective engineering, which ruined up to 10 percent of the ones I bought, has to be compensated for by "positive attitude." To reject a defective Yager tape is Negative; to get your money back for it is a triumph of assertive diplomacy pursued over many weeks. I had to track down the Direct and play the defective portion in his presence, and get him to agree that the defect was in the tape and not in my ears; then I had to field questions like "How do you know your people won't like it?" Finally I might get, not a cash refund, but another copy of the very same bad tape, which obliged me to go through the process all over again. For $3.50 it was hardly worth the effort.

The contents of most tapes are simply recorded Seminars, Rallies, Extravaganzas and leadership training functions. Once or twice a month you drive for hours to sit through the interminable sermons on Love, the advice on being a Winner, the homilies on Attitude, Belief and Commitment, the inspiring personal stories that come to sound like they were all stamped on the back of a cereal box; as if a mad preacher, with a gold cross around his neck, were turning a gigantic wheel that slowly compressed the walls of the church inward on the congregation, squeezing the Negative out of their bodies drop by drop into rows of white polyethylene bottles; and you manage to escape, after holding hands and singing "God Bless America," without screaming and destroying your whole group in one cackling radical fit; and you go to the Direct's house the following week, and his clammy hand shakes yours ("you'll have to firm up that hand-shake") and he grins like a lizard and says "I've got this fantastic new tape. It'll blow . . ." etc. And you pay $3.50 and take it home and plug it in, and it turns out to be the last Seminar and Rally. There is no exit. Amway is watching you. Listen to it before you go to bed. Play it in the car on your way to work. Buy ten more for your people.

By disobeying the crossline policy, I discovered that many non-Yager Directs use only Corporation tapes, or none at all. But in the Yager organization this is difficult to do. Corporation tapes which are disapproved of by Yager people are "not available" when ordered. Every product has to come through the Direct; if he stops the order, you don't get the product. I have seen certain Corporation tapes *re-recorded and re-issued* under that white label and sold to distributors at *double* the Corporation price. Something here must violate even the Amway code of ethics. Perhaps it is, or ought to be, a subject of internal politics on the Board.

To resist buying tapes, or demand them at Corporation prices, is really to resist Duplication. Failure to duplicate identifies me as a "stinking thinker." The way to motivate stinking thinkers to buy tapes is, again, by working depth in their groups. Sell the tape to their people; then say to them, "Hasn't your sponsor heard this tape? You should be able to get it from him. Ask him what's on it." I would not want my people to think I have stopped listening to tapes. Even worse would be to let them think I disapprove of the tapes, or the upline's practices. They would not only quit buying tapes, they might get out of the business.

It must be admitted that the content of the tapes fulfills their purpose as conceived by the leaders. They are not devoid of instruction; but instruction is a secondary goal. The primary goal is to obtain belief and commitment from the distributor. Hearing the same Rallies over and over, the same banalities followed by whistling and foot-stomping applause, the same prayers, the same invocations to God and Country, all work on people's minds to insure that Amway "gets into" them and that they will give unquestioning loyalty to their upline Directs.

Propaganda short-circuits the intellect by acting directly upon the emotions; it relies heavily for effect on repetition. Yager tapes are masterpieces of the art of propaganda—not so much because of what they say, as how they are marketed. The distributors pay for their own brainwashing. If they do not listen to the tapes, they will have wasted their money; and worse, they might be embarrassed by questions about them from their downlines; they might lose their downlines altogether, and months of effort and hope will dissipate into the void.

They can shut off the radio and television, but the tape worms into their cars and bedrooms. "Whenever you have doubts about the business, plug in a tape." I felt disappointed and cheated by the tapes because they did not suit *my* purpose, which was to learn how to build a business as a free agent. Yager's purpose is to catch minds on the flypaper of the Dream.

In order to sponsor people, distributors must believe in what they are doing. At first this is not a difficult leap of imagination. The circles and incomes and boats and homes are still whirling in the vortex of a future reborn; a door has been opened, a way to give form and substance to what was hitherto only an escapist wish: having all the bills paid; getting up at the crack of noon; going on Caribbean vacations any time you want; helping your brother, co-worker and best friend drive out of their financial hole in the car of their choice. These are dazzling possibilities. But the distance between fantasy and act is vast. Many Plan-showings are required to sponsor anyone who will actually stay in, draw circles, sell and use products and build a group.

By the time I had shown the Plan twenty-six times without result, I had already invested over a hundred hours and $600. I wanted a return. I did not blame my sponsor, my Direct or the Corporation; when I blamed anyone, it was the friends and family members who had turned it down. Why couldn't they see the "genius" and "beauty" of the Amway concept? Why didn't my brother, who labored in a factory to meet payments on a 13 percent mortgage—which is cheap now—immediately seize on this Plan to climb out of debt? Why didn't my colleagues, who never stopped complaining about our low salaries, use Amway to create a permanent strike fund—or better yet, buy our College, or retire from it entirely? Why didn't my neighbors collaborate with me to break our dependence on the two or three major employers that dominated the region? Why did friends say they would come to my get-togethers and then stand me up?

Confronted with rejection, I sought to confirm my belief in the business by listening to tapes and upline counseling; I wanted to learn better persuasive technique; and I hardened my determination to beat the odds. These are all highly praised responses within Amway. After a half-dozen rejections, most new distributors give up. The ones who do not are considered Winners. It is ego-gratifying to think of yourself as a Winner, and have your role models in the business agree with you. On the other hand, it is a form of self-entrapment. I wanted to blame others for not letting me sponsor them; and everything in the tapes and counseling sessions helped me to dismiss them as inconsequential. Most people are Losers; they will never join Amway; their opinions don't matter; they don't understand, but I have seen the Light. Already I was detaching myself from my social circle, in order to safeguard my ego—"protect my attitude," it was termed in Seminar. And, relying on the tapes and leaders to accomplish this change, I had opened my heart and home to the daily propaganda and begun depending on the leaders for advice.

The tapes teach that "success is revenge." On whom? On the brother-in-law who laughed at me; on the friend who said it wouldn't work; on all the prospects who stood me up and wasted my time. And what is the revenge? To "pick them off one by one," and to drive a Cadillac or a Mercedes while they are still cranking their rusted Chevrolets on cold winter mornings, and to get up at noon while they go to work, and to park my motor home in the front yard where all the neighbors can see it, and, finally, to leave that neighborhood forever and move into a mansion. In this way I justify being a parasite because I "worked" for it, and the "Losers" deserve to be exploited because they rejected me.

By the time they get a group under them, a couple has a great deal more invested in the business than work and money. The leaders know perfectly well how to use motives like pride and ego to commit their subjects by degrees; I was taught how to use them with my own group when I reached 1500 and 4000: "Don't help your people too much; they should make sacrifices." "Get them to say when they're going Direct in front of their kids." No one wants to let his children down. "Wouldn't you like to fly off to freedom in a helicopter with all those stinking thinkers watching you from the ground?"

In the beginning, then, the couple is drawn deeper into the system by the desire to break even on the kit, samples and tools; then rejection and sacrifice either stop them entirely or toughen their resolve. Their hope is that sponsoring a group will be their ticket to freedom; and in fact repeated sponsoring, sustained over months and years, is the only way to generate a reliable income from Amway. But the group itself becomes the greatest trap of all. Whatever advice from the top they may disregard, the momentum and weight of that group will force them to conform to the Amway mold.

Every person sponsored is not merely an object of manipulation; he or she is a responsibility. With the help of tapes and Seminars I convince myself that I must manipulate this person for her own good. I must help her to overcome her stinking thinking and lead her along, like a child, up the path of success, which is also the path of righteousness. More compelling, when I draw enticing incomes on the marker board, and question the prospects into revealing their dreams, and then claim that those circles will make their dreams come true, I have to deliver on that claim; I cannot sell them a kit and disappear. My own integrity is on the line. First, the PV on a kit is not worth the effort to sell it; and second, almost no one gets anywhere in Amway without help. I have to teach every new person how to make the business work, or else introduce him to the teachers upline from me. A Diamond from Oklahoma describes this process as "teaching people how to teach others to teach people to teach."

I was never tricked into making an *irrelevant* sacrifice, that is, an expenditure which would not in some way help my business, according to the methods practiced by my leaders. No tricks are necessary for these. Anyone who pitches in to build the business in a serious way commits his or her share of blunders without encouragement from above: you let somebody pay for a kit "next week" and she never pays; you take rubber checks, order too many tickets for a big function on a worthless promise, drive a hundred miles to show the Plan for a distributor who is drunk or not home when you get there. A shrewd and realistic assessment of human character can minimize losses of this kind, but there is no way to completely eliminate them. Distributors have no Company expense accounts. It is "your business." If you spend a week sponsoring a fool, who writes a bad check for his kit and is not home thereafter, the entire loss is yours. No hourly or weekly salary pays for your time. No one but you will hire an attorney to get your money back. You wonder which one is the fool.

Aside from the risks, run-arounds and rip-offs, the effort legitimately required to cultivate a productive group calls for a persistence which is sometimes little short of heroic. I might go to a couple's home to conduct a Plan-showing for them, expecting a livingroom full of their prospects, and for the third time in a row no one comes. I know they called thirty people; I know they want the business; I know they feel discouraged and rejected, as though they had to beg their friends to sit through this presentation which I claim is so powerful. They are retailing and using products; I tell them functions and tapes are important, and they attend functions and buy tapes, because they trust my word, although they live from one paycheck to the next. At this point I could abandon them, and write off my time and gasoline as a dead loss, and watch their retail orders dry up, and leave one more ex-distributor in the community to tell other prospects how he was burned; or I could take the husband to the store with me and demonstrate on the spot a method for prospecting strangers; or, using his telephone while he listens, call a few people on his list to illustrate a good telephone approach; and then keep on repeating that if he duplicates what I do, he will get results.

Early on, I was introduced to a tape by Yager that is not normally given to new recruits. If you want to be a Diamond, said Dexter's voice, *fill your calendar.* You ought to be out there drawing circles *six nights a week.* After a solid year of that schedule, if you're not a Diamond, you'll be well on your way.

I had already discovered by experience that building a profitable group was going to involve me in seeing the insides of an endless succession of livingrooms all over the region. Dexter's words came as no great surprise; in fact it was a relief to be told the truth. I chose to fill my calendar. I worked depth anywhere it would lead. I drove from Vermont to Massachusetts, Rhode Island, New York, Maryland and Ohio to extend various lines down to their farthest possible limit. I flew across the country and built a group on the West Coast. Meanwhile my upline Pearl kept feeding me with tales of Diamonds who drove eighty thousand miles in a single year. "So-and-so is making good money now; they just bought a fifteen-bedroom home in Tennessee; they took off on a jaunt to Europe and didn't come back for six months. The Corporation will send your 3 percent checks anywhere you ask." Speakers would say at functions, "A car is just a hunk of iron; it's there to be used. Use it up. When it's gone you'll have the income to buy a better one." My first year in Amway, I put over sixty thousand miles on my car. The year after, sure enough, it was a hunk of iron. But I was no Diamond.

What I had for my trouble was three 1500 groups on different lines, and a handful of other legs in various stages of growth or atrophy; a promising situation financially. If seven went Direct, I would qualify for the Executive Diamond bonus: an extra payment of $100 per month per Direct, in addition to the 3 percent income, profit-sharing, Emerald bonus and Pearl award for Directs in depth. If just three 1500 legs made it I would be an Emerald. In the meantime I had learned a great deal about the totalitarian character of the Duplication principle.

On product pickup day, once a week, I drove thirty miles to my sponsor's house. *His* sponsor, our Direct, lived three miles from me, and I could have picked up at the source; but the policy was to send the goods down through the line. I was moving $2000 worth of merchandise per week. Our upline Pearl wanted to make sure that we had to handle every case and carton. He thought it would motivate us to go Direct faster; the Directs receive products directly from regional warehouses via UPS truck. So I checked off orders, corrected errors, tracked down back orders, carried stuff to my car and packed it in anywhere it would fit. One day I slipped a disc while heaving a 36-pound box into the back seat, and walked around like Quasimodo for three months. On the way home the whole car was fragrant with the lemon smell of soap. I would have to ship a third of it out again, by UPS, to legs over a hundred miles away, who I knew would quit sooner than drive that distance every week just to pick up a few boxes. At Seminars I heard tales of distributors in northern Maine who had to drive down to Portland for their pickup. Some of my legs were crossing into Vermont from New York to get stuff from me.

One must imagine the position of the budding "winners" who have chosen the Amway path out of their rut. They listen to tapes every day in the car, driving to work, and at night before they go to bed. They read only approved "positive" books. Their homes become Amway homes: all the household items, the soaps, shampoos, cookware, smoke alarm, car wash, are Amway products. Christmas, birthday, anniversary gifts are selected from the Corporate Shopper's Catalog. Materialist goals are taped on the refrigerator door. The Direct may drop in any time, usually late at night, and check refrigerators and wallets to review personal goals, and go in the bathroom to make sure they aren't using Crest. All recreations and holidays consist of Amway functions. They take Nutrilite vitamins and eat Nutrilite food bars for lunch. Every month they attend Seminars and Rallies. The wives retail products and keep the home a picture of cleanliness to make a good impression on prospects and downline distributors; these come to see the Plan or pick up orders. The upline offers marriage counseling to straighten out any situations between them (there are no "problems") that might be holding them back in the business.

All their former friends and family members who oppose Amway, or talk against it, have been dropped. They are not allowed to develop friendships with other Amway people in crosslines, that is, in similar circumstances, lest they share some Negative feeling and quit, or fail to duplicate. They see crossline distributors only at upline-controlled functions, where the speakers are carefully selected and the format does not permit unsupervised socializing between groups. Their "friends" from upline tell them only what they want them to hear, and if they refuse to conform, these "friends" will ostracize and bypass them, and transfer their group to a reliable upline influence. The upline "friends" are worshipped as heroes. The distributors cannot say anything to their downlines, or confide any feeling or problem which could be construed as Negative; for downline ears, they love the products, love the business, love the Plan, the leaders are all super people and anyone should give a month's bonus just for an hour on their calendar.

Surely no totalitarian system in the world has ever fastened the puppet strings to its *cadre* of True Believers more thoroughly than this. The Corporation has no torture chambers and forced labor camps (not with the Amway logo on them, at least), and probably does not yet employ hit squads, other than those trained by the political administrations which it supports (readers should note carefully the subsequent fate of this author); terrorism against distributors is not necessary anyway. A far more effective power is achieved by programming the mind and controlling the influences over behavior.

Now visualize the predicament of someone who has turned a good car into a hunk of iron, and left his family six nights a week for months to show the Plan all over Sherwood Forest, coming home at four in the morning to get up at seven to go to work. I call my distributors to arrange a meeting at my house; the Direct calls them and cancels the meeting. In a flash I realize that I no longer have any freedom of association. What are my alternatives? To call the distributors back and involve them in a dispute with my Direct would be poisonous; such an act would fill them with doubts and questions; they might pass the story down to *their* groups, and the legs on the bottom would begin quitting in droves. I could quietly turn in my card and resign, and the effort of months would be for nothing; moreover, the Direct would pick up my lines and profit by them. I could try to wipe out my own group in order to prevent the Direct from getting the benefit of my labor; but I have incurred an obligation to my people; I have been telling them over and over that they can succeed, and stuck by them week after week during meetings to which no one came, and shared their dreams and disappointments, and brought them up to 1500; the last thing in the world I would want to do is pass them anything Negative about Amway. Even if I discover that our upline Diamond is Satan, and Rich and Jay are planning to elect the Anti-Christ for President of the United States, I can hardly go to my people at that point and tell them we wasted our time and the sugared carrot is a withered and revolting vegetable. The Believers would stay in without me. If we make it to Direct, we might indeed stand together on the stage of a Rally and weep. Besides, what if the system is right and I'm wrong?

This predicament is the same in every conflict between upline and downline which involves resistance to Duplication. The model for Duplication comes from the top down, never from the bottom up. "The dog wags the tail." If I passed any good innovations upline for approval, such as new prospecting approaches, the jewels simply stole them and applied them in legs competitive with mine. But downline ideas for basic policy changes are never listened to. A jewel does not let "some guy at 4000" tell her how to design a better system.

In practice the system probably alienates more people than it converts. The turnover in the business, from what I could observe, was staggering. Fifty distributors would sign up and forty of them lost interest in a matter of weeks. A certain percentage in any system will succumb to inertia, excuses and fear; but I sponsored corporate managers, salespeople, teachers—occupational types that I thought would have a high incidence of success in Amway. Again and again I saw the same pattern repeating itself: distributors would feel initial enthusiasm, and then encounter the revivalism and indoctrination methods, and receive pressure to duplicate properly from the upline leaders; then they would complain about the manipulative style of the functions and the expense of the products; and soon after that, they would cease all activity. If I were quick on the follow-up, I could sponsor somebody under them before they were lost, and work with them instead. Many got out, not because I failed to "plug them in" to the system, but precisely because they had no wish to be so thoroughly plugged in.

From the viewpoint of the Corporation and its Diamonds, the system works, because it does what *they* want: it trains a *cadre* of Believers who will remain fanatically loyal to Amway no matter what the adversity, who will find replacements for every drop-out no matter what the complaint, who will go on selling and using the products no matter what the cost. Find a Believer in depth and train him; whether ten legs in between quit is of no consequence, if that one Believer will do "whatever it takes"—use up his car, sacrifice his friends and his freedom.

A distributor with a group to maintain has only two choices: obey the system, in every particular, exactly as given, or do it his way. For someone at 1500, or 4000, or even Direct, the burden of doing it his way is crushing. It is not impossible; but it means that he must personally train, supply and motivate dozens of people, design his own functions, buy products in case lots, answer all questions, finesse personality conflicts in the organization and be everywhere at once. When I tried this, my telephone literally never stopped ringing; I had to furnish, out of my own energy and life-hours, the support that is ordinarily furnished by the system. There were not enough days on my calendar.

What one hopes for is to find recruits who will assume this burden. I want to train others so that they will put sixty thousand miles on *their* cars, and work depth by themselves, and show the Plan six nights a week without me. Let them build, while I watch the kits move out, and the organization grow, and the checks roll in. But no one will do this without Belief. To inculcate Belief I must rely on the

system. Whether I agree with it or not is beside the point. If I want
Believers in my group, then I *have* to agree with it.

The two-edged quality of Duplication is that it takes effect no
matter what. If it is not managed, it works against you. Duplication
exerts an almost mystical force through an Amway group, including
"bad" practices and attitudes. Whatever I do wrong inadvertently
shows up magnified in my business: if I don't retail products, nobody
in my group will retail products. If I criticize my leadership, people in
my group will develop a negative attitude toward the leadership and
lose their motivation. A parent rebels at work and does what he wants,
until he looks up and sees that the child is rebelling in school and
doing the same. The child will take a role model for good or bad. In
Amway, my distributors, if they respect me, will run their business the
way I run mine. Do I really want six rebellious legs going their own
way, or would I rather have them copy a method with a proven track
record?

And so, at Rallies, with my group present, I whistle and applaud;
I stand up when the others stand up; I say nothing when the speakers
make their odious and repulsive Moral Majority statements; I allow
the people I have recruited to be indoctrinated into supporting
Reagan; I hold hands and sing God Bless America; I sell the
propaganda and swear by it; I attend every function and never
complain about the cost or the content, for my income depends on
whether my people in the audience, whom I have worked so hard to
bring this far, can be converted into Believers. I give up my freedom of
association and thought voluntarily; I wear "sharp" clothes, with a
matching jacket for winter; I smile and shake hands and cut my hair
all according to model; my speech is completely formulaic, learned
from "positive" books and tapes, or copied from the upline jewels:

"Hi, how ya doin'!"

"Great! Fantastic!"

"You look sharp! When are you going Direct?"

My whole existence has about as much creative personality as a
McDonald's Happy Meal. My politics, religion, morality, are all
completely predictable.

At Seminar, the speaker asks, "How many of you are in this
business for life? Stand up."

My people are watching me. I stand. I have won the victory over
myself. At last I know that I'm a winner.

TEN

AMWAY
AND THE
FAMILY

Amway leaders claim to believe in the Family.

No married leader (mostly male) will show up at a function without his wife. If the speaker must appear on stage alone, he lets the audience know that this is an extraordinary circumstance, occasioned by a hospitalized spouse or a dying child, and accompanied by profuse apologies from the absent partner. Directs selling tickets to functions in their group usually insist that you buy two, even if you claim that your spouse can't attend. Recognition for every achievement is given to both husband and wife. Pins are always awarded in pairs. Checks are made out to both names. Company—and upline—sponsored trips are planned to include the couple.

For a married man to attempt to buy only one ticket may subject him to a conversation like this:

"You'll need another ticket for your wife."

"She isn't coming."

"Oh? Why not?"

"She has something else to do."

"What's that?"

"Well, she promised to take the kids to the movies."

"Gee, that's no problem, she can go on a weekday."

"But she promised them for Saturday night."

"Won't it be great when you make enough to buy home movies? You could have a whole theater all to yourself."

"Yeah, that would be nice."

"Wouldn't you like the people in your group to go to Seminars?"

"Sure."

"They won't do it unless you go. If people in your group see you at a function without your wife, pretty soon they get the idea that it's not important to bring their wives. See what I mean?"

"But she doesn't want to go."

"Take these two tickets now, you can always sell one of them later if you don't use it. But tell your wife how important it is that she go to Seminar. I know she'll make the right decision."

About 75 percent of Amway distributorships are husband-wife units. It is a major policy goal of the Company to involve both partners of a marriage in the business. One of the selling points of the lifestyle is that it offers families a chance to share common dreams and goals. Achievement in many other occupations means separation from the family: the husband who sells insurance, or gets promoted to an executive position in his company, or goes to the office to drill teeth, cannot, as a rule, involve his wife directly in his job. He may have to be on the road without her for days or weeks, he may go to conventions without her, he many find more in common with women at work. But in Amway, the leaders claim, both partners share the responsibilities and the triumphs.

Operating a "family" business with your spouse as partner also confers several tax advantages: family vacations to functions, dinner dates that become conferences, gifts of furs and jewelry, if these are displayed to motivate distributors, are all tax-deductible business expenses; and the amount of income that can be sheltered by a Keogh plan is doubled. In addition, the chances of being successful are increased if husband and wife work effectively together as a team.

But marital partnership is not advocated simply for tax deductions and business effectiveness. An important mission of Amway is to strengthen the institution of "the Family" in American life.

Rich DeVos and Dexter Yager have both published their views on this subject in books which are on the recommended reading list of all Yager Directs and force-fed, like the tapes, throughout the Yager organization. It is a safe bet that any book by Rich DeVos is read not only in Yager's business but in all the organizations throughout the world of Amway.

Yager's chapter on marriage in *Don't Let Anybody Steal Your Dream* is titled "The Woman Behind the Man"; an accurate short-hand rendition of the Yager view respecting the Woman's Place. A good wife strengthens her husband's career; she uses her sexuality to enhance his ego and prepare him for business success.

The leading industrialists of this country seem to have an extraordinary common denomination. They all have good wives.

But what can a wife do to strengthen her husband's career?...A very powerful force available is her own sexuality...A woman must think positive; believe in her husband and be willing to take a risk with him...

The woman behind the man IS a very important ingredient in his success...If a couple is going to build a business together they must communicate in every area of life.*

DeVos expresses himself in a less patently sexist manner. His words in *Believe!* are a clear and concise statement of Amway policy:

It is time in America for the family concept to be reaffirmed, time for us to be prodded back to our basic responsibilities as parents, time for us to believe in the family so strongly that we will be willing to make whatever rearrangements of priorities are necessary to make our own homes the incubators of the American dream.**

According to DeVos, "Amway has always placed great emphasis on the family as a unit. We do not recruit men alone or women alone to sell our products when we can recruit the entire family." The goal of the corporation is "to make involvement in our busines something which strengthens family ties rather than threatening them." Unlike the more ego-infected jewels at the Seminars I attended, he does not presume that his success as an entrepreneur qualifies him to enter the marriage-counseling field; he speaks from his own experience, and with some attempt at humility; he does not lay down rules for the rearing of children, other than to observe that "There is no substitute for time spent in the home—quality time, when the members of the family are genuinely accessible to one another."***

How do we reconcile this wholesome support for "quality time spent in the home" with the fanatical slogan to show the Plan six nights a week?

As a background for discussion, it is necessary to consider what the leaders mean by "the Family." DeVos and Van Andel do not describe it anywhere with anthropological precision. We must infer what the leaders mean by the teachings and practice of the business

---

*Don't Let Anybody Steal Your Dream, pp. 88, 90-91.
**Believe!, p. 166.
***Ibid., p. 171, 172, 169.

itself. Included in their Family are the spouse and the children. This is
the only unit which has priority over making money in Amway. I may
sell products or show the Plan to my father, mother, brother, sister,
in-laws and cousins, but, as we have seen, if they reject the business,
then I am programmed stage by stage to reject them. We may continue
to associate without ever mentioning Amway; the Direct (probably)
will not follow me around to supervise my visits with my parents.

Amway makes no effort to resurrect the *extended* family, which is
really the old-fashioned traditional unit of American free enterprise
and the foundation of the Protestant work ethic; the brothers who
traded enlistments in the Continental militia, one going off to fight
the British for six months while the other stayed home to tend the
farm; the sturdy clans from Ohio who slugged it out with Johnny Reb
at Shiloh and Vicksburg; the homesteaders who pushed their towns
westward through wild Injuns and cattle baronies into the sunset
from sea to shining sea. Rich DeVos describes "free enterprise" as a
system which "allows the people to own privately the tools of production."* But the only time in American history when the *people*
owned their tools of production was when most of them were engaged
in agriculture, and the family farm or cottage industry was the basic
unit of economic life. That stage of society was dealt a crushing blow
by the robber barons during the Guilded Age, and then destroyed by
corporate capitalism before world War II.

The extended family was gradually replaced by the *nuclear*
family, consisting of a husband, wife and children, supported by the
husband's wage-earned income, with option for the wife to work, and
the number of offspring limited to two or three. This unit is best
suited to a wage-dependent household in a corporate economy; it
allows mobility for the employee to be moved wherever industry
demands, it increases consumption by multiplying the number of
households and reducing the cooperation between them, and it inter-
rupts the continuity of positive labor movement traditions from one
generation to the next. An extended family could get by with one
house, one washing machine and one big kitchen, just as the farm
families of old got by with one barn. Frequent contact between parents and grown children means that if the father and mother were
unionists fighting on the picket lines in 1937, that experience is a
living tradition which the grandchildren hear about in 1985. But sons
who move rootlessly from suburb to suburb in order to maintain their
nuclear families, must each one buy separate washers, dryers, kitchen

Believe!, p. 85.

appliances, cars and homes; moreover, they are much too busy making it in the corporate world to pass on Dad's old tales.

In the suburban household of the 1950s, when the price of gold was artificially fixed at $35 an ounce to make the American dollar the exchange medium of the world, and the United Fruit Company ran Central America with barbed wire and machine guns, and Cuban sugar and Venezuelan oil sold under conditions dictated by the U.S. Marines, the woman's place was in the home, and everybody who didn't hate and fear communism was investigated or locked up, and students did nothing more radical than grow beards, and the dream of life was to own a huge car and a huge television set. This is the period looked back upon with nostalgia and increasing hysteria by the Amway crowds, and this is where their model of the Family is drawn from. The experiments with the family that emerged in the 1970s terrify them: polygamy, polyandry, serial relationships, single parenthood, homosexual marriage, communal living, they see only as "breakdown."

The glue that held the extended family together was economic cooperation. Everybody was needed on the farm, including the old folks. The glue that is supposed to cement the nuclear family is romantic love. Amway leaders have many pearls of wisdom to offer their disciples on the subject of romance. Among the books that distributors "should" read on a monthly basis are *How To Be Happy Though Married* by Tim La Haye (Tyndale, 1968; 1978) and *What Wives Wish Their Husbands Knew About Women*, by Dr. James Dobson (Tyndale 1975; 1979). These authors are not necessarily Amway leaders; but their homilies on maintaining romantic love in the home are considered vitally important to achieving success in the business.

According to Yager, "You have God, man, woman and kids, in that order. When you get that out of line, you've got problems." Women, says Birdie Yager, are emotional, and men are rational. Women need to be led by men. The ERA cause is "junk." Says Dexter, "A lot of you guys don't realize, your gal challenges you because she's waiting for you to prove what a man you are. She *wants* you to take control. And you'll be so happy when he does, won't you, gals?"

The idea of "manhood" is supposed to spur the husband on to higher pin levels. A husband proves his "manhood" by taking leadership in the home and performing in the business. But, the woman speaker warns the wives in the audience, "Gals, don't nag your man if he isn't out there doing it, because it doesn't work, he won't be motivated by your nagging. You've got to let him know you believe in him, even when he doesn't believe in himself. He'll do it, you just have patience with him."

At a leadership training seminar in Portland, Maine, the wives and husbands were divided and addressed separately in different rooms. The male leader told the husbands to be gentle and considerate in their sexual approaches to their wives; the lady should be wooed with furs, jewelry and candlelight dinners in expensive restaurants. The female leader told the wives to submit to their husbands cheerfully, even if they thought it was unpleasant sometimes, because a man needed to feel like a winner in the bedroom as well as out in that livingroom showing the Plan.

The year was 1980. I wondered if I had been caught in some time-warped mirror image of a runaway space colony full of insane Baptist ministers. Maybe they were not really people at all; the ship's computer had mistakenly crossed the prototypes for Charles Dickens characters with clones of Pat Boone and Daisy Duck. Sweet Shot sprayed in the mouth; Amway jewelry jingling on the limbs; personal goals on the refrigerator; and now, an Emerald's advice on how to achieve proper duplication in the bedroom. But within a few months I would grow accustomed to this atmosphere. Soon it would be enshrined in the White House.

As a glue, romantic love is not exactly your perma-grip indissoluble bondo. It must tend to get rather watery under the boredom and oppression of being the Woman Behind the Man, who submits in the bedroom to make her Man feel like a Winner; or being the Winner, who struggles up the corporate ladder in order to woo the Woman behind him with jewels and furs. The use of romantic love as a manipulative device has been adequately analyzed by the feminist movement; the woman of the nuclear family is asked to sacrifice personhood, that is, independence, education, economic and political power, in the name of love. There is no need to rehash that theme here; but in Amway one would never know the theme had been hashed.

A man and a woman can make a free choice to cooperate in building an Amway distributorship, or raising a garden, or constructing a home, without either person being stunted and unfulfilled by the process. They can use all kinds of joint effort to bring out the best in each other. Many couples probably use Amway for their own goals without any sense of loss; indeed, perhaps thousands would claim glowingly that it saved their marriage. The sight of an excited couple working together for an honest goal is an inspiration that only a Scrooge would scorn.

But Amway is not some passive tool that couples pick up and use; it is a social movement that uses and changes them. A definite *model* of the family is held up for emulation; leaders who duplicate that model are heroes to be edified; the model is enforced by the requirement to set an example for the downline. Even a simple thing such as which partner draws the circles is, in the Yager business, prescribed by advice from the top. The business cannot tolerate deviance and creativity. If I babysit and retail products and keep the home clean while my wife goes out to show the Plan, I might start a whole line of woman Plan-showers and male homemakers. People might get the idea that in Amway the woman wears the pants. This amounts to a major policy change, a divergence from the teachings; the tail would wag the dog. Policy changes come only from the top down. Radical deviance, such as group marriage, or open marriage, is simply impossible. An organization which publicly humiliates a woman for wearing slacks to a function that calls for dresses will never have any room for experiments with the family structure. The leaders cannot afford to let their people innovate. Their profits depend on conformity.

Despite their unintentional parody of Bible-school sexual ethics, a great deal of subliminal—and perverted—sexuality goes on at Amway functions. Audiences are led in mass denunciations of soap operas dealing with the theme of adultery, husbands and wives are instructed from the stage to kiss and hold hands. Dexter Yager jokingly refers to the "other woman" in his life, who turns out to be his daughter; the wife of a prominent Diamond calls the ladies to Christ by describing Jesus as a wonderful "hunk" of a man. But just beneath these comfortably square plugs for the monogamous "Christian" nuclear family lurks the tail of the serpent: the men strutting in their suits, leaving business cards on the chairs like dogs peeing on fire hydrants to mark their territories; the women arrayed in alluring and expensive costumes, turning heads as they pass; the equation of attractiveness with pin level ("I'm so glad my man is a *Winner*"); the salacious play on the word "excited" (Are you *excited*? Show me how *excited* you are!); the kind of joke told from the stage by the jewels:

"If you were going to have a baby, would you try it just once or twice, or keep at it until you hit your goal? You might say, 'But Tom, it's fun.' Well, drawing circles is fun too, if you have the right attitude. Am I right?"

"A man is like a lightbulb. You plug in a lamp and it lights up right away. What happens when you pull the plug? The bulb goes out. But a woman is like a flatiron. It takes time for the iron to get hot. But you pull the plug on a flatiron and what happens? It stays warm. Got it?"

Amway has spread to several different cultures and areas, and we can assume that the attitudes toward sex are at least partially adapted to the mores of each locality where the business is built. The American attitude is strict Walt Disney: the only legitimate and "wholesome" reference frame for sexuality is marriage, and even in this context the allusions are circumlocutious and "clean." But the French-speaking jewels in Quebec were much more open about their acknowledgment of the sexual motive. Andre Blanchard, a Crown, spoke from the stage of his shoe-salesman days when he used to position mirrors in the store so that, fitting female customers with shoes, he could treat himself to a "motivating" glimpse under the skirt. An American making such an admission would have his path to the microphone barred by Dexter's gold cross. Male distributors in Montreal would congregate together during intermissions, while their wives were in the ladies' room, and trade appreciative comments about the women in the audience.

What seems perverted to me, in the New England and Southern functions, is the combined suppression/titillation of the sex impulse and its use as a source of energy to achieve PV. The suppression is seen in the denunciations of soap operas and sexually explicit literature, the intolerance of so-called deviant behavior, and the strong, systemic propaganda for the traditional monogamous nuclear family; the titillation occurs in the dress codes for women, the jokes and metaphors, the warm-ups ("Are you excited?"), the skits where a Pearl proves his loyalty by literally dropping his pants, and, significantly, in the fashion-model poses used by the Corporation itself to advertise their cosmetics and jewelry.

There is nothing wrong with voicing opinions about literature and television, or choosing monogamy over alternative arrangements. These are basic civil liberties that we value and respect. Perversion enters in when sex is denied or suppressed, and then manipulated for profit. To program a whole culture to share this "morality" is to couple perversion with dictatorship.

This practice is hardly unique to Amway, but is common throughout the business world. It is one of the many other corporate customs which Amway concentrates and unintentionally parodies by reflection in extreme form. The whole Protestant approach to sex was to convert libido into steam for the Industrial Revolution—and to produce, from the steam, a packaged and economically rationalized sexuality as a marketable commodity. Amway converts it into circles and soap. Napoleon Hill, in *Think and Grow Rich* (Fawcett, 1960), a "positive attitude" book marketed through the Amway system, advises the reader to transmute sex energy into wealth:

> The human mind responds to stimulation!
> Among the greatest, and most powerful of these sti-
> muli is the urge of sex. When harnessed and transmuted,
> this driving force is capable of lifting men into that higher
> sphere of thought which enables them to master the sources
> of worry and petty annoyance which beset their pathway on
> the lower plane...
> The salesman who knows how to take his mind off the
> subject of sex, and direct it in sales effort with as much
> enthusiasm and determination as he would apply to its
> original purpose, has acquired the art of sex transmuta-
> tion, whether he knows it or not. *

The soft-core sexism of advertising, the encouragement of
psychologically destructive competition in fashion, the equation of
excitement with money—Amway amplifies all these features of
corporate capitalism, and worse: the wife belongs back in the home,
ironing her husband's shirts so he can go out and Show the Plan. Her
liberation is henceforth to keep the books, serve him coffee when he
comes home, sell lipstick and foodbars to her friends, and, once a
month, deck herself out like an expensive princess for the upcoming
Rally to advertise and reinforce his success. Her name is on the bonus
checks; "You can't get any more equal than that," said the wife of a
Diamond from North Carolina. Equality is measured, not in rights,
or wisdom, or access to politics and education, but in bonus checks.
Betty Freidan, Kate Millett, Erica Jong, Germaine Greer—and even
further back, Rosa Luxemburg and Emma Goldman—never happened, or were all the result of Negative Attitude, and now we can wave
them away like a bad dream. Mildred Cunningham in *Happy Days* is
the model of what a woman should be.

The televised and printed media have long been used to control
the consciousness of the public; Herbert Schiller, a communications
expert, explains how this control works in *The Mind Managers*
(Beacon Press, 1974). The media put together a "packaged consciousness," composed of a series of myths: for example, the myth that a
market system allows individualism and free choice, the myth that
newspapers and the government are politically balanced or neutral,
the myth that "human nature" does not change, that social turmoil is

*Think and Grow Rich, pp. 184, 188—.

caused by individual problems rather than class oppression, that revolutionaries act from personal hang-ups rather than political motives, or that radical social change always results in dictatorship. These myths are reinforced over and over, in every program from cop-dramas to the six o'clock news.

The design of the programming also influences the mind: fragmenting and delivering, in rapid succession, unrelated bits of terrifying but meaningless information sandwiched between commercials and quiz shows produces a fragmented, alienated, and passive attitude ("Fifteen people were killed today when a bomb exploded in a bus terminal; don't set yourself up for a let-down, use *Lifebuoy*; captain, we see the ship approaching but our sensors indicate that it is not there.") News items, in addition, are taken out of any historical relation that would make it possible to interpret them.

But the control achieved by an impersonal and loveless television tube is incomplete. There is still some diversity in the offerings: animal shows, scientific photography, documentaries, the occasional serious movie, suggest horizons of human interest irrelevant to the PV scale. Amway completes the mind-management process by reaching into the very kitchens and bedrooms of the people. The Directs I met, when they reached a certain level in the business, withdrew their children from public school and sent them to "Christian" schools, where they could be taught a fundamentalist version of history and science.

The nuclear family and the distributorship are designed to coincide within a single package. Every detail of the model has to be copied to avoid the divisive effect that would otherwise result, and does result, when either spouse becomes deeply involved in a new activity.

For the husband to be out showing the Plan five and six nights a week is a potentially disruptive influence. Few wives can afford to hire a babysitter that often; most would not want to leave their children night after night in any case. There must be times that a wife sits at home wondering if her husband is "prospecting" strange ladies, or drawing circles somewhere on the abdomen of a gorgeous blonde. A husband working depth on a distant leg may not come home at all until dawn. He may go from Sunday to Sunday without seeing his children. He may wonder who his wife is "retailing" with in his absence. Walking in the door at four in the morning to greet an infuriated, suspicious wife is a scene that must inhibit many distributors from leaping up to Diamond on the twelve-month timetable. My guess is that more than one Amway home has reverberated with conversations like this:

"Where have you been?"

"Showing the Plan."

"Yeah, I'll bet. To who, that chippie I saw you flirting with in the Mall?"

"Oh, I knock myself out every night so you can quit your job and you ruin my attitude as soon as I walk in the door. Ain't it great!"

"Don't tell me you're doing this for me! *You* were the one who wanted that four-wheel-drive jeep! You're in this for your own ego!"

"The least you could do is iron my shirt before I go out and have coffee ready for me when I get home. How many sales have you made this week?"

"Why don't you listen to those tapes you spend all our money on, you might find out you're supposed to make time for your kids."

"I do, every Sunday. Why don't you read some positive books and get rid of your stinking thinking! We'll never get anywhere with an attitude like yours."

The Direct gets wind of the storm clouds in this home when the couple skips the next function and doesn't buy their weekly case of tapes. A bad sign: sure to follow is a decrease in the number of meetings on the distributor's calendar, and then a drop-off in the flow of starter kits and decision paks, and, worst of all, sooner or later, a decline in their PV. Time for marriage counseling by the upline jewel. This couple needs an attitude Seminar. Sell them *How to Stay Happy Though Married.*

Distributorships are supposed to counteract the effect of repeated absence from the home by involving the children in the business. The couple explains to their children in simple terms what Amway could mean to them as a family: in the future they will have more time together; they will be able to move into a bigger and better house; they will have a better car; they will take vacations together, and maybe, after Daddy reaches a certain bracket, they will take a trip to Disneyworld. Children are encouraged to select "goals" from magazines, or the Amway Shoppers Catalog, such as little red wagons and bicycles, and cut them out and tape them on the refrigerator door beside Daddy's Cadillac and Mommy's fur coat. A child may check off on a calendar the nights Daddy is out showing the Plan, and when a certain number of nights is checked off, the parents buy the child one of the goals on the refrigerator. Absence from the home is in this way turned into a "positive."

Jewels have said at Seminars, "Go home tonight and look at your children while they're sleeping, and say "I'm gonna build this business for you. So that you can have a better life. So that you can go to college. So that you can grow up in a home with positive values. So that you won't get into drugs and promiscuity. So that you'll believe in your country and believe in free enterprise and believe in God!"

"If nothing else motivates you, isn't Amway worth it for your kids? Don't tell them twenty years from now, 'Gee, I could have really done something with that Amway back before it got *saturated*.' What can they say then? 'Yeah, thanks a lot, dad.'"

However much they may be integrated into the Dream, children are rigorously excluded from most business activity. Over and over, Directs tell their people, "When you show the Plan, put your kids to bed or leave them in the next room with a babysitter." Prospects invited to a get-together should be told to come without their children. The standard hour for drawing circles is 8 or 8:15, after a small child's bedtime. Distributors should not bring their children to their sponsor's house during product pick-up. Children are not allowed at Seminars and Rallies, Extravaganzas, Family Reunions, Free Enterprise Days and Dream Nights. Directs may arrange special Christmas parties for children, but otherwise, the rule is, children and business do not mix.

It is sensible to make such a rule: anyone who has ever stood in front of a marker board delivering a sales pitch while dogs paw his leg, and four-year-olds erase his circles and run around the livingroom jumping on chairs, would not wish it to be changed. A dozen cowboys and Indians romping through the kitchen can transform product pick-up day into a monkey house. Likewise, children may be excluded from Seminars for the same reasons they are excluded from conventions and hearings.

The policy concerning children, however, reveals the difference between Amway and a healthy social movement. In a healthy movement, bent on enriching and humanizing the quality of life, children would be the concern of the whole community; their creativity is a precious resource that needs to be fed. Children must have contact with all races and classes of people, and all kinds of ideas, to keep their minds and their curiosity alive. They deserve more than red wagons and bicycles and trips to Disneyworld. Having them put material goals on a refrigerator is teaching them to relate to objects, not people; the object becomes the explanation for the parent's absence, and then a substitute for the parent, and finally a means for controlling the family. It is a form of "behavior mod," suitable perhaps for pacifying a child, but not for helping her to grow into an autonomous and spirited adult. Then to take the child out of public school and enroll her in a "Christian" school, is to restrict and narrow her view of the world to a single dimension; she need not have any exposure to the working-class poor, evolutionary science, atheism, sex education, minority races and cultures or "subversive" books and teaching methods. She will grow up safely protected from all pernicious influences; she will have little or no sexual experience before marriage, and need not ever feel doubt, skepticism, uncertainty, or the kind of value conflict that must attend any creative response to the cosmos. Her father and husband express love for her by giving commodities. A "nice" life, paved, boxed, made up, straight and orderly, like a clean white chapel, with all the windows closed, on a hot day. And what she ought to pray for is that the air conditioning never breaks down.

This treatment of children accurately reflects the *ethos* of the organization. Just as upline manipulates downline through propaganda and behavioral control, so parent manipulates child through goal-setting and scheduled reinforcement. Duplication, the highest virtue in the business, is transferred and internalized within the home. Just as "love" between sponsor and distributor is conditional, depending on the distributor's willingness to edify and obey his upline role models, so "love" between parent and child is expressed as a function of money and deferred to the future: someday "we" will have that big house or motor home, but in the meantime, be good while Daddy shows the Plan thirty more times and you can have that tape deck from the Shopper's Catalog.

Neither the Corporation nor my particular upline arranges day care centers for children while distributors are attending functions. Such an idea, in any case, contradicts the Amway value system. The concept of a day care center, though usually inadequate as practiced in America, at least begins to recognize that children are a social responsibility; but in Amway, children from different lines would play together in a day care center; parents would meet there and the barriers against crosslining might erode. Day care tends to be viewed by jewels as a form of creeping socialism which the whole point of Amway is to reverse. It is considered the responsibility of the individual couple to hire babysitters. Although vastly more expensive than a simple unified day care system, hiring babysitters is more consistent with the ideal of the nuclear family motivated by the pursuit of wealth: couples provide for their own, the llines are kept apart, and the distributor must strive harder to boost his PV in order to meet the cost. But it is a rather interesting paradox to leave children with a babysitter on a family holiday, in order to attend a "Family Reunion" and listen to sermons about preserving the sacredness of the Family.

No doubt the children of many Directs would come onstage in a chorus to tell the world how Amway changed their indifferent parents to loving Moms and Dads. The comment "Before Amway I didn't know I had a father" was made by the son of an alcoholic, who was cured and "born again" as a result of joining the business. In some families children grow up and break off from the parents as Directs and go Diamond, adding to the family Crown. Others name their children after prominent Corporation figures, or the headquarters town—Rich and Jay and Ada. This kind of devotion serves to illustrate an earlier point: Amway is a "born again" religious experience which thrives only by securing a perpetual flow of converts. For an alcoholic whose life is on the rocks, the business can be a practical application of amazing grace: a purpose to live for, a faith to live by, and a chance to make a living, all wrapped in the same box of soap. To save his marriage, and his income, and give his children a reason to respect him, are admirable and worthwhile achievements, certainly better than lying drunk in the gutter; but the logic of the business demands that he must carry it to others; he must bring them a mold, and fit them into it, and change their values and minds too. He may be rehabilitated, but the hundreds of families in his organization pay a price for it which, if fully understood, they might not be willing to pay.

The ideal distributorship is a kind of polyethylene bottle which contains, and preserves, the nuclear family by assigning clear roles to each member and tying the performance of those roles to the receipt of a bonus. The role of the wife is to retail and handle products, do the paperwork, manage the children, handle telephone orders and messages, keep the husband's suits and shirts clean. The role of the husband is to develop prospects, show the Plan, sponsor new distributors, work depth and be the leader of his group by being a faithful follower of his upline. The Functions accentuate both roles by dress code, association, order of appearance onstage, and by subtle cues which amount to a body of mores and folklore. A male speaker jokes, for example, that his wife's capacity to dream big always exceeded his own capacity to keep up with her spending habits. A joke like this conveys indirectly the message that the wife *should* spend a lot of money, and the husband should work hard to sponsor new Directs so that his wife can have the cars and clothes and diamonds and travel that other Amway wives have. Then the speaker's wife appears to show off her furs and boast that her man is a Winner.

This is the model of approved behavior, a role expectation for each partner; if they fulfill the roles, others will assume that they are in love and have a secure marriage. The role offers security and ego reinforcement, and a simple definition of "love" which allows no surprises and makes no deeper demands on the intellect and spirit.

The Plan is the same: easily and quickly learned, broken down into eight or twelve steps; a husband need only keep repeating that Plan night after night, month in and month out, to demonstrate that he cares for his Family. When the roles get boring, the wife can look forward to hiring a "girl" to answer the telephone, clean the house and manage products; the husband can hope someday to quit his job and go full time in the business.

The indoctrination into the belief system is a process shared equally by both partners: they should listen to the propaganda and attend the functions together; the rewards are part of the indoctrination, and serve to attach their self-contained bottle to the great uterus of the Corporation. After going Direct, the couple travels to Ada for additional Seminars and a tour of the Corporation facilities: "Then," say the leaders, "you'll see what you've really got behind you." At the level of Pearl, the couple attends special events, with titles like "Go Diamond Weekend," which take place at luxury hotels and vacation resorts; diamond merchants may come to display selections of jewelry, which the Pearls can only afford by going on to the next pin level. At Diamond, the couple goes on a yacht cruise, or an excursion to a Corporation-owned Caribbean island. Trips like this are then described on tape and marketed throughout the organization to motivate the great mass of rank and file distributors:

"And then you lie there on that white beach under the palm trees, and listen to those warm waves wash up on the sand; and then a servant boy brings you a whole pineapple, and he slices that pineapple in half, and you smell that fresh pineapple aroma; and he puts a scoop of ice cream right in the center, and you bite into the real thing, not like it tastes in the can; and that juice oozes down over your chin, and that's what I call *First class living*."

The product supply, the income, the family roles, the rewards, the future, the Dream, are all contained, defined and dispensed within the life of the Corporation. The Family is not so much held together by the distributorship, it *is* the distributorship. In the beginning, the Family spends the PV checks on expenses; later, if they are one of the very few who make it to a profitable level, the husband and wife spend the bonuses on Corporation and upline-designed recreations and luxuries. For some of these events the Corporation will pick up the tab.

The incentive for an Amway couple to stay together, no matter what their incompatibilities or independent paths, must be powerful: divorce could mean dissolving the distributorship, and then litigating which legs belong to which party; the example might send a Negative ripple down through the group and threaten the stability of the whole edifice. Indeed, jewels brag that the divorce rate in Amway is 1 percent.

The Family that the leaders believe in is not quite the same as the real American family beyond the fences of the business. The real family is fluid and takes many temporary forms. It is partly a nuclear family, partly recombined; it includes single parents, divorced parents who trade the children, older relatives and communes.

John Naisbitt, in *Megatrends* (Warner, 1982)* estimates that one-fourth of all American households are occupied by a single person; "More than ever before, people live alone." Furthermore, it is likely that "at least thirteen separate types of households will eclipse the conventional family, including such categories as 'female head, widowed, with children' and 'male head, previously married, with children.' "

Amway sponsors will recruit among all these diverse types. The proportion of singles in Amway is about the same as the fraction of single households in the country at large. The pages of the *Amagram* reveal that many single distributors of both sexes make it to the level of Direct, even Pearl and Emerald. Occasionally one sees a male/male or female/female partnership in the magazine. But the Amway version of the Family is nonetheless believed in and proselytized. Among the Diamonds, the vast majority of distributorships are married couples. Almost always, the featured Crown on the cover is a husband/wife team. The leaders believe in a Family *reconstituted* by the business, and held together by the prescribed roles. The Amway Family is not fluid; it must be stable, and patented, everywhere the same, in order to coincide with a reliable distributorship and present a uniform model.

The tree-like structure of the sponsorship lines, on the other hand, is an artificial kinship system which replaces the extended family. Each leg added to a line is a "generation." The circle maps that leaders draw to lay out their organizations on paper resemble, and are sometimes referred to, as family trees. Distributors hero-worship the prominent figures in their upline just as the scions of a great family might take pride in descending from a famous ancestor. Some leaders, like Yager and his lieutenants, consciously play the role of Big Daddy to the thousands in their downlines, surrounding themselves with a mystique of authority and inaccessibility; to get an audience with Big Daddy is a supreme privilege; advice from Big Daddy is precious gold; his decisions are irreversible and only a loser would disregard them. Yager seems to enjoy projecting himself to the

Megatrends, pp. 261-262.

public as an Old Testament patriarch, drawing an implied parallel—in his book, *Don't Let Anybody Steal Your Dream*—between his career and the Biblical Joseph.

The paternalism of upline/downline relations, discussed previously, transfers to the business the psychodynamic pattern of dependent child and authoritarian but loving parent. Each of my legs is like a son or daughter. When they succeed, I not only feel personally vindicated, I become literally enriched. My favorites are the ones who follow the role models and do whatever it takes; the black sheep are the distributors who refuse to conform. The prodigal son may lose interest or do it his way until he drives his business into the ditch, and then comes home and asks for help. And just as, in a family, a man may develop closer ties with a nephew or grandchild than with his own son, so by working depth, I may find a protege several legs down the line who duplicates better than my personally sponsored leg.

The tough but loving father image emanates from no less a figure than Rich DeVos, who describes himself in *Believe!* as an "authoritarian" parent, willing to compromise on unimportant issues: "I don't believe that a few inches of hair over a boy's collar is worth a major family hassle...If I have to put my foot down, I want to do it on something that is really worth it!"* He projects this image to distributors on tapes like *Try or Cry*, which upbraids listeners for complaining about their jobs, and admonishes them to perform cheerfully or quit and start their own business.

From one perspective, the Amway use of the Family is only another means to control distributors and maximize consumption; the long-range political effect is to strengthen the power of big business over the life of the nation. The value system of corporate capitalism in general is insured a direct conduit into the minds of the people by converting the family into a miniature corporate model, whose reason for being depends on the parent company.

To some temperaments, this lifestyle may be suffocating and stultifying beyond any repression enforced by a Communist regime; it seems a cruel parody of American freedom, which has always included the elements of chaotic excitement and creative diversity of thought, not merely of product; to the unindoctrinated observer it feels creepy to meet Amway families and see the same code of dress, and hear the same formulas of speech, and the same morality, and encounter the same smiles and handshakes, and the same Dream in

Believe!, p. 171.

couple after couple; and then be saturated with the same political views preached by leaders from the stages of the Rallies. Once you learn the duplication model, you can usually spot Amway distributors the minute they open their mouths.

But others find security and predictability in a model that tells them exactly what happiness is and how it is to be pursued; how to dress for any occasion, how to please your mate, how to keep your children away from disruptive influences, how to achieve status and worship God.

In "Stepchildren of the Moral Majority" (*Psychology Today*, November 1981), noted psychological consultant Daniel Yankelovich observed that many American parents feel drawn to the Moral Majority because they "are increasingly uncomfortable with the sweeping permissiveness that their own pursuit of permissiveness has created for young people....Uncertain and confused about the full import of their own values, they fall back upon simpler, less individualistic, less *ad hoc* principles—values that exist, as it were, 'out there': patriotism, duty, sexual fidelity."* Amway exerts the same authoritative influence over divided minds; it tells families how and why to stay together, and what to strive for, and how to give their children a good life; and, to a region beyond that polyethylene bubble, it seeks to banish the tragedy, impermanence and terror of the "Negative" world.

*Yankelovich, p. 6.

ELEVEN

THE
INCREDIBLE POSITIVE
MIND-BLOW MACHINE

The value system taught in Amway is a cousin of the whole modern "consciousness transformation" movement, which includes an amorphous flux of loosely related ideologies and groups: scientology, *est*, mind dynamics, psychocybernetics, success motivation institute. W.W. Bartley III, in his biography of Werner Erhard (N.Y.: Clarkson Potter, 1978), traces the common roots that many of the recent transformation programs share in the earlier work of Maxwell Maltz, Dale Carnegie and Napoleon Hill. The Amway positive attitude training descends from the same ancestors. To these names may be added David Schwartz, whose *Magic of Thinking Big* (1959) has been a basic success handbook for over two decades.

Amway people prefer the word "attitude" to "consciousness." The language presumably relates better to the broad spectrum of middle America which the Corporation aims to reach. The basic principle of their training is that mind, not environment, determines achievement and direction in life: "Attitude, not aptitude, determines altitude." Heredity and social circumstance both play their part, but for most normal people, mind, or attitude, if properly cultivated and acted upon, is a sufficient power to realize whatever we can dream. With the right attitude, mind is not defeated by obstacles, but uses them as stepping stones and sources of energy.

Amway borrows from motivational principles that have been known for centuries, and breaks this knowledge down into simple bold-face topics: action conquers fear; believe you can succeed and you will; never accept excuses from yourself; set daily and monthly goals, write them down, program your subconscious to attain your goals by surrounding yourself with images of them and connect the images with emotion; whatever the mind can conceive and believe, it can achieve; persistence wins where talent only watches; happiness is found in doing; speak only positive thoughts, for you are hung by the tongue; if you don't know where you're going you'll end up somewhere else.

Positive attitude is not unique to U.S. business philosophy: the conquest of Mexico and Peru by the Spanish, the political system founded by Lenin, the survival of the Soviet nation during the Nazi invasion, the victory of the Vietnamese, were all triumphs of belief, persistence and will, directed toward clearly defined and imagined goals. The power of disciplined belief has been known to Western civilization since before the March of the Ten Thousand. Amway, with its genius for packaging intangibles, like dreams, religion, love, and the Family, puts success principles together into a packaged ideology and delivers it to Seminar audiences in memorable and duplicable form.

For what end? Any ordinary person of normal intelligence, by applying the system faithfully, has a slender chance of acquiring a ten-bedroom ranch, servants, a Jaguar and a private plane. The fact that the vast majority of distributors will never do anything of the kind does not obviate this possibility. It can be done. This much must be granted. I saw it done by others. But Amway is not the only way to change class. It can also be done with Shaklee, Stanley, religion and the Mafia, among thousands of other "vehicles." The key to the process is Mind.

To change class using the Amway vehicle, one must change the mind—utterly, completely. To go the whole nine yards in the vehicle means to get out of the working class. This hope is the main appeal of the Plan. The Dream is a collection of images from a leisured lifestyle, and the rut is none other than a prospect's own traditional cursing complaint about working-class existence. We would rather not have to answer a bell and punch a clock every day, or be on a roof nailing shingles. We would rather paddle a canoe down a good fishing stream while living off someone else's work.

Every person of leisure—everyone who is able to live on profits and need not hold a job—must have laborers somewhere generating his wealth. Amway from this perspective is a ready-made instrument for recruiting and organizing those laborers, and living off them. Of course I must work very hard to recruit and organize, but once the organization is properly built, I need not spend time in it. When I work the hardest in Amway I am probably making the least money— in fact I may have to subsidize the business from a salaried income. Years later, if the work pays off, I "enjoy the fruits of my labor"—that is, the labor of those "legs" I have sponsored, whose sales generate my commissions.

In order to change class, I must root out and obliterate from the self every attitude of a low-income mentality and replace it with the consciousness of a corporate manager. I must discover in the self all the "Negative" mental habits inherited from being brought up to hold a job and get rid of them. I must cut away every thought and association belonging to my former class identity. To become rich, I must dress and think the role, seek out friendships with rich people (in this context, the Amway jewels), act the way they act, read the books they read, take their advice, ape their attitudes and language. The ultimate meaning of the ABCs taught in the Seminar (Attitude, Belief, Commitment) is to kill off the class identity I wish to reject, and create, by imitation, the class identity I wish to assume. Total commitment to this Pygmalion act will energize all the forces in my world that might help me make it, and draw them to me. People will notice the change. The "losers" will drop away from my company, but other "Winners" will recognize one of their own. They will begin to identify me with the class I have decided to join.

This is the essential message of the self-help literature marketed to distributors. "Positive" consciousness, when examined for the class values which it conveys, is utterly contemptuous of wage earners and inimical to their identity. Holding a job is the mark of a loser, unless it is merely a stepping stone to higher things. Taking welfare is even worse; you might as well be a petty crook. A job is called a J. O. B., which, in the words of Bill Britt, prominent Diamond in the Yager organization and a member of the Amway Board of Directors, means "Jackass of the Boss." Speeches by Kay Fletcher and Don Held, also prominent Yager Diamonds, imply that corporate employees are suckers who are too frightened to let go of their security blankets and exercise their own ability to perform.

But what is lost when I root out a wage earner's values from the self and replace them with corporate management thinking and belief? What values am I giving up? Is there something vital and positive about the attitudes on the lower end of the social scale that workers need in order to safeguard their own interests as workers? What does it mean in social terms for the Amway *ethos* to be vigorously, persistently, and with missionary zeal, propagated throughout a working and middle class population? What long-range effects will this have on support for public schooling, the strength of organized labor to resist oppression and paternalism from big business, the level of wages and benefits for all employees, the preservation of civil liberties, national resource land and social

services? The time to answer these questions is now, before Ronald
Reagan appears the most liberal of the candidates to hold office in the
United States of Amway.

The effect of "positive" indoctrination on wage earners must
surely be to make them ashamed of that status. Everything possible is
done to encourage them to reject their class. This means that all the
common traditions and experience built up by workers over generations must be nullified. Attitudes that serve the useful function of
resisting rich parasites are held up for ridicule. If I do not bow to my
upline jewel and let him run my life, I am a stinking thinker.
Somewhere inside my memory banks, the warning bell goes off: this is
precisely what every boss I have ever worked for, and my father worked
for, and his father before him, would like us to believe. They all want
loyalty, commitment, lots of free overtime and maximum productivity for minimum wage. In Amway they want it for no wage at all.
They also want me to silence that warning bell. That bell is a sign of
stinking thinking, and if I don't silence it then I will never be a
success.

The attitudes of wage earners are not all heroic, certainly. Anti-
intellectualism, bigotry, resentment and envy of status, fatalism and
cynicism toward any prospect of healthy social change, are well-worn
mental grooves which have prevented us for years from acting
collectively on our own behalf to revitalize the U.S. political process.
Many of my prospects rejected Amway for the same non-reasons they
reject everything else. They have no hope. They would rather watch
television and drink than help their community wake up. If their
comatose spirits were the only alternative, then anyone with a breath
of life in them would be quite right to ride the vehicle of Napoleon
Hill, Dale Carnegie and Rich DeVos out of that vegetable morass as
quickly as they could start the motor and kick in the four-wheel drive.

But what the Amway "positive" programming does is throw the
baby out with the bathwater. And this is deliberate. It is one baby that
corporate managers in general do not wish ever to see grow up. That
baby is labor consciousness in its own positive aspect: egalitarianism,
respect for good work, mutual aid, solidarity, the will to find social
solutions for social problems. Amway gives lip service to some of these
values—work especially—but only for its own goals, which are
anything but egalitarian.

Rich DeVos, in *Believe!*, devotes a whole chapter to the worth and
dignity of the working "man," without whom, he clearly recognizes,
production and wealth would be impossible. Coming from a working
background himself, he is sensitive and alert to the ways in which
academic intellectuals demean workers with status labels. Mechanics

and salespeople are "warm, giving, highly complex" human beings, doing their jobs with "pride and competence," for which they deserve respect and gratitude.* One might see in Amway certain persuasive egalitarian themes: anybody can join, anybody willing to work and learn and change can make money; garbage collectors can make it to Crown Ambassador, and build a castle on the seacoast, if that is their dream. But it is not by practicing egalitarian values toward their distributors that they will get there. The structure of the business, although open to expansion by people of any class, mirrors, as we have already noted, the hierarchy of the corporate world. Amway offers a vehicle for a few people to enter the upper middle class economic bracket who might otherwise have remained "non-professional" workers; but overall the business reinforces class differences and defends extremes of wealth.

Believers advertise Amway as "people helping people," and on the surface this concept resembles mutual aid; but mutual aid in the business occurs in the context of upline-downline relations, which are parasitical, on the one hand, and demeaning, on the other. Amway reflects the way mutual aid is practiced between classes in "free enterprise" society. The rich help the poor through charity and welfare, by benevolently offering the "chance" for employment. These forms of condescension elevate the giver and degrade the recipient. There is no welfare in the Amway system, but the condescension appears in the paternalism of downline management, the hero worship of upline success models, and the idea that I am doing my prospects a favor by giving them the chance to be sponsored under me.

Mutual aid among workers is untainted by the profit motive. Workers help each other because it is the neighborly thing to do, not because one will get a bonus check for the other's effort. Many hands make light work. I fix your car today because you might unload a cord of wood for me tomorrow. Neither of us is degraded, used or hero-worshipped in the transaction. I earn your respect as a mechanic and you earn mine as a woodcutter. Then we might go fishing or shoot some pool to confirm the friendship. We make no assumption of inferiority and superiority between us. I am not your upline, downline, crossline or competitor, just your friend; we have the same problems; we might even have the same boss. From a network of such mutual ties could grow a union, a community self-help organization, a rent strike or a new political party with the goal of power for

*Believe!, p. 101.

workers. The Amway structure would never lead to concerted action of any kind unless it was controlled from the top.

Amway might be valuable to workers if any significant number of people could use it to solve their economic problems—to pay the bills, educate the children, provide quality medical care for the family, break the wage-earner's total dependence on the job, and still afford sufficient living space, a reliable car, time off to enjoy life and expand the mind. One major test for the value of Amway is to examine how many people can make a living at it. If not more than a small fraction of distributors ever achieve the level of a jewel, then it is clear that most workers will never benefit from the business.

No distributor is able to replace the income received from a job at least until he or she goes Direct. With a well-balanced organization of multiple legs, and provided that no single leg does more than half the volume, a Direct might make a net PV bonus, after payments to the group, of around $1200 to $1500 per month. This estimate assumes a monthly volume in the range of $12 to $15 thousand. The bonus on that figure is 25 percent of BV, approximately half of which would be paid out as bonuses to the group. From the remaining figure must be deducted costs for gasoline, mileage, advertising, inventory, bookkeeping, telephone; the Internal Revenue Service also allows deductions for business use of the home, which is a short-term tax advantage, but in the long run represents an actual loss, and is part of the total cost of running the business. At $1500 per month, net profit, the Direct has another wage-size income, equivalent to a second full-time job, very helpful, certainly, but not enough to change class.

How many distributors reach the level of Direct?

The Corporation does not publish statistics of this kind, but one may arrive at a reasonably accurate figure by examining the data in its annual reports. The *1980 Annual Report* put the number of active Amway distributorships world-wide at 750,000. The *1981 Annual Report* gave a figure of over one million. For the year 1981, then, about 250,000 new active distributors joined the business. According to the 1981 *Report*, there were 6433 new Direct, Voting Member/ Profit Sharing, Ruby, Pearl and Emerald Direct Distributorships. This figure does not reveal how many new Directs were unable to maintain volume for the six months required to become a Profit Sharing Voting Member, or how long each new Direct took to get there. But, using the figure of 6433, we discover that a possible 2.57 percent of all new active distributors, in the best year Amway had ever had to date, reached the level of Direct. If we subtract the Directs who did not maintain volume, the percentage may well decrease by more than half.

In 1980, the Corporation-financed survey to determine the mean-average sales of products sold by all "active" distributors to only retail customers, plus products retained for personal or family consumption, disclosed a figure of $150 BV per month.* Using this figure, an average Direct would require an organization of at least 75 to 100 active distributors to produce a PV-BV sufficient to remain a Profit Sharing Voting Member. The percentage of Amway people who will *ever* make it to Direct in any given year, then, is between 1 and 2 percent of the total. In the structure of the system, the size of the distributor force is about 75 to 100 times greater than the number of Directs. So 98 to 99 percent of all Amway distributors are not, nor can they ever be, at a level where they make enough to replace the income of a single wage-earner in the family. For, regardless of how many go Direct in the future, each person or couple can only get there by adding 75 to 100 new active distributorships to the total sales force, under their own downline.

Moreover, at Direct one cannot be said to have changed class, but merely augmented the family income. To change class, a distributor must get into the Diamonds; a Diamond with a strong organization may turn a respectable $50 to $100 thousand a year net profit. How many distributors actually do this? And what are the odds of success?

Again, using the same annual reports, we find that in 1981 there were 120 new Diamond, Double and Triple Diamond, Crown and Crown Ambassador Direct Distributorships relative to the same total of 250,000 new distributors for the year. The individuals who made Diamond that year may have actually joined years previously, but in order to reach their new pin level, they, or their groups, had to recruit the additional 250,000; it is therefore appropriate to measure the odds in terms of current figures. The percentage is .048. For one person to change class using the Amway vehicle, at least 2083 new active people must be brought in, trained, motivated, programmed and supplied. The odds of any particular distributor attaining Diamond are, using these figures, approximately 1 in 2083. They would have a much better chance playing a three-digit state lottery number. Of course anyone may increase the odds by location, persistence, attitude and other intangibles impossible to quantify, but if we assume that every distributor has access to attitude training and indoctrination, the intangible factors over the long run would tend to follow a law of diminishing returns.

The 1982 and 1983 *Annual Reports* would not change these conclusions. For 1983, in fact, the Corporation, for the first time, did

The Amagram, February 1982.

not publish the graph showing its growth rate and did not give figures on the number of new distributors, Directs and jewels in the business for that year. The reason is easy enough to discern: revenues were less than for 1982. In 1983 the total number of distributors remained at 1 million.

It is fair to say that over 97 percent of all "active" distributors, using the Corporation's own definition of "active," are not making any money. If they buy tapes, attend functions and keep inventory, they are actually losing money and must subsidize their Amway business from other income. Further, this condition will always obtain in the business as a whole, because, for one person or couple to make money, they must bring in dozens of others at the bottom of the pyramid.

What motivates that 97 percent, clearly, is the ideology taught throughout the business by means of mass Rallies, books, tapes, television commercials, magazines, conventions, tours and propaganda events of all kinds: old-fashioned "free enterprise" in the Benjamin Franklin mode. Keep thy shop and thy shop will keep thee. In a period when small business has been supplanted by the corporate monopoly, it would appear to a superficial observer that Amway has revived traditional American values by giving millions of people the opportunity to set up a small business of their own, with hope of wealth and prosperity down the road.

But the Benjamin Franklin mode, like the Family, has been revived *in a corporate context*. No distributorship is a truly independent business; all exist only at the mercy of the Corporation, which controls ethical codes and rules, research and development, plant location, supply and wholesale price. No business which depends on a single source of supply is anything but a marketing agent for the parent company. In Amway, Voting Member Direct Distributors elect the Board of Directors, and so have some input into the overall policies of the Company; otherwise, the relationship of the Direct to the Company parallels the relationship of small business generally to large corporations: the small business takes the risk of opening a new market, does the work with the customer, pays the local overhead and is the first to be wiped out if anything goes wrong. When a small business succeeds, it is usually bought outright by a large corporation, or drawn into its gravitational field as a satellite. To advertise this system as "free enterprise" is like a giant company using the symbol of a Minuteman in a three-cornered hat to sell insurance policies.

The distributors below the level of Direct, that is, the 97 percent, are not even recognized by the Corporation for purposes of income and supply; they deal with Amway only through the Direct, except for catalog orders and customer returns, which may be processed by mail. The Company and the FTC define them as independent entrepreneurs, but they are in fact corporate workers. These 97 percent, not the jewels, perform the actual labor of recruitment, sales and distribution. The Corporation as of 1983 had about seven thousand employees on the payroll, worldwide. This is a strangely small number for a billion-dollar company, until we remember that the real work force of Amway is not defined as such, and is therefore invisible in the employee total: that is, the one million distributors who market, store, transport and deliver the products.

These "entrepreneurs" are, from a corporate point of view, the ideal labor force. In fact they are every employer's dream. They work for less than nothing. They get no regular wage. Every nickel they receive is tied to productivity. They pay all their own expense accounts. They lift and tote the cartons, carry the soap to the customer, pay for the advertising. They are incapable of concerted action to improve their compensation or working conditions. They cannot socialize with their peers. In fact they compete for market outlets, bonuses and pin awards. They have no legal standing as employees, and so cannot unionize, bargain collectively or make importunate demands on the Company for medical and insurance benefits. If they are injured or killed distributing products, in a car accident, for example, the Company is never liable. If one of them slips a disc lifting a box, the Company will pay nothing. They are controlled by a military hierarchy that extends into their homes. They need not be fired; they fire themselves. They cannot collect unemployment benefits when they leave. They recruit their own replacements. Best of all, they are fanatically loyal to the Company and believe religiously in the system that exploits them. They are eager to extend the influence of that system everywhere, and the most energetic, when they reach a level where they finally begin to make an income which is commensurate with their effort, absolutely depend on the Corporation for everything they have: lifestyle, identity, belief, role, sense of worth.

The distributor force is the real triumph of "free enterprise." Amway has achieved what other corporations dream of and spend billions to accomplish, but, for all their propaganda and manipulation, can only approximate: a completely powerless army of servants, with no independent organization and no revolutionary capability whatever. This remarkable product has been manufactured by the very methods which the Company leaders profess to abhor, as being inimical to the freedom and dignity of human beings: behavioral

138   AMWAY

modification, through operant conditioning and differential reinforcement. Amway must mark some kind of watershed in the history of
applied political thought. To glimpse what a Reaganite future would
mean for working people, perhaps we can regard the Amway plastic
bubble as a crystal ball.

This system may well indicate a trend which is being accelerated
generally throughout the corporate world. *In Search of Excellence* by
Thomas J. Peters and Robert H. Waterman, Jr. (Warner Books, 1984)
describes eight basic principles applied by so-called "excellent"
companies which have enabled them to achieve outstanding business
success. Peters and Waterman attempt to identify an American
management style which corporations can use and build on in the
future. The authors are specialists in "management consulting," a
business which advises employers how to get the most work out of
their staff for the least cost. Motivation, they say, is the key to
productivity. People "want desperately to be on winning teams" and
need to feel that "they are in at least partial control of their destinies."
They thrive on the intimacy of small-group settings.

An "excellent" company gives its employees "transcendent
values," that is, a reason to live and a faith to live by. The company
treats the employee like a "winner," reinforces achievement with
recognition and attention and uses rallies and rah-rah events of all
kinds to generate excitement. According to these authors, "many of
the best companies really do view themselves as an extended family."
They cultivate heroes and myths to teach role models of achievement
to the new recruits.*

The general object of "excellence" in management is to get the
employee to identify with the company in a self-transcendent way, so
that she will make sacrifices for it without expecting more money.
"Excellent" management policy also has an important long-range
political effect: it prevents employees from becoming conscious of
their own interests *as workers*. To act on their own behalf as workers,
they must find self-transcendent values by identifying with each
other, not with the company. The ultimate result of this kind of
consciousness would be to form organizations which represented the
interests of all workers, and "transcend the self" by working for the
success of those organizations. The "reason to live" and the "faith to
live by" which is taught in the "excellent" companies is basically the
corporate economic system. For workers to find a "reason to live" in
collectively serving themselves, is, from the viewpoint of the

In Search of Excellence, pp. 60, 76, 57, 68-69, 247, 261, 266.

"excellent" employer, a terrible catastrophe, to be averted by in-
doctrinating the masses into the joys of corporate rah-rah.

Peters and Waterman studied forty-three successful American
companies to reach their conclusions. Amway was not one of them;
but all the methods which they analyze and represent as the wave of
the future are applied in the Amway business with religious passion.
The illusion of control over personal destiny is the biggest single
enticement of the Amway dream.

The ultimate purpose of the positive attitude training is to attain
the goal of a productive loyal, perfectly exploitable and expanding
labor force which believes in the Corporation and the product,
including themselves and their families as one of the products. What
kind of message does this active, missionary *cadre* of believing Amway
products carry into unions, elections, shops and schools? Having
raised this question in various ways throughout the book, let us now
consider Amway as a political movement, with definite aims respecting public opinion, government policy, collective bargaining law,
education and economics.

The tapes and recruiting literature seek to frighten people with
the specter of Communism and Socialism. Unless we act now,
according to them, our "American way of life" will be swallowed by a
collectivist "bogeyman." "Take up Amway as a cause," urge the
leaders, "believe in Amway as a principle and you will succeed." The
"cause" they are talking about is the corporate political ideology,
dressed in Benjamin Franklin clothes, which, they say, is our only
hope of staving off disaster.

Promotional brochures used in the Yager business treat the
reader to a full-page cartoon sequence depicting what will happen to
America when "profits become illegal." Each successive panel reports
a dire consequence worse than the last; in each, the American flag is
drawn smaller and smaller until it disappears altogether: corporations cancel all programs for reinvestment; new plant and equipment
orders are halted; manufacturers announce lay-offs affecting five
million workers; machinery builders close down; automobile factories lay off one million; the Dow Jones Industrials plummet 750
points; trading is suspended; by the afternoon of the second day,
unemployment rises to 47 percent; the Federal Government prints
more money to pay swelling public welfare costs; inflation rises to 100
percent per day; people riot in the streets; politicians begin fleeing the
country.

The Corporation makes a similar point with a play, *Tom Smith
and His Incredible Bread Machine*, currently going the rounds of
shopping malls across the country. Tom Smith invents a machine

which produces bread for a penny a loaf; he is about to end world hunger with this invention, when "socialistic" government interference turns his dream into a nightmare. Free enterprise will solve our problems if only the "bureaucrats" would leave Tom Smith alone and allow him to operate his bread machine without regulation.

During the elections of 1980 and 1984, Amway leaders spent lavishly to get Ronald Reagan and other right-wing political figures into office. Every Seminar and Rally that I attended in 1980 (twelve, plus Free Enterprise Day) was turned into an occasion for campaign propaganda. Conservative politicians gave speeches in a format which mandated applause and approval as a "positive" example for one's downline. Douglas Wead, Yager's public relations agent and the ghost writer for *Don't Let Anybody Steal Your Dream*, produced a campaign book about Reagan, which was sold to distributors at functions and marketed through the organization as one of the books that "positive thinkers" should buy. Literature tables were set up in the foyers of civic centers, offering advertisements from "Citizen's Choice," Van Andel's conservative pressure group, to the audience attending the events. The drive for Reagan within Amway had all the histrionics of a Billy Graham crusade. The pressure and practice of Duplication in effect dragooned masses of distributors into supporting it.

During the election campaign of 1984, Yager "dream-building" literature urged its readers to finish the defeat of "liberalism" by electing Reagan for a second term, so that he and his supporters would have a chance to control the appointments on the Supreme Court. Such an outcome, they anticipate, will affect the American political process for the next forty years.

From the stage, leaders constantly program their audiences to favor complete unregulated freedom of corporations to invest, make profit and do business as they see fit. Yager attacked the "Windfall Profits" tax and defended the "right" of oil companies to charge whatever price they could get for gasoline. Other Directs frankly urge distributors to fill their communities with Amway people so that "we" can revoke all the government red tape that interferes with business. Political power is a definite objective for the upper echelons, which they are going after with the same persistence and cheerful optimism that they applied to earning their pins.

The statements of various jewels, in personal conversations and at leadership training seminars, reveal that they all have more or less the same political opinions. They want massive cuts in Federal programs to aid the working-class poor. They are anti-union; they stereotype unions as defending low productivity, protecting incompetence and ruining the economy with inflationary demands. They favor so-called "right to work" (for less) laws, which mean that a legitimately elected union could not collect an agency fee from non-members in the shop, even though it must represent non-members in contract negotiations with the employer. Some jewels were looking forward to the Reagan welfare cuts because that would mean more competition to get into Amway; in the same spirit, corporations appreciate high unemployment rates which produce long lines of applicants for even the most menial subsistence jobs. One Direct asked me what my Dream was, and I quipped that I would like to live in a gigantic pyramid. "Then," he said, "after Reagan gets elected you can have all the people on welfare build it for you." Such are the comments that pass for humor in Amway circles.

The political attitudes expected of Amway people emanate from the top of the Corporation. DeVos and Van Andel support such anti-labor organizations as the Committee for the Survival of a Free Congress, the National Conservative Political Action Committee, the American Conservative Union Victory Fund, the National Right to Work Committee and the Public Service Political Action Committee. Van Andel urged publicly that the Comprehensive Employment Training Program (CETA) be terminated; he wants the Department of Energy dismantled, and more money for the Pentagon. Like Yager, he supported the big oil companies in opposing Carter's windfall-profits tax. He has opposed the Consumer Protection Agency, Universal Voter Registration and regulation of natural gas prices.

DeVos contributes heavy financial support to the Religious Right: the Christian Embassy, the Christian Freedom Foundation and Third Century Publishers, among other similar groups, all favor cuts in Federal programs to help the poor, handicapped, unemployed and minorities; an end to the political power of unions; withdrawal of American support for the United Nations and a return to Cold War politics. The National Association of Manufacturers, of which DeVos has been a Director, formed in 1977 the Council on a Union-Free Environment, whose purpose is indicated by its name. The victory of Reagan must have been planned and coordinated long in advance within Amway.

Diamonds tell their groups that Amway leaders should keep current, "educate" themselves and be well read; they should subscribe to *Fortune, Business Week, The Wall Street Journal, U.S. News & World Report*. The recommended reading matter is obviously prescribed, not to educate, but to shape the distributor's political opinions. It would be unusual to hear a Direct recommend *The New York Times* to their people, much less *In These Times, Mother Jones* or *The*

Guardian; but an educated citizen with an open mind would want access to different sources of information, not only the views of the conservative business world.

Typically, Amway leaders know little about history or political science; often they simply make up facts to justify their opinions and pass the most outrageous misinformation on to their audiences as "positive thought." Jay Van Andel, a rather well-informed man, if we are to believe Charles Paul Conn and *The Saturday Evening Post*, may be an exception to this statement. But an Emerald in my upline once explained to his listeners, in a brief "history lesson," the reason that people had jobs: around the turn of the century, Americans got lazy and did not want to be in business for themselves anymore. Workers, in short, were in the working class because they "lost their Dream." The equation of Socialism with "government regulation" is an old fallacy, brought to life by Amway people and painted with the face of the devil. The idea that any serious person on the Left wants to make profits "illegal" is pure fanciful rhetoric. Even a Communist system makes profit, or surplus; the question is what will be done with the surplus, and who determines the allocation. But a movement which relies on conditioning and repetition of doctrine to secure agreement does not trouble its adherents with questions of this kind.

A principal target of influence for jewels is the public educational system. All the ones I heard speak on the subject criticized public schools for being Negative about America; they were not teaching children to respect men of great wealth; they did not require students to pray or to read positive-thinking books; they were exposing teenagers to smutty reading matter; they were programming students to fail. One remedy for these deficiencies, they suggest, is to sponsor teachers and school administrators into Amway. Imagine the curriculum of an Amway-controlled school; a perpetual Seminar and Rally. But an alternative remedy, advocated more and more openly and practiced by some Directs in my line, is to withdraw support for public education, by withdrawing funds, removing one's children from the school, and lobbying for Federal measures allowing tuition tax credits for parents who enroll their children in private academies.

What dangers does Amway pose for wage earners?

Quite simply, Amway threatens everything the public fought for in the last hundred years: Medicaid, Medicare, the rudiments, however inadequate, of public transportation and housing, occupational health and safety, social security, unemployment compensation, access to public education all the way up through the university level, and the right to bargain collectively, from a position of strength, over terms and conditions of employment. Few wage-earners would deny that other gains of this nature, not yet achieved, would also serve their needs: low cost quality medical care, adequate and safe public transportation and housing, day care centers for working parents, and, most important of all, power to allocate resources for public interests.

The American people have also fought to preserve wilderness areas for future generations. We have not done near enough to protect the environment from the ravages of private exploitation, but, as with Medicaid, Social Security and unemployment compensation, a beginning has been made; existing controls on air pollution, the national park system, the creation of environmental protection agencies, at least afford a place from which to start. We need to go further: to create, or revitalize, community political structures which would give us a vehicle for halting corporate pollution of our back yards.

Amway as a political movement opposes all these forms of collective action. The underlying assumption of Amway is that private enterprise will solve all our problems, and if private enterprise won't do it, then they are insoluble and must be endured until the coming of Armageddon. The Amway Dream in social terms is a *petty bourgeois* imaginary paradise, in which deserving winners produce wealth from their own little business, and the Job is either a temporary stepping stone, or a self-inflicted punishment reserved for losers. In practice, the Dream means absolute power for corporate monopolies.

The experience of humankind with Marxist-inspired dictatorship has given the population in the West good reason to think twice about supporting Communism. It seems a poor trade-off to work for an oppressive state as a means of escaping an oppressive corporation. But it is not therefore true that every social problem should be left to private enterprise. The wanton spoliation of ocean, air, and forest, the proliferation of deadly energy sources whose waste cannot be safely disposed of, the shortages of food and oil and arable land, are all primarily the work of corporations, cheerfully and positively pursuing their profits without adequate control from any agency representing the needs of the whole people. The major policy decisions that have to be made in the next generation, concerning the use of the oceans, the land, the wealth under the land, the air and the sun, cannot be left to private companies. Workers must get involved in these decisions, collectively, through organs of real political power, or they are certain to be victimized by the outcome, just as they were victimized by the Industrial Revolution.

If Amway leaders have their way, and we cast out all this "bureaucratic" interference with business, and curtail the power of unions, and relax what little public custody of the environment exists, and cut our social services, then it is difficult to see what freedom will be left to working people, other than to join Amway and achieve the "self-transcendence" of the Corporate path. Occupational health and safety regulations will be unenforceable, if not simply repealed; the workers who are injured and diseased as a result will not be able to get disability payments, either from the government or their employers; unions will have no strength to bargain effectively for benefits; retired workers, having little Social Security, will have to sell soap to survive; one in a hundred will make it to Direct. New employment opportunities may open up as a result of further corporate expansion, but only at the terrible cost of new recessions and wars, new famines and new forms of pollution. Perhaps we may console ourselves with the message of religious network television echoed now from Washington—that we are living in the Last Days.

Finally, it must be asked, since positive attitude training is cloaked in the garments of the Personal Growth movement, whether any mind-expansion or spiritual consciousness happens to you as a result of submitting to the Amway indoctrination process. Jewels are convinced that spiritual growth is the most precious aspect of their business; they are all willing to testify in droves how much more spiritual they have become since they joined Amway, how they give money to churches and support missionaries to foreign lands and discovered the healing efficacies of prayer.

The power of prayer and genuine spiritual consciousness in human life is evident in all of the planet's great religions, and has been manifested repeatedly for thousands of years. Equally evident is how the self-interest and self-aggrandizement of the ego may use this power for its own ends. In the name of religion, missionary schools destroyed the cultures of countless Indian and African peoples and programmed the survivors with the Protestant Work Ethic: it is holy to serve your boss.

In the Christian tradition, the spiritual ideal is represented by the *saint*, a man or woman who loves even enemies (especially enemies), will wash and cleanse lepers at the risk of getting the disease, cares nothing for wealth and status, does nothing to harm others, and will even offer his or her own life, like Christ, to save people he or she does not even know. In the Buddhist tradition, this ideal is transmitted by the *bodhisattva*, an awakened being who surrenders all the benefit of enlightenment in order to serve as a bridge for others to cross over into the awakened state. The *bodhisattva* likewise cares nothing for wealth or power and will take on the harmful karma of others in order to alleviate their pain.

These ideals set a tough standard for ordinary mortals seeking to expand their consciousness by taking a correspondence course in mind dynamics. Christ said that if you will be perfect, give all you have to the poor and follow him. We might well reply with Chaucer's Wife of Bath, that it takes all kinds to make a world, and the brass pots are not needed less than the gold. But when an organization purports to bestow spiritual illumination on its adherents, and turns out to be recruiting and exploiting an army of willing slaves, we are entitled to measure it against known spiritual criteria. By their fruits shall ye know them.

What are the fruits of Amway?

TWELVE
THE
CULT OF
FREE ENTERPRISE

Bill Emerald, my fictional name for a prominent Yager jewel in the Northeast region, stood on the stage of an auditorium telling the 1500 pins in his organization that "the outside world just doesn't understand us; they call us a cult..."

Other Pearls and Emeralds of that leadership function came out to say that Amway was America's only hope. Without Amway this country was in deep trouble. Commitment to Amway meant commitment to ourselves, our families, our country and the free enterprise system. Only Amway could effectively stop all this bureaucratic government interference in our lives. In Cuba and Russia and China and Eastern Europe we would not be allowed to have an Amway business, we would all be slaves of the government. If we believe in freedom, and God, then we must take up the cause of Amway. We must get out there and fill our communities with new distributors.

"If my tax return is audited, you know what I hope? The IRS agent will be an Amway distributor. And if I have to go to court, I want the judge to be in Amway too."

The leaders made everyone in the audience stand up. "Now point to the stage," they said. All hands pointed to the stage. The rows of hands looked like a mass salute. "Now repeat after us," they said. "Where you are is where I will be!" The crowd repeated the line in unison. "Now repeat: I can do it too!" The crowd chanted "I can do it too!"

Again the speakers said "Dexter is Our Leader! Isn't that right?" And the crowd responded "Right!"

"We've got the finest Leader in the business! Isn't that right?"
"Right!"

146

"If you don't think so, then what are you here for?"

"Ain't it great!"

"I tell you, I love Dexter! I'll never be able to describe how I feel about Dexter! Without Dex, none of us would be here in this room today! Dex gave us freedom! Do you know how precious that is? He gave us freedom!"

And now, said the speaker, it was time to announce who was going to be at the next big Extravaganza. He unrolled a screen. From a slide projector flashed a huge statuesque image of Dexter, twenty feet tall. The Afro hair stood out around his head like a halo. From his neck hung that gold cross. The crowd screamed and cheered. Row after row stood up and poured out their applause. A standing ovation for the Leader's picture.

> Cult: 1. A system of religious rites and observances: 2. Zealous devotion to a person, ideal, or thing. 3. The object of this devotion. 4. The followers of a cult; a sect. L. *cultus, colere*, to cultivate, cherish, worship. (*Standard College Dictionary.*)

Around the time I passed the zenith of my career in Amway, the Reverend Jim Jones, leader of a cult in Guyana, ordered his followers to take poison in a grisly paroxysm of mass self-destruction. This is probably what we think of when we hear the word "cult."

Amway compares favorably with the cult members of Guyana. For one thing, save the escapees, they are all dead. Amway people are bound to look good next to them. The live distributors are still walking around showing the Plan. So far as I know, they are not armed, and will not shoot Congresspeople and reporters who investigate them. Neither are they likely to drink poison. But they certainly show "zealous devotion to a person, ideal or thing," and practice "a system of religious rites and observances."

The term "cult" is usually reserved for newly formed religious fringe organizations which lack the respectability and tradition of the long-established churches. Otherwise it might be hard to put together a definition which would not also include Methodists, Baptists and Catholics. We tend to forget that these sects were all regarded as cults in their youth, and looked on by their early contemporaries with grave suspicion and distrust. The groups that we call "cults" practice indoctrination with such telling effect that some parents of their members are filled with fear, and go to extraordinary lengths to rescue their children—kidnapping, bondage, discipline, counter-indoctrination by means of the lockup treatment. The Unification Church, led by the Reverend Sun Myung Moon, seems to fit most people's image of a

publicly tolerated cult. Modern cults also resemble certain features of
totalitarian parties: Leader worship, regimentation, adherence to a
single point of view, intolerance of dissent, the demand that members
express active agreement with the Leader and give their whole lives to
the organization.

What distinguishes a cult from a genuine spiritual path?

A cult diminishes the awareness of its members; a spiritual path
enhances awareness. A cult narrows perception and programs the
mind with an ideology, a simple-minded, one-dimensional view of
life. A spiritual path expands perception, undermines all ideologies
together with the conditioning that creates them, and exposes the
sojourner to the mystery and complexity of life. A cult limits choice
and tells you what to think; a spiritual path begins in choiceless
silence. A cult demands the surrender of your intelligence to the
Leader; a spiritual path awakens it, and demands only the surrender
of ignorance, aggression and greed. A cult is a product of ego; a
spiritual path exposes ego as a source of pain.

Members of the Unification Church are not supposed to marry,
or make important life decisions, without the blessing and permission of the Leader. The member who brings in a new recruit is
considered that person's spiritual parent. Recruits are indoctrinated
with a new ideology; they must attend special seminars for this purpose, and consent to being separated from their former social group.
They give up their possessions to the organization and must listen to
tapes and read tracts which re-program their consciousness. They are
convinced that they belong to the children of light, as opposed to the
forces of darkness. They are prepared for a complete break with their
former friends and family members. The cult members become their
new families. They are trained to reject any thoughts which go against
cult doctrines.

The troops of the Church, who fill its bank accounts, pay its bills
and enrich the Leader, are called Mobile Fundraising Teams, or
MFT's, members who are expected to make any sacrifice for their
faith, even going down into hell, if need be, to sell flowers to the
Devil. They work eighteen to twenty hours a day sometimes, travel in
vans or on foot from city to city, sleep on floors, spend time in jail and
endure other hardships, including personal abuse, to raise money on
the streets for the Faith. But they are not permanently hypnotized and
they are not zombies; like Amway distributors, at some level their
adherence to the cult is a matter of, albeit uninformed, choice. If they
knew more, they could choose differently.

The similarity between Amway and Moonies is so profound that
one wonders if the two are in cahoots. Maybe at the top of the ladder

they scratch each other's backs. I know distributors who, upon reading this description of Moonies, will light up and clap their hands and exclaim "Fantastic prospects! Think of what they could do in *our* business!"

Both groups have a Leader who offers himself as an object of edification and devoted hero-worship. The Leader and his teachings are the guide for the major decisions of a member's life. Both claim to be the salvation of America, a purpose to live for, a faith to live by. Both indoctrinate their followers with books, tapes, and special mass meetings. Both provide a substitute for the extended family, and simplify human contacts into basic categories. Both groups aim to regulate the influences over members and reconstruct their identity and their consciousness. Both practice thought control. Both expect recruits to endure hardship to win the prize in the end. Both are anti-Communist and use patriotism for personal gain. Religion and money in each are closely allied; each organization claims to exist for Love, but also is a means to enrich the Leaders. The profit motive is much more frankly acknowledged in Amway, being the center of the cult.

But even if Amway is a cult, so what? Is this not a land of religious and political diversity? Are we not free to worship God, say whatever we like, and make money as we see fit, within the limits of the law? Doesn't the protection of the First Amendment extend to cults?

These questions cannot be answered apart from the context that creates them. In practice, the right to be heard is bought with the price of media control. The effect of a cult is to enhance the power of the leaders and diminish the freedom of others to oppose them. Cults are a threat as long as people do not understand how they operate. There is no First Amendment unless we are free to unmask religious hypocrisy, expose rip-off enterprises and combat pollution of the mind. Freedom works only so long as this second freedom is cherished and preserved—"Like a casket of precious jewels." For it is only by means of a second freedom that we can prevent the first from being a mere tool of corporate dictatorship.

The Amway Plan is not an inherently evil scheme; it would be an honest living, if all members and prospects were fully informed of the odds against making the incomes, and if the leaders did not attempt to turn it into a political cause, and if they did not claim to be offering a religious path. But the harm actually done by the practice of Duplication is of the worst kind: it withers the growth of human wisdom. Far down on the Tree of Life is a dead-end branch, where the leaves are greenbacks, and the Presidents' faces dangle like balls on a Christmas tree. To get stuck there is to be out on a limb indeed.

Amway diminishes awareness and narrows the perceptions by
wrapping brains up in box-size flags and spitting them off the end of a
production line. The business smothers compassion for the poor; they
are "always with us," even Jesus said that; it is their choice to be poor,
so we don't have to look at greedy landlords, low wages, overpriced
medical care and astronomical interest rates as causes for poverty.
Wage earners who reject Amway are suckers, and corporations ought
to be able to pursue their insane illusions and selfish ends to the limit
of their capability. Amway demands the surrender of intelligence to
the upline leaders. The Dream, the reason for being in the business,
strengthens ego, by the acquisition of status, individual power, and
materialist objects. To say this is not to oppose the objects, but their
anti-human use as symbols of personal aggrandisement and substi-
tutes for compassion.

Finally, the whole central thesis of the Amway cause is a lie.
There is nothing free about this brand of corporate "free enterprise";
except, perhaps, the free Labor donated by the distributor to the
Company.

Wage earners discovered long ago that without collective bargaining, they are in no position to exercise much freedom of choice on the
job. Unions do not guarantee freedom; some of them are worse than
the company (some of them *are* the company); but the existence of a
large, active labor movement in any country makes it possible,
sometimes, for wage earners to deal with employers on a level
approaching equal terms. The Wagner National Labor Relations Act
recognized this principle nearly half a century ago. Indeed, the
Wagner Act gave unions the protection of the law specifically in order
to strengthen free enterprise:

> the inequality of bargaining power between employees
> who do not possess full freedom of association or actual
> liberty of contract, and employers who are organized in the
> corporate or other form of ownership association substan-
> tially burdens and affects the flow of commerce...
>
> Experience has proved that protection by law of the
> right of employees to organize and bargain collectively
> safeguards commerce from injury, impairment of interrup-
> tion, and promotes the flow of commerce by...encourag-
> ing practices fundamental to the friendly adjustment of
> industrial disputes...and by restoring equality of bargain-
> ing power between employers and employees.*

*Preamble to The National Labor Relations Act.

Amway Corporation has deliberately designed a system that makes collective bargaining impossible, either for distributors or wage employees.

The wage employees of the Corporation are centered in the home plant headquarters in Ada, Michigan. According to Mike Johnston, in "The American Way—Really" (*Grand Valley Labor News*, Dec. 1981), Amway employees have been asking unions for help since the firm began. Several attempts have been made to unionize the Company. The Retail, Wholesale and Department Store Union AFL-CIO (RWDSU) tried it in the middle '60s. DeVos nipped that effort in the bud by holding weekly in-plant meetings which everyone was required to attend; he ran them like Rallies, preaching to the multitude on the Company's virtues and the evils of unionism. Anti-union workers stood up and gave testimonies on what Amway had done for them. The International Chemical Workers AFL-CIO (ICW) tried again in 1967, and was receiving bunches of signed authorization cards from Company employees, when a pro-union worker was transferred to nights, and Amway "filed charges with the NLRB accusing the ICW of forcing three people to join the union against their will." The Board later found that there were no such people. Rumors and half-truths circulated: workers would no longer receive their uniforms free if they joined a union, activists would lose their jobs. Several departments "suddenly received unexpected pay raises." Both foremen and shop-floor workers were pressured to wear the "vote no" buttons that were freely distributed throughout the plant. DeVos and Van Andel called all employees together during working hours and read them a six-page letter, according to union files, giving the impression that, if the union won, the Company would not work with the employees. The RWDSU tried again in 1971, but several pro-company lead people formed a "Committee Against the Union" and were allowed free run of the plant during working hours. "The Committee was allowed to hand out flyers attacking the union while asking people to sign petitions showing their support for the company." One union supporter was intimidated when she refused to sign.

The class and sex divisions maintained by the Company make further organizing efforts highly difficult. Much work is done by temporary job services, like Manpower and Kelly Girls. These employees are used often for 40-hour weeks, without benefits, over periods of months, Johnston writes. About 300 workers are employed in "pools" where every new person must start. Wages here in 1980 were $3.85 and $4.85 and hour. To get out of the "pool," you have to bid on a posted job, but "the decision on when a person leaves to fill that position is up to the company." Amway has an "incredible" employee turnover rate: a five-year employee is an old-timer, honored with a pin and a dinner. Wages vary greatly from job to job. Amway leaders boast that employees don't need a union, because the Company gives benefits and wages that top union shops. But this is true only for a few long-term employees.

Apparently, if Johnston's information is accurate, the approximately 7000 workers in the corporation are organized like the distributors: a great deal of turnover on the bottom, class and sex divisions, and carefully groomed loyalty at the top. There is not much free enterprise to be found here.

The "entrepreneurs" who market the products are, as we have seen, totally dependent on the Corporation for supply, research, development, commissions, policies, rules and regulations, wholesale price. Even the fantasy Amway-World lifestyle is supplied by the Company. There is not much free enterprise to be found here.

One of the largest organizations within the business, Yager Dream-Builders, civilizes its members like pupils in a missionary school: determines what clothes they wear, what books and magazines they read, what values they believe in, how to run their marriages and homes, how to spend their money, who to associate with, how to manage their downlines, what to say and what to think and, by suggestion, what political candidates to support. There is not much free enterprise to be found here. Perhaps we should look for it in the two-week summer workshops which Amway has arranged for teachers in sixty cities, or the Amway audio-visual aids used to get Corporation views into the classroom.

Discovering Amway to be a cult, we may be tempted to go one step further and describe it as a fascist movement. We should not resort to this label, obviously, unless Amway itself has taken that step, past the cult phenomenon, to become a home-grown American brand of fascism. Labels are useful only if they are accurate.

A fascist movement is a totalitarian or authoritarian organization, supported primarily by an alliance between large corporations and the middle class, which preserves corporate power by attacking Communists, Socialists, Social Democrats and unions. Fascists practice the Leader principle and employ violence and police-state methods to gain their objectives. When they win state power, they suppress dissent; they jail or kill their opponents and outlaw competing parties. They wield government authority, sometimes under a guise of left-wing rhetoric, but actually to serve the interest of big business cartels and large landowners. Sometimes, in Spain under Francisco Franco, for example, fascists enter into alliance with established religion. But they may be actively opposed by the church; many German Catholics resisted the Nazis, just as many priests and nuns resisted the Somoza regime of Nicaragua and the dictatorships that currently control Guatemala, El Salvador and Chile. Fascists think that a woman's place is subordinate to a man. They enforce a subordinate woman's role by sharp curtailment of her opportunities for career and political life. Fascists also tend to be racial bigots. If the context is right, they do not hesitate to stir up race-hatred against minority groups. This particular strain reached a kind of apogee in Hitler's crazed massacre of the Jews, but fascism and racism often attend each other in various countries. Batista, the dictator of Cuba in the 1950s, discriminated against Black Cubans, partly in order to please American businessmen who went there on vacation and did not wish to see Black faces in the luxury hotels and beaches of Havana. Blacks, Jews, and Latins are also quite capable of a fascist mentality on their own.

To what extent does Amway fit this image of fascism?

The fairest way to answer this question is to break the comparison down into categories, and discuss any fascistic tendencies in the business point for point. My categories are: 1) class basis; 2) attitudes toward organized labor; 3) use of violence, regimentation and dictatorship; 4) the Leader principle; 5) racism and sexism; 6) suppression of dissent and single-view indoctrination.

1) *Class Basis*

Amway distributors will recruit from any social level, but the movement is led by the Corporation and based solidly in the middle class. The political objective of the business is to create a middle-class alliance with corporate power. They serve the same constituency served by fascists; but this alone does not make Amway a fascist outfit. It merely means they have a common goal.

2) *Attitudes Toward Organized Labor*

Amway propaganda is explicitly anti-liberal and anti-left. The leaders are contemptuous of wage earners, although they make a show of respect for the hard worker. They are hostile to unions and all forms of collective action by employees on their own behalf. The jewels react with near hysteria to any measures of alliance between government and wage-earner organizations, such as OSHA legislation, tax-the-rich schemes and social service programs for the unemployed.

3) *Use of Violence, Regimentation and Dictatorship*

I never saw any violence or threat of bodily harm applied within an Amway group to enforce conformity. But violence is not the only, or even an especially effective, way to keep members in line. The upline-downline system, and the ban on crosslining, regiment distributors perhaps more completely than the command chain of a fascist party. Positive and negative reinforcement work much better than punishment as a means of maintaining dictatorship over the behavior of others. Amway leaders quite consciously program their downlines, through the Duplication process, to conform totally to the Company system, accept everything they are told, and respect the upline's authority in all matters pertinent to the business—that is, pertinent to the Amway life, which is all-inclusive and extends even to marriage, friendships, dress codes and trips to the store.

Moreover, because violence is not used against distributors is no argument that Amway jewels love peace. They invested heavily to elect a President who hires assassins to kill anti-corporate rebels in Central America, and who is openly attempting to "de-stabilize," or overthrow by subversion and force, a successful anti-fascist government in Nicaragua; Reagan also rattles missiles at the Soviet Union, and surrounds himself with advisors who believe that a nuclear war can be won. In the arena of world politics, Amway leaders are about as peace-loving as the men who "civilized the Indians."

4) *The Leader Principle*

Reverence and adulation for the Leader seem to be characteristic of fascist methods. The Leader of course has a partnership with God. Hitler and Mussolini were both cult figures while they lasted. Roman emperors proclaimed themselves gods.

It is valuable to respect and learn from merit, in whatever category. The Leader principle, however, demands surrender and obedience, and relies on building a fantasy image of the Leader and surrounding his person with an aura of mystical devotion. Objects that he may have touched are invested with power. His house and chair are places of pilgrimage. His picture is an ikon. His every word is cherished as a guide for living. This kind of surrender is needed and required only by a movement which cannot afford to rely on the intelligence of its members, and must capture their emotions instead.

"Edify your upline" is an Amway slogan which members should follow *without question*. Forget about whether the jewels deserve to be edified. They may have got ahead solely through the anonymous persistence and sacrifice of Believers in their groups, but the pin alone qualifies them for lordship. They are the best leaders in the business *no matter what*, just like the products and the Company are the best in the world *no matter what*. Keep saying it and it will be true.

5) *Racism and Sexism*

We have already discussed the sexist role assigned to women in the Yager organization. The fact that Diamond wives like the Amway system does not make it any less sexist; slaves can be found to defend the master and his rights. A Diamond wife in any case is not going to resist the system that gives her mink coats and Cadillacs and travel to the "beaches of the world."

The public attacks on ERA that came from Amway leaders throughout 1978-81, during my career in the business, and the role of women within Amway, show quite clearly which side the movement takes on feminist issues.

From appearances, Amway seems to have a much better record on the issue of race. I never heard a single overtly racist comment by anyone at an Amway function. It was not "positive" to be racist; it was not professional or courteous and would only harm your business. Rednecks, crackers, even Klansmen, would willingly sponsor Blacks, Chinese and Chicanos whenever they had the chance, and vice-versa. Any Black person who could wear a three-piece suit and earn a pin was assured of a warm welcome at Seminars and Rallies. If he or she became a jewel, they got on the stage and received standing ovations from white audiences, and their tapes were marketed throughout the business right along with Dexter's. In the Amway environment, whites could relate with Blacks and not get sweaty palms. Smile, offer a Dale Carnegie handshake and talk about Family, Occupation, Recreation, Money. Then punctuate the conversation with "Up your PV!" and you can't go wrong. A "deep" exchange might include your Dream, your Rut, a few topics of the day from *Fortune* magazine and the *Wall Street Journal*, words of gratitude for the racial harmony and progress contained in a little box of SA-8. There is nothing to prevent a Black couple from going Diamond.

Joy Duckett, in "Is Amway the Blackway?" (*Black Enterprise*, October 1981, pp, 80-84) quotes Black distributors who praise the business in the highest terms:

> In this community, what Amway has done more than anything else is give our people some hope.

> W.E.B DuBois said that the problem of America is the problem of the color line—and a lot of that is based on economic reasons. In Amway, you look past skin color because you look at people for what they're doing, for their actions.

I have heard George and Ruth Halsey, Amway's highest ranking Black jewels, speak at Yager functions; they are featured in the Duckett article as Double Diamonds earning $250,000 a year. It took them five years to reach this level, starting from his J.O.B. as a policeman. A steadily expanding parade of Black success stories is following in their footsteps. But what the Halseys say to their audiences is really no different from what is said by any Diamond. Their Blackness, after the first few minutes, is irrelevant; their language is poetic but they nevertheless give the Amway line, sparkling with humor and precious gems; you must Believe. You must commit. You must get the Negative out of your life and Duplicate.

Amway, then, will take a Black distributor on the same terms as a white. The plant was picketed a few years ago for not hiring more minorities; but so far as I could observe, neither the Corporation nor the Yager leaders practice any form of racial discrimination in pricing, bonus payments, sponsoring, functions and awards.

However, the business can make no claim to a solution of racism in this country. Just as it justifies and reinforces class division and extremes of wealth, so, in the long run, it will probably create ghettoes much faster than the inhabitants will ever be able to escape from them on the graph of their PV.

W.E.B. DuBois pointed out, in *The Philadelphia Negro*, as far back as 1899, that the problems of Black people in the United States are fundamentally economic; they do not control enough resources to end their second-class status. DuBois in *Dusk of Dawn* (1940) and again in his *Autobiography* (1968), deepened and broadened this perception by showing how racial oppression, generally in the form of poverty, resulted from the unrestrained power of big business to invest profits and exploit colonies in the world market.

E. Franklin Frazier, in *Black Bourgeoisie* (1957) and Malcolm X in his *Autobiography* (1968) reveal, to those with ears to hear and eyes to see, that the existence of a few prosperous Blacks does not do much to ameliorate the condition of the many; in fact the few often participate in keeping the many where they are. The Black American poet Langston Hughes, in *The Big Sea* (1940) described how his father, a wealthy "Negro" entrepreneur in Mexico, hated ordinary poor "niggers and Mexicans" worse than any Texas redneck. As we have already seen, even if every Black family in America joined Amway, not more than 2 percent would make any money at it—unless they could somehow persuade all the whites to be in their downlines.

Urban Black communities are poor and jobless because they are powerless—they cannot allocate resources to build their own schools, hospitals and housing projects, train their own doctors and teachers in sufficient numbers, or produce and control their own wealth. They will remain powerless until they organize on a community and neighborhood level, to serve their own interests, by means of collective politics, and until white workers do the same. A doctrine which blames poverty on the poor, and offers a Plan for one Diamond to become rich on the sales of three thousand distributors, simply perpetuates the forces that created poverty in the first place. In its overall effect on U.S. social conditions, the Amway doctrine might be more racist than the Ku Klux Klan. To say this is to take nothing away from the very laudable and decent racial attitudes of individual distributors, or the achievements of couples like the Halseys. But racial oppression is a systemwide economic and political legacy, not merely a personal hangup of white bigots. It cannot be resolved by "free enterprise," or by anything less than collective action on the part of all victims, whether Black or white; male or female.

For Black people as a whole to change their status fundamentally within the U.S. is clearly a formidable task. The first step is to have a positive attitude toward themselves, and each other—to find "self-transcendence" by identifying with the value of Black Liberation. Real progress was made in this direction in the 1960s, but a major counter-revolution has occurred in America since that time. The most visible leaders were killed. The overall message of television and newspapers to Black people has been, "there may be a place for you on the police force, in advertising and entertainment, possibly even in management, if you work hard and join the corporate system. Do not resist it or you will die." The Amway message is not very different: "there may be a place for you, selling our products and ideas, if you dress, think and act like us, and believe in our Company and our God, and recruit others into our way of life."

Despite the increase of Black membership in Amway, it cannot be said that any serious racial integration has happened within the business. Whites generally do not go into Black neighborhoods to show the Plan. As noted in Chapter One, the Blacks who become distributors, typically, already had some kind of middle-class position before they joined. They do not maintain a Black culture, or ideology of Black Liberation, in Amway; they are indoctrinated in corporate "free enterprise" right along with the whites. If the ban on crosslining prevents real friendship from developing between whites, it would also act as a barrier to interracial friendship. White Directs, in fact, although they may wish to sponsor hardworking and productive Black distributors, prefer to send their children to all-white private academies and locate their new homes in all-white neighborhoods. Many individuals may not object to having a Black family move next door, provided that family was high enough on the income scale to afford a luxury home.

At all-Black functions, the application of the system would have the same general effects it has among whites: to erode the social networks which already exist and reconstitute them according to the

Amway "family tree." The movement as a whole is thoroughly counter-revolutionary in root and branch. It can have no "positive" effect on Black communities, other than to help convert them to the corporate cult.

The final category in our comparison of Amway and fascism is:
6) *Suppression of Dissent and Single-View Indoctrination.*

Fascist movements usually suppress dissent by means of assassins, threats and prison camps. They indoctrinate their members to a single view in order to gain power. Since their slogans and ideas will not stand the test of intelligent criticism, they must secure agreement and complicity through propaganda in the worst sense of the term: manipulation of irrational motives and prejudices.

Amway deals with dissenting members in a "humane" and "positive" manner, but, nevertheless, the business does not tolerate nonconformity of dress, ideas or lifestyle. You must conform in order to succeed. It is a gradual conditioning process, not a command dictated by thugs; but you must adopt the single view in order to get along with your upline and convert your downline into Believers. You must let Amway "get into you."

A distributor who cannot agree with the ideology will probably sooner or later leave the business. It is unnecessary for the Company to enforce discipline by expulsion and punishment, except for outright violations of the Code of Ethics. Dissenters will simply stop recruiting and retailing. That person's Distributors, if they agree, will stop too; if they Believe, they will avoid dissenters and model themselves after the upline jewels.

A new member can drop out anytime and lose nothing but the price of the starter kit and a few gallons of gasoline. People are kept in and converted by making it expensive for them to quit. The more often they show the Plan, the more people they sponsor, the more sacrifices they make, the harder it is for them to resist the doctrine. I have seen 4000-pins and Directs so roughly handled by their superiors that they were trying to conceal their tears in the middle of a function. When I resisted the system, I was called up and threatened with ostracism over the telephone; my upline leader verbally abused my nonconforming downline and transferred the Believers to his influence. The higher your PV, the more crap you have to take—until your resistance is worn down, and you Believe or get out.

The absence of prison camps in the world of Amway does not mean that jewels are filled with sweetness and light. They support politicians who approve of guns, clubs, barbed wire, jail cells, poison gas and neutron bomb radiation as proper means to deal with the enemies of free enterprise.

The Amway business, in sum, scores rather high on our fascism test. The movement builds alliance between corporate power and the middle class, actively combats worker organizations, regiments and indoctrinates followers, supports the use of state violence against left-wing political enemies, inculcates the Leader principle and converts or ostracizes dissent in its own ranks. Agreement is secured by appeals to fear, chauvinism, greed and God. The same cold-war "free enterprise" ideology is repeated over and over (never intelligently discussed) until behavior is conditioned to the desired mold. Amway does not discriminate racially against distributors and prospects, but supports an economy which victimizes the Black poor along with the white.

So many warm handshakes and happy smiles—how can we use a dirty word like "fascist" for these people without coming on like scraggly, long-haired, speed-crazed, pot-smoking, sign-carrying, sandal-flapping, guitar-banging leftist scumbags, green with envy of their wealth, throwing clods of mud on their clean suits and lovely gowns? Yet reasonable analysis leads to the conclusion. If Amway is not fascist, it is hard to imagine what a fascist movement in the U.S. would look like.

The vast majority of distributors bear no resemblance to the drooling, bug-eyed Nazi or the hooded Klansman of our paranoid nightmares. They are pleasant, polite next-door neighbors, who pat their dogs, and polish their kitchen floors with Mopmate, and serve coffee late at night to excited prospects. They would like to go to Disneyworld and have fun driving expensive cars. Many never even discuss politics. They might say "This business has nothing to do with politics," and be perfectly sincere. They are *innocent*.

They cannot understand why a Central American peasant would pick up a gun rather than go on enduring the free enterprise of the Somoza family and the United Fruit Company; or why a Palestinian refugee would rather die, or be exiled, than continue under a "Christian" phalange or a zionist dictatorship. All guerrillas must be seduced and brainwashed by the KGB.

Amway people want free enterprise to work so much that they design a whole hierarchy of payments and exchange, a whole support system of advertising and a whole existence around the sale of soap, when they could produce and distribute soap cooperatively at a fraction of the cost. They put bumper stickers on their cars that say "free enterprise works." Their innocence is like the concern of church members who donate money to the starving children of other lands, unaware that the food packages they buy will probably be sold to drug dealers and black marketeers, and the missionaries they support will teach Africans to slave meekly in diamond and copper mines. It is the Cold War innocence of Free World vs. Communist World, when the Americans were good guys, and the Russians were the bad guys, and poverty was the result of Negative Thoughts, and wars were caused by evil tyrants who lived in foreign countries.

Every social system, near the end of its lifespan, turns in on itself and begins to gaze in the mirror and repeat, "I am strong, I was never so powerful as I am today, I will last a thousand years." It can no longer take itself for granted; an element of hysteria creeps into the philosophy and transforms it into cult doctrine.

The noblemen of eighteenth-century Europe went on practicing their rituals of chivalry and aristocracy, just as though they would ride forever in coaches. They no longer bothered to summon Parliamentary advisors and their women took to playing "milk-maid." Southern masters, approaching the apocalypse of the Civil War, began asserting that Negro slavery was a positive good, ordained by God and the Bible as the foundation of a free society. Americans in Vietnam went on digging harbors and pouring their resources into the country, just as if most of the people had not united in determination to throw them out, and Saigon was still a representative government after all; though much of the population had been uprooted and confined behind barbed wire. Americans passed out cigarette packages to the refugees, printed with the motto, "The Government of South Vietnam cares for its people."

When "free enterprise" was a progressive system, in the eighteenth and nineteenth centuries, it did not have to be maintained as a cult. The energy of trade was clearly and visibly liberating; new ships resulted from it, new inventions, new railroads and industries, whole new cities and fields of thought. In the twentieth century, the "freedom" is already gone for most of us, monopolized by the giant corporation. The evidence of a decaying system surrounds us: bad water, foul air, encroaching deserts, oceans littered with the trash of a thousand companies, violent death. Alternative systems have appeared in the world, and are thriving. Corporations have to justify themselves continuously to keep from being taken over by the public. The cult is part of that effort. "Free enterprise" becomes a cult because it has already ceased to be a viable reality. The less real and workable it is, the more it needs to be preached. The question is whether we can let go of this concept before it destroys us.

When innocence must be continually maintained by pro-paganda, hysteria is taking hold. We gaze worriedly in the mirror, as the world heaves and changes around us to the rattle of automatic weapons fire; we want to see the old-time religion, the red, white and blue, clean suits and hard work and haircuts and soap. We want *something* to be the way it always was, even if it was never that way; but our very demand is a sign that it is already gone. In this moment of vision we can wake up; or we can Dream the great American Dream, which resembles more and more an Obsession, that, if we just Believe, just Say and keep Saying, will, on the strength of our faith, like Victory, come true.

Disaster is brought on most frequently, not by skeptics who agree to live under flawed and cumbersome human laws, but by "men of principle," who cannot be satisfied with anything less than the Law of God. Kurt Vonnegut compared the Thomist hierarchy of laws to playing cards: "Divine law, then, is an ace. Natural law is a king. The Bill of Rights is a lousy queen."* Dictators, according to Vonnegut, have fistfuls of aces and kings to play. What troubles him about our country "is that its children are seldom taught that American freedom will vanish if, when they grow up. . .they insist that our courts and policemen and prisons be guided by divine or natural law." The groundwork for this vital lesson is that "no one really understands nature or God." American freedom will end "as all freedoms end: by the surrender of our destinies to the highest laws."** In fact we would argue that it never existed for workers and the unemployed poor; but Vonnegut's metaphor of playing cards is useful to summarize what Amway is all about.

Aces and kings. "You have God, man, woman and kids, in that order," said Dexter Yager. "When you get that out of line, you've got problems." Amway plays with aces and kings. The free enterprise cult is inspired by God, the answer to our prayers, but yet fully in accord with Nature too, which has made us all greedy and selfish and motivated only by the hope of profit.

Aces and kings always beat queens. In any conflict with a God-inspired Leader, not only the Bill of Rights but critical intelligence becomes a lousy queen. And there will be a struggle between the holders of highest cards "until somebody plays the Ace of Spades. Nothing beats the Ace of Spades."***

The main reason Amway people worked so hard to elect Reagan is that he is one of their own; he plays with aces and kings. He also holds an Ace of Spades. There is more than one in this particular deck.

---

*Palm Sunday, Dell 1981, p. 10.
**Vonnegut, pp. 11-12.
***Ibid.

Other people hold them too. But even so, he is not afraid to trump any card on the table. His advisors tell him that you can play the Ace of Spades and not get trumped in return. That is the danger, and terror, of the Amway innocence.

THIRTEEN

FEAR
AND LOATHING
IN CHARLOTTE

Free Enterprise Day was the most important celebration on the Amway Path. It was the climax of the summer, the essence of all Seminars and Rallies, the *noumenon* of the business itself. Going to Free Enterprise Day meant that you had taken the plunge; you had transcended hesitation; you were willing to commit yourself to becoming a jewel—"whatever it takes," It meant that you had made a decision to let Amway get into you. What distinguished the casual distributor from the future Leader was attendance at Free Enterprise. If you went to this mighty gathering, you were almost certainly destined to go Direct within the year. Free Enterprise was like a salvation experience. It was like agreeing to take *est*, or surrendering to a revival meeting. If you could come away from it and still not Believe, then you were truly a cold fish, a deeply entrenched skeptic, you had not seen the Light. You would have to really dog it. You would have to pretend Belief, and keep listening to tapes and going to Rallies, until one day the real thing might creep up on you and maybe you would go Direct after ten years, in spite of yourself.

Local lines began preparing their groups for the Day as far back as January. "Last year Dexter filled two coliseums," said my leaders; "they sold so much cookware, they caused a shortage of stainless steel in Ada." Films of previous Free Enterprise celebrations were shown at every Seminar and Rally: cheering crowds, continuously popping flashbulbs, glittering diamonds; the Leader, like the Pope, waving to the multitude. "Wait till you see what goes on, you'll never forget it." "Your mind will be *blown*."

Charlotte, North Carolina, the home territory of the Leader, was the only logical place to hold such an event. You had to reserve motel rooms months in advance. Those who could afford it flew. Those who were driving might be asked to share rides with members of their own downlines—never with crosslines. Tickets went on sale some time in June. The cost of the whole trip varied between $200 and $500, depending on the accommodations, distance traveled, and mode of transport. You paid your own way. You also paid for the speakers. It had to be planned for well in advance and it certainly represented a high level of commitment, or curiosity; for you were also expected to attend Family Reunion in July and Dream Night around Christmas, both of which had similar price tags.

I had made up my mind in the Spring that I was tired of wearing a 4000 pin all the time and I was going Direct by Christmas no matter what. I had already reached 5500.

"Are you going to Free Enterprise?" asked my upline Pearl.

"Of course."

"Good, then you won't have any trouble meeting your goal. What about your people?"

There were over sixty active distributors in my business at that point, but only a handful had bought tickets.

"Move those tickets out. Go down in depth and move them out to the new people. Don't trust the legs in between to do it."

I took personal checks for ticket orders. This was customary up and down the line. The Direct asked on the phone, every order night, "how many tickets for Free Enterprise do you want? Could you let me know by Monday?" The pressure was on; sell those tickets. When the time came, some of the checks I had taken developed elastic propensities, and the check-writers were nowhere to be found. The rule is, when you order an item from the Direct, and it comes, you are stuck with it, even if your own customer or downline distributor cancels the order and refuses to pay. You must follow all the rules; Directs would never do anything to hurt your business; they would only be hurting themselves. I had six tickets to Free Enterprise and I only needed two. No matter, I could sell them on the sidewalk outside the coliseum door. If all else failed I could take the loss as a tax deduction.

"Be sure and get your tickets now while they last," said the Seminar speakers, "we can't guarantee there will be any left at the last minute."

Dexter's Home was going to be a principal shrine of pilgrimage during the weekend. Bus trips and visitation times were arranged for those who wanted to take pictures and touch the emblems of the Leader's success: the mansion, the swimming pool, the motor coach, the antique cars, the Rolls Royce Silver Ghost. Most of us had handled color photographs of these cult objects over many Plan-showings;

they were put together in a compendium titled *Profiles of Success*, which we were urged to buy from the upline and pass out during Dream sessions to whet the prospects' appetites for the Plan. Many times I had given out those pictures at livingroom meetings, saying "Look, here is Dexter's red brick mansion with the white pillars on the front; here's the swimming pool in the back yard with the green grass, he must hire a gardener to keep the lawn so trim; he can walk out of his bedroom and jump right into the pool, it's huge; here's the Rolls Royce Silver Ghost; this is the motor coach, I saw that when he came up to Portland. Not bad for a little soap business. He started out driving a beer truck in Rome, New York; they lived in a trailer with cracks in the walls."

This was the Legend of Dexter; short, fat, stuttering truck driver who lifted himself up by the Amway free enterprise gospel to become the Joseph of a whole sub-culture. The Legend of Dexter was learned faithfully by Yager Plan showers and repeated, from Nova Scotia to Florida and California, as the songs of Joe Hill were once sung in lumber camps and factories, and the deeds of High John the Conqueror were recited by Black slaves. The Legend was so prestigious that Charles Paul Conn had given it part of a chapter in *The Possible Dream*. The Corporation had given it a cover story in *The Amagram*. Free Enterprise was the day when the Legend of Dexter came alive; you could walk in his yard, and stroke his cars, and stand in front of his mansion and gaze at the white pillars. At the coliseum you saw the tens of thousands in his business. On that day it all became real.

It was late August of 1980. Rumors flew that Ronald Reagan might show up as a surprise guest speaker. I had naively objected, a few months previously, to the constant political references at functions; I said they represented, under the guise of duplication, an attempt to determine what candidates and issues a good distributor should support. Tom Pearl had nodded sympathetically; the Corporation had frowned on political speeches at Rallies, he said, but it might take a while for some Diamonds and Emeralds to get the message.

"Reagan!" I said to another leader. "How can you claim to be non-political and have people like him speak at the biggest function of the year?"

It was a silly question. I was in business now, he said; Reagan was the candidate of business. He was a natural choice. Of course they would want him to speak.

"You're fighting the system," said another leader. "If you fight this thing, you'll never make any money."

I shared ride and room with two of my downline people in depth.

Being in the same car and motel with legs in depth imposes certain unspoken rules on the conversation. Sam and Pete were not sponsored directly by me, but descended through intervening legs from John and Betty (the names are fictional), one of our 1500 pins. I had worked long and hard with John and Betty to extend their lines, and we had developed a characteristic Amway friendship: never say anything Negative, and dream together of goals that become real only through showing the Plan. They trusted that I would never do anything bad for their business; I was their upline, and they had confidence in me. I must not share any misgiving about Free Enterprise Day in front of their people; that would be passing Negative downline. I must say only positive thoughts that will inspire Sam and Pete to produce. Even if I did not care personally whether they got discouraged and quit, they were not personally sponsored by me; they belonged to John and Betty. One episode of stinking thinking on my part might cost my friends immeasurable future PV bonuses. Driving 800 miles in virtual silence with a carful of people, I had plenty of time to reflect on the wisdom of the ban against crosslining. It was a perfectly sound and reasonable policy. If these fellow travelers were on crosslines, no one in *my* Amway family would be hurt by frank talk and I could have said whatever I liked. But honest discussion in this setting was an act of treachery against my disciples, my own Amway children, the parents of my passengers; I might undercut, not just my Dream, but theirs.

> Congress shall make no law respecting an establishment of religion, or prohibiting the free exercise thereof; or abridging the freedom of speech, or of the press; or the right of the people peaceably to assemble, and to petition the government for a redress of grievances.

Congress did not have to make such a law. Group loyalty and positive attitude did the job.

How close your motel was to the Charlotte Coliseum depended upon how much you wanted to pay and how early you had reserved the room. Hierarchy seemed to be reflected in this detail: the Directs and jewels stayed right across the street, or slept in the motor homes that had begun filling acres and acres of the adjacent parking lot the day before. Others scrambled for space in the outlying districts; our group stayed near the Interstate system, on the edge of a ghetto. The city police cruised the streets here in force. You didn't go out walking alone after dark.

At the coliseum, long lines of suits and gowns converged on the main gate. Dozens of hawkers, oversold on tickets, stood on the sidewalk offering them to the crowds. It was clear that I would be stuck with my extra four. Groups of adolescent kids danced in the halls, clapping hands and singing "Keep on doin' it to it! Keep on keepin' on! Keep on doin' it to it! Keep on keepin' on!"

The floor of the coliseum was at least the size of a football field, and it was set up with row after row of folding chairs. The surrounding tiers went back so far that a spectator at the top needed binoculars to see the stage. The whole vast area was filling with gowns and suits. Some sections were draped with banners representing groups from the same state or province: Nova Scotia, Connecticut, Maine, New Brunswick, New Jersey. This particular Free Enterprise was only for distributors north of Charlotte. The southerners were having a separate Free Enterprise the following week.

I looked out at the thousands upon thousands of faces, rock-concert size choirs in a huge bowl, and the acres of tiny flames from cigarette lighters whirling circles in the air; I considered the fact that every sponsorship line in that massive deep-dish mob went up through twining distances of space and time and class to the Leader, and before the first speaker had opened his mouth, my mind was properly blown.

Dexter's Coach had been driven through a main gate right up to a space behind the stage, and sat there for the entire function, almost smiling, decorated with banners and lais. The Coach and the Flag were silent witnesses to all that transpired, visible emblems of salvation, like jeweled lions on either hand of a throne.

Performing first was the Sammy Hall Band, greeted by a prolonged and approving roar. Sammy Hall began with his Personal Story. He had been a confused and strung-out rock musician. He had taken drugs. He was a hippie. He was nowhere. Then he found the Lord, and he found Amway. Now he hated decadence. Decadence was the ruin of America. Decadence had nearly destroyed a whole generation of our youth. But Amway was the Answer. He had come home.

We saluted the flag. We prayed. We thanked the good Lord for this Free Country of ours, and for the opportunity to build our Amway business.

Then the familiar circle pattern of the Plan was flashed on a huge screen, in strobe-light rhythm, and Sammy launched into his first number. The Band gave him a thumping backup; he jumped in the air; he sang, shouting, "I'm excited, how about you?!" The crowd yelled back, "I'm excited too!" People danced in the aisles. The line became a hypnotic refrain, punctuated by drums and bass and flashing lights: "I'm excited, how about you?! I'm excited! I'm excited! I'm excited, how about you?! I'm excited too!"

Dexter finally came to the microphone, preceded by jewel awards. He deliberately understated himself. On other occasions he had whipped his microphone around, waved his cross, bent over and growled that critics of Amway were stupid and we, the distributors, were "the only hope this country's got"; he had scowled and snarled and paced and danced, numbering off his possessions on his fingers and describing them item by item, to the whistling cheers of the throng whose sales had bought them; "now I'm gonna hit heavy," he had told his people, hammering fist into palm; "You know I don't lie! Ain't that right!" And the crowd would stand and cheer and beg for more. But tonight he walked quietly to center stage and talked to his people as if the coliseum were his livingroom and they were all invited guests.

He introduced Gloria Wead, wife of Doug Wead, his own personal public relations agent. Gloria was going to sing a song for us. Gloria had first presented this song to Dex in the Yager livingroom, beside the piano, and Dex had been so moved he said "Ohhh, Gloria, you've got to sing that at the next Free Enterprise." Gloria came forward, glittering with jewels. The Motor Coach smiled in the background. Dex told all the men in the audience to "reach over and take your gal by the hand. And you gals, you look in your man's eyes and pretend this song...is from your heart, right to him." A rustle of moving hands washed up and down the tiers. Gloria crooned, and the entire mass fell silent and swayed gently in their seats: "Darling, I knew you were a Winner from the start...yes, I knew you were a Winner from the start."

One of the speakers that weekend was a Black politician from the South. Dexter, introducing him, said "a lot of people may not want to hear a Black Man. I know some folks think that a Black Man shouldn't be heard. Well I think *this* Black Man ought to be heard, and I'm happy to share the stage with him."

This Black Man said that we need laws putting homosexuals in jail, where they belong. "All this talk about 'gay rights!'" he snorted. "One of them said to me 'you're fightin' for the same things we are,' I said 'Oh no I'm not! You oughta be ashamed of yourself!'" General laughter. "Some people say you can't legislate morality! Well, we got the Ten Commandments, that's legislating morality! We got laws against stealing and murder, that's legislating morality!" This Black Man passed on to the subject of busing: "Some people say we gotta achieve racial balance in the schools, we gotta send Black kids over to this school and white kids over to that one whether they like it or not! Don't they know when the government tells you where you can go to school, that's slavery! That's what it is, slavery!" Then he attacked the media for focusing on militants like Stokely Carmichael and H. Rap Brown. Stokely had left the country ten years ago at least; Rap Brown was unknown to the new generation of students on my campus; but This Black Man Who Ought to Be Heard saw their ghosts still hovering over the newspapers, and he wanted them exorcised; he warned us that they did not represent anybody but the lunatic fringe. Their names should be expunged from textbooks on Black history. What kind of school was it that taught the words of these lunatics instead of Booker T. Washington and Mary McCleod Bethune? Booker T. was the mainstream of Black America. Students should be compelled to read *Up From Slavery* and forbidden to read trash. It was time school boards started exercising more control over the stuff that went into their kids' minds. Abortion was a crime. Banning prayer from the schools was sin. Welfare should be abolished. Free lunch programs were a joke on the taxpayer. "There ain't no free lunch." We needed bigger and better police forces; the only way to deal with muggers and thieves was to get tough.

It was indeed a great and progressive gesture to share the stage with This Black Man; by inviting him to speak, Dexter had advanced the "Negro cause" almost as far as it had been advanced by the Atlanta Cotton Exposition in 1895, when Booker T. Washington had won over his all-white audience by supporting their views on segregation. In that speech Washington was offering to Southern businessmen their own terms for reconciliation with "the Negro." The races could be "as separate as the fingers of a hand," and still work together in all things necessary for mutual progress. "Cast down your buckets where you are..." Washington had said; that is, hire Negro workers, for they will produce without unions and strikes; they are faithful servants, and will work for low pay. Employers in 1895 were not entirely convinced.

"I like him," said the distributors in my group, when This Black Man had made himself heard. "He has a lot to say."

In the morning our pilgrimage to Dexter's Home was arranged. We wound across the city in an automobile caravan, into a posh neighborhood of maze-like driveways, lined with hedges and trees. Close to the Shrine, a parking attendant directed cars into a lot; tour buses stopped at the bottom of the driveway and the passengers walked up the hill, cameras over their shoulders, to the Great House.

There it was, red brick, white pillars. I might have been more impressed if I hadn't seen so many pictures that made it look like a palace. It was of modest suburban size; behind the trees I could glimpse many others like it, in varying shapes and styles. The whole area seemed as if it had been developed since the end of World War II. For neighbors you might expect to find corporate lawyers, insurance salesmen, fast-food managers, junior executives gone to the Sunbelt during the War on Poverty.

I walked around the back, to the swimming pool. Amway people were clicking their cameras. There was not enough room for them in the small space around the pool, and groups were already moving off toward the garage. A wooden ramp led from the sliding door of the Master Bedroom to the diving board. The lawn wrinkled under my shoes. I was standing on a green mat. The yard was layered with artificial grass.

I went up to a window and pressed my nose against the pane. I was peering into Dexter's Study. The room was decorated with flags and American eagles. A huge eagle would greet the guests as they entered the doorway from the hall. Everything was orderly and spotlessly clean, except for the pool which had a bad case of ring-around-the-tile. Perhaps I had committed a desecration by leaving an imprint of my nose on the glass; but others had done likewise, and I knew Dex would have plenty of See Spray Window Cleaner on hand for the occasion.

The cars impressed everyone. We walked through the garage like tourists in a museum, studying the antique silver Ghost, the Model A, the vintage designs from the 1950s. It was like being in a giant hobby shop. When I was twelve I used to get excited about bringing home plastic models of cars and assembling them at my desk. After they were finished there wasn't much else to do with them, and they sat on shelves, waiting to be admired, like these grownup models, on display in their showcase. Distributors waited in line to photograph wives, husbands, downlines and uplines in front of this or that car.

I drifted back to the front portico. I looked through the window at the chandelier in the stairwell. I leaned on one of the pillars. It was cold to the touch. Rapping on it, I discovered it was hollow metal painted white.

This was the top of the mountain. The meadows of freedom. The lake of fulfillment toward which all our energies flowed. This was the great Dream.

We drove down off the knoll to the expressway. In the other lane, parades of cars were still arriving to see the Shrine.

The program at the coliseum continued all afternoon, and far into the night. I sat in a different section, away from the members of our group, so that I could slip out the back any time unnoticed. Leaders at various functions had warned distributors repeatedly that it set a poor Duplication example to leave, for any reason, before the end of a speech. Even if you had to go to the bathroom, you were supposed to wait for a natural break to occur. Sometimes, when too many conversations were going on in the halls, a jewel would go out and yell, "You 1500 and 4000 pins who think you can teach your people out here better than we can inside, wait till you go Direct; if you had anything good to say you'd be on the stage." At the coliseum, people came and went freely to get hotdogs and Cokes from the concession stands, but Directs frowned on too much moving around. You were expected to sit still and listen.

One Diamond after another came to the microphone and delivered a Personal Story. Amway saved one from alcohol, a second from bankruptcy, a third from depression and suicide. Dex figured prominently in some of these tales as the Saviour.

A husband who married a woman already in Amway recounted the story of his proposal to her:

"She asked me, 'Do you want to get in this business in order to marry me, or do you want to get in for its own sake?' And I said, 'Well, I'd want to join in order to win your hand, but from what I've seen of this business, I would have to get in whether you'll have me or not.' That's when she knew I was the man for her."

Doug Wead told a long anecdote of how he met his wife Gloria and won the respect of her mother. She was rich and he was poor; naturally, her family worried about whether or not he was a loser, trying to marry into money. He drove an old clunker of a car; sometimes when he shifted gears, the lever came right off in his hand. This happened when he first met Gloria's mother, and had to give her a ride somewhere. The point of the story seemed to be that he proved himself worthy of her by achievement in Amway. It was another illustration of Dexter's benevolence. Dexter did not need him, having broken off eighteen Directs already; but nevertheless the Leader had consented to sponsor him, and teach him how to build.

Toward evening a country western band came on, and a team of dancers in hayseed clothes did some fancy clogging on the stage. Dexter appeared, wearing a gigantic cowboy hat, at least ten feet across. From the upper tiers, the effect was truly bizarre: the mite-like figure of the Leader, almost hidden under the spread of a western hat as broad as a room. His head looked smaller than a pearl.

He introduced another political speaker, a paraplegic in a wheelchair. Any obstacle could be surmounted. The Yager business had blind Directs. I thought he might urge us to vote against government programs for the handicapped.

Literature from *Citizen's Choice* was passed around through the audience, with solicitations for membership and money. This election year was our big chance to turn the bureaucrats out of office and elect "men" who believed in God, free enterprise and a balanced budget. We heard speeches on the astronomical size of the Federal debt. What we needed was a Constitutional amendment mandating that the Government spend within its means. Too many people were taking handouts. The leaders did not mean, of course, the handout takers of the Pentagon, who would consume $231.6 billion in 1983 for defense appropriations, but the jobless poor, the old people who needed winter weathering for their homes, the crippled children on Federal grants for special education, the ripped-off consumers who needed agencies like Legal Aid to stick up for them in court. It was time to stop coddling these swillers at the public trough.

Someone else took the microphone and talked about the vital importance of reading the right books and associating with the right people. If you want to succeed you have to program yourself for success. Good distributors take every opportunity to get close to their upline jewels. An hour on their calendar is priceless. If a jewel calls you up and asks you to be somewhere, you should go, period; don't be an idiot and question him. If he says you need a particular book for your business, then buy it and read it. Everyone in the coliseum should buy at least one copy of the books on sale in the lobby. They were put there for us, to help us succeed. The secret of success is Faith. Have Faith in your upline.

A man opened an ice cream stand one summer and he was doing a prosperous business. Then his father said "Haven't you heard there is going to be a recession? You'll never make any money this year." And the son said "Gee, I didn't know that," and he cut back on orders for ice cream, and passed the word around: "recession coming." When the customers saw him do that, they stopped buying, and other stands began to close, and the makers of ice cream were thrown out of work. Before long, as the panic spread, sure enough, there was a recession. So there you have it: recessions are caused by stinking thinkers who lose their Faith. If you want to Duplicate properly and strengthen your Faith, then read the positive books that we recommend.

The seats were hard, and the speeches repetitious. We had just heard a confirmed report that Reagan would not appear. Sometime late in the afternoon I decided to take the chance of missing the very Word that would enable me to go crown. I slipped out the back door.

In the halls were distributors wearing sweatshirts that said "I'm excited! How about you?" In the foyer the members at the literature tables were marketing the "positive" books that only stinking thinkers would refuse to buy. One of them was Wead's campaign book about Reagan, the movie actor's face smiling up at me from the cover.

I went across the street to a restaurant. There, hidden away in a back booth, munching on a hamburger, sat Tom Pearl, conversing with a Direct from one of his Canadian legs. I had sinned; I had left a Rally before the end; I had walked the halls during a speech; and not merely to go to the restroom, but to feed myself and escape from the Word. But I felt better about it, knowing that I was duplicating Tom, the man who had worn his bathing suit to a leadership function simply because his sponsor had told him to do it at seven o'clock in the morning. I waved hello to him. For some reason he could not see me. Perhaps it was the light that made me invisible.

I waited hours for the festivities to conclude. I could not return to my room without the members of my group; they had to ride with me. It grew to be two a.m. and I crept, like an outlaw child skipping church, across the lawn, to the coliseum walls. Dexter's motor coach was sticking out the side of a vehicle gate like the rear end of the Wizard of Oz behind his cloak. A door had been left open and I peeked in, directly onto the stage.

The Leader had taken over. He was leaning into the microphone. It seemed to me that he wore a white suit, but that may have been the dazzling effect of a dozen powerful spotlights following his every move. I had a profile view. Behind him were thousands and thousands of tiny faces, all in rows. In all that great coliseum the only sound was the Leader's voice.

"If you Beleeeeve," said the voice, echoed and amplified by the sound system until it came back from every tier. "If you just Beleeeeeve ..." "You know," he said, "it's such a simple thing, even college minds often can't understand. This business is not complicated. It will do whatever you want. But you gotta have a Dreeeeem. You gotta Beleeeeeeve that you can have Diiiiiimonds." Man was not born to be poor. Jesus said Whosoever believeth in me shall have eternal life. And Thomas said Unless I touch his wounds, and put my hand in his side, I will not believe. And Jesus, when he rose from the dead, he told Thomas, touch my wounds, and put your hand in my side. And Thomas said Lord, I Believe. And Jesus said You Believe because you have seen. Blessed are those who have not seen, and yet Believe. Faith will move mountains. The apostles cast out devils, and healed the sick; what did they do it with? Belief. They Believed. "Set your heart on Diiiimond! Dare to Dream! The Bible says that a man without a Dream is a dead man! You will be a Diamond if you Beleeeeve. You gotta Beleeeeeeve."

He leaned over toward the crowd. The microphone cord whipped behind him, like a tail.

I sat on the wall, waiting for him to finish. Near three in the morning, the crowds began to spill onto the sidewalk. A group from New England danced along the street in unison, clapping and chanting "Five and six! Nights a week! Five and six! Nights a week! Five and six! Nights a week!"

I passed rows of tenements and shacks and crumbling roads and empty lots. Poverty went on for blocks, patrolled by the city police.

In the motel, the members of my group had spread their Amway products out on the dresser: Whisker Whiz, Reasons Cologne, Satinique Shampoo, Family Bar Soap, Glister Toothpaste. I had made my percentage on all of them. I should have been proud.

On the road home, for 800 miles, I said almost nothing. I thought about Tom Pearl's *exemplum* of crossline distributors from his group, riding home in the same car, who had talked each other out of the business after Free Enterprise Day because nobody from upline had been there to set them straight. I could not pass Negative downline; I was too well trained.

"I'm gonna make it," said Sam, "I'm gonna be a Diamond. Did you see this book on Reagan? It's good, it's real easy to read."

He saw that I had not bought the book. What if he inferred that I was Negative about buying the "positive" books? Would his resolution to be a Diamond cool off? Would it weaken his Belief?

"What did you think of Dexter's speech at the end? Wasn't that fantastic?"

I fell back on an old prospecting technique: answer a question with a question. "What did *you* think of Dexter's speech, Sam?"

"That did it for me. If all those people on the stage can do it, by gosh, I can do it too. Wait till I get set up in my new apartment, I'm gonna show the Plan five nights a week. I've got a hundred names on my list."

I leafed through the Reagan book. Wead said that he was warm and wonderful and tough. He would never allow this country to be humiliated by a foreign power. I believed him. Somehow I derived no comfort whatever from the fact.

I knew that Reagan would win. And I knew that the triumph of this crusade, far from doing anything about poverty, would fill the land with unemployed poor. The Amway leaders knew this too. Months prior to the campaign, a New Hampshire Emerald had confided their political goals to me at a leadership party. "This is not just a little soap business," he said. "When we get big enough, the first thing we're gonna do is force the Federal government to balance the budget." He did not mean cuts in military spending.

"Then you must mean massive cuts in social services," I said. "That's the only way you could do it."

"That's right."

This man would later choke up and weep on the stage during a speech about Amway love.

I should have been excited about the impending Reagan victory. The vision of all those unemployed poor and all those desperate retirees and wage earners looking for a second income was causing the leaders to lick their chops in anticipation. They were so excited they could hardly sit still. They were reading *Amagrams* with the kind of eye-gleams normally elicited only by *Penthouse* and *Hustler* Probably they had acquired Napoleon Hill's art of sex transmutation. "I tell you," my Direct repeated over and over, "the people who are getting into this business now... five years down the road... are going to be millionaires! This thing is gonna explode! It's exploding all over the place!"

I also knew that my fellow passengers, and all those tiers of faces, and thousands like them in the coliseums and motels from coast to coast, would not see the limits of "free enterprise" until they had drunk this cup to the dregs—if they even saw it then. As for me: I was through fighting the Duplication process from inside the business. The jewels were right—Amway depends on it. There may be subtler and more human lines, but without Duplication there is no Amway system. It was time to get off the bandwagon and look around. "Realize what you've got in your hands."

I was almost a Direct. I had been trained for leadership and built a good skeleton of a business. I had even started to make money. I was paying off old debts, and putting on weight from eating in gourmet restaurants. One of my PV checks was over $1500 for a single month. When I said the word "excited," my mouth tasted foul. I gave it a squirt of Sweet Shot but it tasted worse.

It was entertaining, on that long ride home, to *imagine* becoming a jewel by creating a special unit in the business called the Loose Goose Brigade. Boxes of soap in the Loose Goose Brigade are stamped with the face on the Shroud of Turin. To encourage self-use (as opposed to self-abuse, which is Spending without return, a waste of economic potential), every member is required to wear every piece of Amway jewelry, simultaneously, at all times, even during visits to public restrooms; for you never know what downliners might be peeping through a hole. To make room for all the earrings, cufflinks, tie-clasps, bracelets, necklaces, stickpins, and brooches, the ears, nose and lips would have to be pierced multiple times. At *my* Rallies, besides the squirting of innumerable Sweet Shot cartridges, you would hear the incessant jingling of 12-karat gold up and down the rows.

At leadership functions, to demonstrate faith, I would ride my Directs around the stage like camels and beat them with leather from the Shopper's Catalog. I would take the new Silver Producer and stand him up and say "What would you do to show your people how well you practice Duplication? Strip to the waist, please." Then, using Silver Producer pins, I would put him through the ritual that Richard Harris endures in *The Return of a Man Called Horse*. He would be required to sing "I'm excited! How about you?" as the Believers lifted him ceilingward, in front of the red, white and blue banner inscribed with the motto, "Thank You For Teaching Us To Be Free."

When the group was ready, I would plan the Free Enterprise celebration of the century. Surmounting the stage would be a gigantic portrait of George F. "Divine Right" Baer, the coal operator who asserted, during a miners' strike in 1902, that wages would be set, not by the Union, but by the property owners, to whom God, in His infinite wisdom, had entrusted the affairs of the world. Distributors must kneel and kiss the Flag as they pass the Father's portrait.

The featured speaker would be Big Tex, played by a fat midget. He squeals and jumps up and down and shinnies up a cross the size of a telephone pole, and sits on one of the arms, where he croons to the audience, in a falsetto voice, "You gotta Beleeeve, you gotta have a Dreeeeeem." Distributors make pilgrimages to his Doll house during the afternoon; they have a chance to snap pictures of his HO gauge model railroad, and pass them out during Dream sessions before they proceed to the circles. The yard is landscaped with green Easter Bunny fluff.

Award receivers come onstage and have their bodies anointed with LOC. The moans of pleasure are taped, and the distributors required to buy the tapes and plug them in at bedtime. Reaganomics in the mental health field is relieved by sponsoring unemployed therapists to adjust the attitudes of the stinking thinkers. Clients are encouraged to woo their spouses with toy motor homes. Before love-making they should listen to a tape of Big Tex getting his Triple Diamond pin. Then they should visualize his HO train set.

To encourage Plan-showing, a special behavior-mod facility is built for shy types. Each time they draw a circle on a board, an electric heart beats faster, like the sound effects of a pinball machine. Then, as they draw the Directs breaking away, Big Tex's face flashes on the marker board, the eyebrows popping up and down, the lips pursed in a circle, cooing "Ooom, ooom," and the eyes rolling from side to side;

then, when they unfold the Amway poster, the board jingles like a slot machine and paper bills pour onto the floor. They are printed "Not Negotiable" and stamped with the face of Rich DeVos.

During Free Enterprise, the Direct wives dress up like flatirons and, holding their plugs, dance in a chorus line opposite their Direct husbands, who are dressed up like lightbulbs. They weave circle patterns around each other, swapping Hee-Haw gag routines:

"Honey, how can I prove that I'm your man?"

"Why, get out there and show that Plan."

As they dance, they plug themselves into Big Tex's cross, and then suddenly run fast across the stage, kicking heels and doing a little shiver and going "Woooo! Wooo!"

"Honey, how can I keep my light turned on?"

"Why, that's easy, silly, just Stay Plugged In."

"But you don't stay plugged in."

"Well, honey, that's because a woman is not rational like a man; you only have to plug her in once and she'll keep warm for hours. *Got it?*"

Then Believers open soap boxes from the high tiers and scatter clouds of white powder over the audience; bubble machines inundate the whole building with suds.

After the function, distributors dance along the street, clapping and chanting "Five and six! Times a night! Five and six! Times a night!"

The next time I met with a Prospect, I spotted a guitar and a banjo in the corner of his livingroom. I had not touched a musical instrument for over two years. According to the thinking of Tom Pearl and Bill Emerald, I should earn the right to this Dream by first winning my Gold Profit Sharing Pin.

"You play these?"

"Yeah," said the Prospect, who was moved out of that category into the category of Musician. Before the night was over he would become uncategoried.

"What kind of music?"

"Blues, folk, bluegrass."

I picked up the guitar. He broke out some beer and we jammed. I never got to the circles that night, or any night thereafter. It was like dumping an ugly master off your back, and no longer having to fear his spurs, or go sniffing after his carrot.

> Amazing grace, how sweet the sound
> That saved a wretch like me
> I once was lost, but now I'm found
> Was blind, but now I see

And there I was, following my Rut, going back and forth, showing the Plan every night, carrying my board and easel on my knee,
home to work, showing the Plan, showing the Plan.

Nothing here should be taken as a slight to the intelligence of
Yager jewels. They do indeed "know how to put this thing together."
Most of their predictions came true. They said my people would
duplicate me; they were right. When I stopped retailing, the sales fell
off in the whole group. When I stopped booking meetings and sponsoring new prospects, the orders in the group for starter kits dried up.
When I stopped going to functions, my Belief, what was left of it,
evaporated. When I gave friendship priority over Amway, I lost the
desire to draw circles. My leaders said that you get paid years down the
road for work you do now, and to some extent, they were also right
about that. The PV checks kept coming in on the products sold or
used by a handful of hardcore legs who never grew, but never quit
either. There is no question that if I had really been willing to do
"whatever it takes" for the rest of my life, I would have joined Dexter's
Diamonds. They are not personally at fault because 97 percent of
Amway distributors make little or nothing, any more than Ronald
Reagan is to blame that 95 percent of actors are unemployed. It is
simply the nature of the business.

FOURTEEN

THE
FACE OF
THE DRAGON

Late in 1984 I got a phonecall from a young man in his mid-twenties—call him John Shire—who had decided to look me up after an interval of five years and find out if I was still involved in Amway. I had hooked John by saying "If you ever want to make some good money, let me know." His trust in me was unquestioning and completely naive. When I showed him the Plan, he thought about it for one day and got in. A year later he dropped out of sight, and his group, never much more than five or six distributors, faded away. Now he had joined again under a Diamond from the South. He had made a decision to build the business. But he wanted to know why I had quit.

"If you're serious about building the business, why do you want to know? Aren't you afraid it will mess up your attitude?"

"Because you're just a loser," he laughed, "and I want to find out what motivates losers."

"Why did you get back in?"

"Well, it's an opportunity, it works if you work it. I tried a lot of other things that I thought would be easier and they weren't."

"You really want to make it in Amway?"

His answer was yes.

"You remember Duplication, don't you? Follow the system 100 percent. Do everything your upline tells you. Don't deviate from it in the smallest detail. If you do that, you've got a chance."

"Why didn't you do it?"

"Because it's a disgusting, destructive process."

John leaned back and roared. "And because," I continued, "nothing they could offer me made that worth my while. Also, the longer I did it, the less I did of anything else. I wasn't doing any research, or playing any music, nothing, just going to rallies and mouthing that inane collection of phoney dreams.''

"But anything you really care about, that's what you spend your time on, right? A carpenter talks about tools, a broker talks about dividends..."

"Well, if you care about it, go for it."

"I wanted to tell you how much I appreciate you for showing me the Plan. That you thought enough of me to want me in your business..."

"Yeah, you know what I said the night after you signed? The same thing you say: 'Wow, I got another one!'"

John laughed. "It's the smell of the SA-8. I couldn't forget that, you know, I got in my car and took a whiff of that stuff and it was just like yesterday, you were drawing circles for me in my little dorm room..."

"Yeah, there's a drug in it. Scrambles your mind."

"What do you think of Amway now?"

John's interview with me tells a lot about distributors who have been through the revolving door: many get back in two or three times. It is a possible, though improbable, dream, and also a nightmare. John had made up his mind to do it again, but he wasn't completely happy with the decision. He still wanted to hear from a critic. And he still thought a genuine conversation was worth risking his attitude for.

"Are you trying to sponsor me?"

"Hey, I'd love to sponsor you," he said...

"But your calendar is full," I finished, "and you won't be able to get back to me for at least a month." We both laughed.

I thought, if all of them could only keep laughing at themselves, and each other, then maybe they would stay sane, and the business might mellow into a harmless marketing venture. No, that won't happen. Because the real product is not soap.

In the beginning of the Personal Story, I described Amway as perhaps "the most successful and frightening" center of reaction ever to appear on the American scene. It is large, it is well-financed, it is skillful in method, it makes use of the latest discoveries in behavioral technology, it taps into traditional American values and seems to tell people what they want to hear. Unlike the Ku Klux Klan or the various American Nazi splinter groups, Amway does not isolate itself from the mainstream culture by coming on to the public in a mean and threatening style; the image of the movement is carefully tuned to maximum sales. Amway is a selling business. It is only when you contemplate what the leaders are selling that epithets like "formidable" and "frightening" appear to be justified.

The face of the dragon, the real product behind the sales pitch, is power: the power of the corporate few to rule over the many. Religion, patriotism, smiles and handshakes, "positive" thought, the debasement of national politics into a grade C movie fantasy presided over by the grandfather of television commercials, are all techniques to sell the product.

In the long run, what is the likelihood that Amway will continue to thrive?

The multiple-marketing system itself, in which each person may accumulate profits by retailing a small amount of merchandise and sponsoring others to do likewise, has been imitated by a wide range of companies: Yurika foods, Old World, and Amzoil, to name a few. In fact, established major corporations appear to be entering the field under different names. Some Yurika distributors, for example, say that their food products come from General Mills, although the central office of Yurika will not divulge this information. Multiple marketing has caught on; as we have seen, it seems to give the average person a chance for self-transcendence and financial success. It is also an enormously effective vehicle for corporate propaganda.

In many respects, multiple marketing through person-to-person sellers is quite compatible with several long-range trends in American society. According to John Naisbitt, author of the best-selling *Megatrends*, people want more personal involvement with each other in their work, a trend which he calls "high touch." They want more decentralization, more opportunities for self-help, more networking, less hierarchy and more participation in the economy. By "networks" he means informal social structures that cut across traditional institutions and do not have clearly identifiable leaders and followers. Person-to-person selling is a "high touch" activity which brings people from different occupations in direct contact with each other. "Our response to the high tech all around us," writes Naisbitt, "was the evolution of a highly personal value system to compensate for the impersonal nature of technology."* At a time when marketing is dominated by huge shopping malls and computers, this form of retail exchange appears to provide precisely the "human" component which is missing from the giant enterprise. The mythology of "your own business" gives the illusion of an immediately available chance for self-help; the fact that you begin a multiple-marketing business in

Megatrends, pp. 36, 219ff.

your home tends to decentralize buying and selling away from the super-store.

It is dangerous to take *Megatrends* very seriously as an objective "roadmap to the 21st Century." Long-range trends in society are not impersonal roadmaps that descend magically from the sky; they are the result of deliberate decisions by individuals and groups. Naisbitt's book is a useful statement of what people want: more genuine contact with each other, and more control over their lives. It is also an excellent summary, unintentional perhaps, of what *corporations* must do in order to maintain their power. A corporate economy, by its very nature, cannot give people genuine control over their future. In a corporate economy, resources are exploited for the private profit of the few, at the expense of the many. Because of this system, people suffer and die in vast numbers. They endure unspeakable maiming and are terrorized when they resist. Whole forests disappear, killed by acid rain or leveled to raise filet-mignon steaks for successful businesspeople to enjoy at their tax-deductible dinners. To maintain a system which is so profitable for the rich and so destructive for everyone else, corporations must give people the *illusion* of control. If "high tech" is dehumanizing, they must respond with the "high touch" of the personal growth movement, which will show how you, too, can become rich, smart, generous, excellent, happy, loved and successful. Throughout the marketing process, of course, human relationships go on being conditioned, in a very intimate way, by commodity exchange. If workers sense they are dominated and powerless, then corporations must provide "self-help" opportunities that reinforce their system; otherwise, on their own, people are sure to create "self-help" organizations which challenge that system and create alternatives to it.

Amway will give the illusion of high touch, and the reality of Duplication; the illusion of self-help, and the reality of mind-control; the illusion of decentralized small business units and the reality of personal dependence on Big Daddy; the illusion of participatory capitalism, and the reality of hard work for little reward; the illusion of networking and the reality of domination by a few leaders. In this sense, once again, Amway focuses the "megatrends" in our society and reveals their true nature in microcosmic form. It is as though the business projected the ideological skeleton of the corporate system on a screen.

Amway will continue to thrive, for the time being, because it is riding, and helping to sustain, a wave of reaction which has not yet run its course in the U.S. But Amway has a fatal weakness. The fact that I could recruit fifty distributors and lose forty of them in a matter of weeks suggests that the real product is more transparent than it seems. The basic intelligence of the public is not so easily hypnotized. The leaders run a tight act, but if the distributors on the bottom were to quit, the whole paper castle would start collapsing from the ground up. Jewels need Directs to stay in business; Directs in turn need distributors. The whole edifice depends on the Belief of that person on the bottom who just bought a kit. Once that person, and her prospects, sees that the system is based on a lie, then it begins to fall apart.

"If Amway is so bad," a Believer might respond, and rightfully too, "then show me something better." There is no use taking someone's opportunity away if you have nothing to put in its place.

Genuine self-help, positive attitude and participatory economics are all worth dreaming for. But "positive attitude" has to mean something more human than Belief in my ability to make a million dollars. At some point I could take my eyes off the picture of the motor home taped on my refrigerator and actually look out of the kitchen window. I might be shocked by the garbage. Or I might enjoy the squirrels in my neighbor's tree, or the shape of the clouds in the afternoon sky. Life is not so mean that it has to be justified with motor homes. I might try talking to my neighbor about something besides an Exciting Business Opportunity. I could learn to trust my own intelligence and teach others to do likewise. I could begin the never-ending process of getting to know my mind. This is a positive attitude. There is no need to manipulate it as a tool for personal exaltation. A real appreciation for the gift of life results in a loss of attachment to commodities. In the pursuit of happiness, we are all overtaken repeatedly by greed, aggression, ignorance, jealousy, envy, arrogance. I could pursue the objects of my greed with dogged unconcern for anything that gets in my way, because I envy others who possess these objects and would like to be better than they are, and then call my belief in this vain chase "positive attitude." Who am I kidding? Who wants me to do this, and why? On the other hand, I could sit down and learn, from the movement of ambition in my heart, what it is to be arrogant, and greedy and envious. Which is a genuinely positive choice?

Real self-help, unless we choose to be isolated in the wilderness, requires the cooperation of other human beings. It is positive to develop informal contacts with others outside established institutions, because those institutions are largely corrupt and obsolete, and it is very difficult to maintain them and at the same time do anything meaningful for anybody. The corporation is one of those institutions. The basis of truly positive self-help must be a cooperation between people which is honest, and open, and unconditioned by the requirements of any institution outside themselves. The Believer who denies that this cooperation is possible is the negative thinker, not the Amway dropout.

Participatory economics could take many forms. Whatever the form, it would have to include a vehicle for the public to decide what is produced, in what quantities, at what total cost and for what purpose. These decisions are made presently by a handful of profiteers, operating through giant companies and governments, guided by little else than their own desire to be rich. To say that we can't do any better than this is the ultimate negativity, the doomsday attitude that the end of the world is just around the corner and we better use it up now.

The world will not change for us overnight, but those committed to the task will find each other in all kinds of unpredictable "networks." We should act, when action is called for, without preconceptions. At certain times, for example, a good way to resist a cult might be to join it. Certainly if the cult were leavened by an influx of well-informed and deviant members, it would be less reliable as a reactionary movement. Sometimes aggressive energy can be dissipated by a passive, sluggish, noncommitted agreement that acts like sand on the tires of a speeding truck. In any case, whatever action may be appropriate, it is necessary, at all costs, to avoid Belief. The fire of Belief is the dragon's funky breath.

LIST OF REFERENCED WORKS

Amagram, The.   Periodical published by Amway Corporation.

Bartley, W.W. III, *Werner Erhard.* N.Y.: Clarkson Potter, 1978.

Carnegie, Dale, *How To Win Friends & Influence People,* Pocket Books, 1982

Conn, Charles Paul, *The Possible Dream,* Berkley Publishers, 1977.

    The Winner's Circle, Berkley Publishers, 1980.

    An Uncommon Freedom, Berkley Publishers, 1982.

DeVos, Rich, *Believe!,* Pocket Books, 1975.

    Try or Cry, cassette tape, Amway Corporation.

Dobson, Dr. James, *What Wives Wish Their Husbands Knew Aout Women,* Tyndale, 1975; 1979.

DuBois, W.E.B., *The Philadelphia Negro,* 1899.

    Dusk of Dawn, N.Y.: Harcourt, Brace & Co., 1940.

    Autobiography, N.Y.: International, 1968.

Duckett, Joy, "Is Amway the Blackway?" *Black Enterprise,* October 1981.

Frazier, E. Franklin, *Black Bourgeoisie,* Macmillan, 1962.

Hill, Napoleon, *Think and Grow Rich,* Fawcett, 1960.

Hughes, Langston, *The Big Sea,* N.Y.: Alfred A. Knopf, 1940.

Johnston, Mike, "The American Way—Really," *Grand Valley Labor News,* 1981.

La Haye, Tim, *How To Be Happy Though Married,* Tyndale, 1968; 1978.

Naisbitt, John, *Megatrends,* Warner, 1982.

Peters, Thomas & Waterman, Robert H. Jr., *In Search of Excellence,* Warner, 1984.

Profiles of Success, Compendium used in the Yager business.

Schiller, Herbert, *The Mind Managers,* Beacon Press, 1974.

Schwartz, David, *The Magic of Thinking Big,* Cornerstone, 1962; 1959.

Vonnegut, Kurt, Jr., *Palm Sunday,* Dell, 1981.

Waterman, Robert H. Jr., see Peters, Thomas.

Yager, Dexter, *Don't Let Anybody Steal Your Dream,* W. Douglas Wead, 1979.

Yankelovich, Daniel, "Stepchildren of the Moral Majority," *Psychology Today,* November 1981.

About South End Press

South End Press is a nonprofit, collectively-run book publisher with over 150 titles in print. Since our founding in 1977, we have tried to meet the needs of readers who are exploring, or are already committed to, the politics of radical social change.

Our goal is to publish books that encourage critical thinking and constructive action on the key political, cultural, social, economic, and ecological issues shaping life in the United States and in the world. In this way, we hope to give expression to a wide diversity of democratic social movements and to provide an alternative to the products of corporate publishing.

If you would like a free catalog of South End Press books or information about our membership program—which offers two free books and a 40% discount on all titles—please write us at South End Press, 116 Saint Botolph Street, Boston, MA 02115.

Other titles of interest from South End Press:

Breaking Bread
Insurgent Black Intellectual Life
bell hooks and Cornel West

Necessary Illusions
Thought Control in Democratic Societies
Noam Chomsky

Prime Time Activism
Media Strategies for Grassroots Organizing
Charlotte Ryan

Old Nazis, The New Right and the Republican Party
Russ Bellant

Rockin' the Boat
Mass Music and Mass Movements
Edited by Reebee Garofalo